EDUCATING THE CHRONICALLY ILL CHILD

Susan B. Kleinberg

Mount Washington Pediatric Hospital
Baltimore, Maryland

AN ASPEN PUBLICATION®
Aspen Systems Corporation
Rockville, Maryland
London
1982

Library of Congress Cataloging in Publication Data

Kleinberg, Susan B.
Educating the chronically ill child.

Includes bibliographies and index.
1. Chronically ill childen—Education—United States.
I. Title.
LC4580.K53   371.9   81-20560
ISBN: 0-89443-652-X   AACR2

Copyright © 1982 Aspen Systems Corporation

Library of Congress Catalog Card Number: 81-20560
ISBN: 0-89443-652-X

Printed in the United States of America

1 2 3 4 5

To Ben and Allen and Leah
who have helped to keep me centered
within the love and community
of our family circle

Table of Contents

Preface

This project was undertaken in order to attempt to bring together a number of lines of inquiry relating to the issues involved in educating the chronically ill child. Against the background of the developing child within the family, the following strands are interwoven: law and policy in regard to the educational rights of the chronically ill child; the psychosocial effects of illness; medical perspectives in diagnosing and treating the chronically ill child; and educational strategies and approaches. This book was written primarily for those who encounter the chronically ill child in an educational context—teachers of the homebound or hospitalized, special education teachers, regular teachers with a chronically ill child in the classroom, and hospital-based educational staff. It is my belief that a full awareness of these interdisciplinary issues is essential if one is to attempt to provide to chronically ill children coordinated educational programs that can fully meet their cognitive, social, and vocational needs.

A major impetus in writing this book has been my desire to share with others the model of coordinated interdisciplinary care of the chronically ill child that has been developing at Mt. Washington Pediatric Hospital. Change does not occur easily, especially when it threatens the roles and territory of health professionals. Often, these barriers act to build a wall around the child, with each professional peering into his or her own window, diagnosing the child and determining the child's needs from the professional's own perspective.

I have been active, with my colleagues at Mt. Washington Pediatric Hospital, in trying to tear down these walls. The task has been formidable and the process continuous, but well worth the effort. Again and again, our reward has been to see children improve medically, socially, and educationally and to maintain their gains after discharge.

Part I provides a historical background of programs designed for the education of the child with chronic illness, a discussion of the current legal perspective, and a review of normal growth and development as it pertains to psychosocial issues affecting the chronically ill child. Chapter 3 examines the overall effects of chronic illness on children and their families.

Part II clusters common diseases by category in terms of their common distinctive impacts upon the child's development, rather than in terms of medical diagnostic categories. This allows for a continuing focus on educational issues and strategies, reflecting the book's main emphasis on the application by educators of strategies appropriate for a given setting and age-graded population. Short medical summaries are provided for each disease, including likely age of onset, symptomatology, usual diagnostic and treatment procedures, effects of the illness and of its treatment on the child's behavior, prognosis, and any special considerations or restrictions, such as required bracing or dietary limitations. These medical summaries can serve as a handy reference tool for teachers, without requiring that they have an extensive medical background. Educational strategies and special techniques are described in detail in each chapter for preschoolers, school aged children, and adolescents in home, school, and hospital settings.

The choice of which disease entities to present and which to ignore has been a difficult one and one that is necessarily subjective. An attempt has been made to include those conditions most often encountered by educators that fall broadly under the definition of chronic illness. Burns and spinal cord injury have been included, since they are conditions that usually have an effect upon the child's educational and vocational needs. Cerebral palsy and mental retardation have been omitted, since these conditions are widely covered in other educational sources.

Part III focuses on the teacher's role as a member of an interdisciplinary team and provides guidelines for effective communication with health professionals. The need for teachers of the chronically ill child to recognize and deal with their own feelings and to act as advocates for chronically ill children is addressed. Suggestions are made for creating a supportive environment for the chronically ill child in school settings, along with ways to use the hospital as a learning environment.

Throughout the book, emphasis is placed upon the complex interplay of genetic, environmental, familial, and social factors as they affect the chronically ill child.

Acknowledgments

Mere words cannot adequately thank all those who helped in the development of this handbook, yet they will have to suffice. A number of colleagues contributed their ideas and expertise and deserve a special mention. Carol Rabin, senior teacher, Home/Hospital Services, Baltimore City Public Schools, shared the writing of Chapter 5 and contributed the specialized knowledge she has acquired in working with chronically ill children. Deborah Meehling contributed to the section on stress-caring for the caregivers and provided some of the text based upon her research on the effects of stress on special educators. Celeste Klima, reading specialist and former child life teacher, prepared the material on educational strategies for the school aged hospitalized child. Her contribution, based upon years of practical experience with this population, represents ideas that work in practice. Paul Burgan, M.D., Ph.D., F.A.A.P., Medical Director at Mt. Washington Pediatric Hospital, Assistant Professor of Pediatrics, Johns Hopkins School of Medicine, and Assistant Clinical Professor of Pediatrics, University of Maryland School of Medicine, acted as medical advisor, reviewing all the medical sections for accuracy and clarity. His thoughtful reading of the material and his comments and corrections proved to be invaluable. All illustrations were done by Sharon Guertler, Child Life Specialist and Director of Volunteer Services at Mt. Washington Pediatric Hospital. Along with her drawing talent, Sharon shared her sensitivity and insight in her reading of the text. Her knowledge of child development and her recognition of the emotional needs of hospitalized children were immensely helpful.

Gratitude is extended to Mr. Brooks Major, chief executive officer of Mt. Washington Pediatric Hospital, for his consistent support, and to the patient care staff of MWPH for providing a working model of a caring, coordinated, health care team. Many of the ideas suggested in this text originated from the staff's daily management plans. A special thanks to the physical therapy department, for sharing their ideas on breathing exercises and adaptive equipment; Claudia Sick, clinical dietitian, for her diabetes diet information; Eileen Washington, for her summary of nonvocal communication techniques; the child life department for their consistent modeling of high quality care of children in hospitals; and the patient care department heads, for their help in completing the survey of roles in the health care team.

The text could not have been readable without the tireless efforts of Laurie Grammer, child life secretary, who accomplished the herculean task of turning my scrawls into typed manuscript. The entire text was read with critical insight and edited by a very dedicated, caring person, whose vision of the whole, and attention to detail combined to help make this handbook a reality—that person is Benjamin Kleinberg, my husband and partner.

Thanks to my children, Allen and Leah. To Allen, for working diligently to develop the glossary as a high school research project; to Leah, for always being patient with me; and to both, for teaching me the special joys that accompany parenthood.

A final thank you to Curt Whitesel, my editor, for his consistent support and encouragement in spite of personal travail.

This book would not have been possible without the incredible spirit, courage, and stamina of chronically ill children and their families and the untiring dedication of their teachers and counselors.

Chronic Illness: Theoretical Perspectives

OVERVIEW

Part I provides a discussion of two major theoretical dimensions involved in educating chronically ill children. Chapter 1 presents an examination of the policy issues involved in the delivery of services. Chapter 2 considers the child within the system and provides a theoretical model of psychosocial development. This dual perspective sets the stage for understanding the effects of chronic illness on the child and the family, explored in Chapter 3.

These issues form the basic framework for educating chronically ill children. Educational strategies need to be developed within the context of the environment, and the child's and family's unique needs. Without such a framework, there is the danger of developing strategies that are unrealistic, unworkable, and thus unused.

Chapter 1

Chronic Illness: Policy Issues

OVERVIEW

The development of appropriate, comprehensive educational programming for the nation's chronically ill children is a formidable task, yet one that is essential from both a legal and an ethical perspective. Over the years, home/hospital programs designed to serve the needs of the physically handicapped seriously ill child have increased in both quantity and quality. Beginning with a few hospital schools on the wards of large, innovative children's hospitals and informal home visits made by regular classroom teachers, home/hospital teaching programs have evolved to take their rightful place in the continuum of special education services. Yet for the child with chronic illness, who may, after an initial period of disability, attend school sporadically, home/hospital services have yet to make significant inroads. This chapter will examine the availability of such home/hospital services around the country, the requirements for certification for teachers engaged in this kind of special education programming, and the laws relating to the education of the chronically ill child.

Before beginning this examination, however, it is essential that the population that will be discussed throughout this text be defined. Who is the chronically ill child? Is there a standard definition of chronic illness? Which conditions fall within this definition?

CHRONIC ILLNESS DEFINED

Chronic illness is not a single disease entity but rather an "umbrella" term (Travis, 1976). It is not equivalent to a long-standing physical or neurologic handicap, such as cerebral palsy, for these children can be either ill or well, independent of their handicap. It is a set of conditions that affects one or

3

more body organs and represents an active disease process. It may last many months or a lifetime. It may be secondary to an inherited disorder, such as hemophilia, or it may be acquired at birth or in early childhood or be the result of an acute illness or injury (e.g., seizures following closed head injury) (Myers, 1975).

Chronic illness may be life-threatening or relatively benign. It may leave the child permanently damaged, as in the scarring from burns, or may be resolved with little or no aftereffects or sequelae. In many cases, psychological effects may be present long after the disease process has been resolved.

Can chronic illness be defined by certain features common to all? The Commission on Chronic Illness in the United States (1957) defined the term as including all impairments or deviations from normal that have one or more of the following characteristics: are permanent; leave a residual disability; are caused by nonreversible pathologic alteration; require special training of the patient for rehabilitation; or may be expected to require a long period of supervision, observation, or care. Ake Mattsson (1972), who has researched chronic illness and its effects for many years, provides this definition: "Long term or chronic illness refers to a disorder with a protracted course which can be progressive and fatal, or associated with a relatively normal life-span despite impaired physical and mental functioning. Such a disease frequently shows periods of acute exacerbations requiring intensive medical attention" (p. 108). For the purposes of this book, chronic illness will include those conditions that usually require homebound or hospital instruction, such as burns; trauma from physical injuries that are long-standing, such as spinal cord injuries or closed head trauma; and conditions more classically defined as chronic illness, such as asthma, diabetes, cystic fibrosis, and cancer.

Acute Versus Chronic Illness

Children suffering from a short-term acute illness or a self-limiting physical disability such as the fracture of an extremity receive intense medical treatment over the course of their disorder. They often are absent from school during this time. Educational programs can be provided for these children on a short-term basis at home or in the hospital so that they can maintain their academic progress and return to the mainstream when their condition is fully resolved. Whenever children are seriously ill or are involved in an accident in which bodily injury results, developmental continuity is broken. Children must adapt to strange surroundings and undergo the trauma and stress related to the accident or illness and concomitant treatments. Often, the actual effects of the condition are less serious than the child's perceptions of them. With careful preparation and sensitive handling by parents and professionals, permanent damaging physical or psychological effects of short-term accidents or illness can be minimal. Children and their families can "get on with" their lives and return to their normal patterns at home, at school, and in the community.

This is often not the case for children with chronic illness. For most children and their families, the condition does not get better and disappear. Even with good control and years of remission, the threat of a recurrent crisis is everpresent. Children with chronic illness have long-term educational, social, and emotional needs that must be addressed. These children are not confined to beds or hospitals except for occasional flare-ups of their disease. They attend local schools and are involved in after-school community activities to the extent that their limitations permit them. They are at home, in the community, and in the schools for a much more significant proportion of their lives than they are in hospitals.

Yet these children have frequent bouts with acute stages of their illness and are often hospitalized or homebound for significant numbers of days during their school career. For example, the asthmatic child may have near normal attendance during the bulk of the school year but spend most of the spring and early fall months in the hospital or at home due to increased allergenic conditions in the environment. The child with rheumatoid arthritis may miss a number of school days during the cold, damp months in northern climates, while having near perfect attendance on warm dry days. Clearly, the inconsistent and unexpected nature of their absences is a factor to reckon with in planning for their educational continuity.

CHRONIC ILLNESS: SCOPE OF THE PROBLEM

It is impossible to state with certainty the number of chronically ill children in the United States today. Definitions vary, and statistical computations are often made for particular disease entities or by specific localities rather than nationally. Infants are particularly vulnerable and often die in the early weeks of a potentially life-long chronic illness, although medical technology has made remarkable progress in this area. Infants born with serious heart defects or meningomyelocele were often unable to survive the neonatal period until the last few decades. Neonatal surgical techniques and modern technology have changed this picture dramatically. J.P. Reichmeister (1980), a Maryland physician specializing in meningomyelocele, estimated that 30 years ago 90 percent of those children born with the condition died in infancy, whereas today 90 percent are saved through a series of medical interventions.

Unfortunately, many children thus saved remain impaired to one degree or another and face a lifetime of coping with the limitations imposed upon them by their condition. There is general agreement in the literature that 7 to 10 percent of all children suffer from some form of chronic illness (Mattsson,

1972; Pless, Satterwhite, & Van Vechten, 1976), and the combined prevalence of chronic illness and other handicapping conditions such as cerebral palsy and mental retardation is estimated to be 20 percent (Green & Haggerty, 1968). The most common conditions cited are asthma (2 percent of the population), cardiac conditions (0.5 percent), and diabetes mellitus (0.5 percent) (Mattsson, 1972). Some conditions affect special populations differentially; sickle cell disease is most prevalent in black populations, and hemophilia is most prevalent in males. Additionally, mortality rates have decreased dramatically in the past 50 years. M. Green and R. Haggerty (1968) report a drop in death rates from 5 per 1,000 in 1935 to 1 per 1,000 in 1960 for ages 1 through 4, and for children ages 5 through 14, the mortality rate has declined from 1.5 per 1,000 to 0.5 per 1,000.

With the advent of antibiotics, modern public health programs, and highly skilled medical teams, deaths from acute illness and from acute recurrences of chronic illness have decreased dramatically. On the other hand, since children are dying less frequently of acute illness or acute episodes of chronic illness, the proportion of children with long-term chronic illness has tended to increase (Holt, 1972). Today, many of these conditions can be treated only symptomatically because modern technology has not yet discovered either cause or cure for diseases such as leukemia, muscular dystrophy, diabetes, or cystic fibrosis.

Prevention

Prevention may represent one solution to reducing the numbers of chronically ill children in this country. The advent of prenatal monitoring techniques such as amniocentesis, sonograms, and fetal monitors has increased the ability of the medical team to predict and occasionally prevent the births of severely damaged children. Careful prenatal care and the monitoring of the pregnant mother's exposure to dangerous drugs, alcohol, and x-rays also aid in prevention. It has been well documented that the risk of disability or disease in a child increases dramatically given a number of factors: extremes of age of the mother; poor prenatal care; low income level, which often affects the pregnant woman's nutritional intake; frequent pregnancies; and untreated illnesses of pregnant women are but a few. A goal would be to reduce these risks wherever possible through adequate public education, extensive health education curriculums in the public schools, and a variety of community efforts. This goal has yet to be achieved in spite of available medical knowledge.

Immunization programs based upon new medical findings in the last few decades have dramatically reduced the incidence of specific diseases such as poliomyelitis, measles encephalitis, and the sequelae of German measles (rubella). Furthermore, tests in infancy to diagnose a number of inborn metabolic disorders, notably PKU (phenylketonuria), have gone a long way toward preventing the devastating retardation that results from untreated PKU. Research continues in the fields of diabetes, cancer, and other diseases, lending hope for future scientific breakthroughs.

Large numbers of chronically ill children, their disease entities well-managed by combinations of diet, medication, and other therapies, attend school daily with little or no apparent difficulties in their school attendance or performance. For these children, the prospect of a near normal life span and life experiences is quite good, and educational strategies to enhance their potential should be within the scope of any well-designed academic setting. For countless others, specialized programs, equipment, teacher training, and/or service models are required in order to provide to chronically ill children the appropriate educational opportunities that are mandated by law. In the following sections, the law will be reviewed as it relates to chronic illness, and then the current status of home/hospital services nationally will be examined.

LAW AND CHRONIC ILLNESS

In 1975, Congress enacted landmark legislation assuring all handicapped children the right to education. This law, PL 94–142, states: "It is the purpose of this Act to assure that all handicapped children have available to them, within the time periods specified, a free appropriate public education emphasizing special education and related services designed to meet their unique needs (PL 94–142, 1975, Section 3, c). Based on traditional categories of disabilities, the law defines as handicapping the following conditions:

- emotional disturbance severe enough to be disruptive to the learning process

- learning disability in one or more of the basic psychological processes involved in understanding or using language

- mental retardation, defined as below average general intellectual functioning that originates during the developmental period and that is associated with impaired adaptive behaviors

- visual handicap

- hearing impairment

- speech disorders that interfere with communication and/or cause maladaptive behavior

- multiple handicaps, with children exhibiting one or more disabling conditions

- physical handicaps, which include neurologic and orthopedic conditions, as well as other medical conditions that result in serious health impairment. Specifically, *other health impaired* is defined as having limited strength, vitality, or alertness due to chronic or acute health problems such as a heart condition, epilepsy, tuberculosis, rheumatic fever, nephritis, asthma, sickle cell anemia, hemophilia, lead poisoning, leukemia, or diabetes, which adversely affects a child's educational performance (PL 94-142, 1977, p. 42478).

PL 94-142 thus puts the chronically ill child within the scope of the special education law. It requires that those children identified as health-impaired receive appropriate programming, as well as all the other due process rights to which children in other special education programs are entitled. This federal law requires that each state educational agency develop detailed guidelines and bylaws for program implementation. It outlines those aspects of the regulations that are mandatory and that must be included in each state's plan.

Child Identification

Recognizing that many children in need of special education services were not enrolled in any public program, the law requires that each local educational agency develop a method of identifying children in need of such programs. This entails considerable financing of public education campaigns, as well as the staffing and training of assessment teams to screen such children once found.

Nondiscriminatory Testing

In order to ensure that children are properly identified, testing must be done with a variety of assessment tools by a variety of professionals. Parents retain the right to request independent evaluations by professionals employed outside the public education agencies, and these results must be considered in any program planning. The requirement that a variety of assessment tools be utilized provides the framework for a multidisciplinary team approach to program planning in the educational system, which includes the parents and, when applicable, the child as well.

Least Restrictive Environment

Placement decisions must be made so that the child receives the most appropriate educational program in the least restrictive setting. This requirement is especially crucial for the chronically ill population, since homebound and hospital programs are generally considered to be the most restrictive settings.

Development of an Individualized Educational Plan

The individualized educational plan (IEP) is perhaps the most essential and least understood aspect of the special education law. The IEP can be seen as a process by which a team of professionals and parents, using an array of standardized assessment data, observations, and knowledge of a child's needs, develops a working plan to provide the most appropriate educational program for each child. The IEP is developed gradually, in screening meetings and by diagnostic/prescriptive teaching, so that its written form can be viewed as a blueprint for a child's education. IEPs really represent current needs and program approaches, so that they should be reviewed periodically for revisions and updated on an annual basis. The development of the IEP and the need for meetings to write, review, and update the results can be time-consuming. A frequent dilemma faced by teachers can best be summed up by one colleague's complaint, "I spend so much time in meetings, and writing up the necessary documentation, I hardly ever get to teach anymore." Hopefully, as teaching staffs and local educational agencies become more familiar with the process and develop streamlined approaches, this problem can be resolved. In-service instruction and preservice training may also aid teachers in this area. It is essential for the child that the IEP function as a working document that improves the quality of the educational program, enhances its implementation, and facilitates interaction between the child and the service producers. An IEP that only satisfies the law (paper compliance) and does not achieve these goals is all but useless in providing optimal education.

A concern raised by teachers of the homebound/hospitalized population relates to the issue of whether an IEP is necessary for the child temporarily disabled by an accident or illness who will return to a home school with normal programming. Such issues need to be addressed by the administrators of homebound/hospital programs. Specialized forms that document the temporary change in educational programming due to medical considerations may resolve this dilemma without the necessity for the development of a detailed IEP. This may provide a solution to the sporadic placement in homebound/hospitalized programs of chronically ill children who have no other special educational needs.

Related Services

All services related to the appropriate education of the child with special needs can and should be included in the IEP. Transportation, speech, or physical therapy services are the usual categories included. A teacher and parent may well find that other services, less well-known, are essential and can be provided for under this category. A child in a wheelchair may be able to return to school with the addition of ramps or an elevator pass. A child who is gradually losing the ability to perform fine motor tasks can be included in school if a tape recorder or a teacher aide is provided to record the work and if oral tests are allowed. Short rest periods in the health suite or a shortened school day may allow a leukemic child the opportunity to remain in school many more days. All of these requirements can be written into the IEP, thus assuring compliance. Parents can be especially helpful in this area, suggesting alternative or additional services for the child.

Parent Rights

Parent involvement must be an essential component of program planning and implementation. Parent rights are clearly spelled out in the law and involve each aspect of program development. For children with chronic illness, parent involvement, as well as the involvement of the health professionals caring for the child, is essential in appropriate programming.

DELIVERY OF SERVICES

States are thus committed by law to provide adequate, appropriate educational and related services for health-impaired children in the least restrictive environment. The impact this has on special education generally and on home/hospital services specifically is enormous. Major changes in state laws, funding mechanisms, certification procedures, and program alternatives are required and are slowly being implemented nationally. This need for a reevaluation of homebound/hospitalized programs arises at a particularly crucial time in the development of the home/hospital service model. Beginning in the 1950s with the recognition of the need for hospital schools and comprehensive programs for homebound children (Newman, 1950; Plank, Archer, & Crocker, 1959) school administrators and teacher-training institutions have attempted to develop uniform standards for the certification of home/hospital teachers and have grappled with the continuing problem of a scarcity of funds to adequately provide home/hospital programs.

The critical issues raised in the 1950s have yet to be resolved (Connor, 1964). They include certification standards for home/hospital teachers, funding mechanisms, the administration of home/hospital programs under special education or regular education, the instructional time available to home/hospital teachers, and the competing need to comply with requirements for documentation. The direction and scope of home/hospital services in the coming decades will be determined by the way in which education administrators resolve these issues. The present status of these issues nationally will now be examined.

Certification Standards

In a study of home teaching provisions at the state level conducted in 1958, R.R. Simches and E.F. Cicenia noted that state legislators were directing their attention to the provision of educational services for those handicapped children able to participate in groups in regular or special school settings. They expressed concern that adequate funding and quality of education for the homebound population would suffer. This concern was echoed in F. Connor's monograph on the education of homebound or hospitalized children in 1964. She noted a move toward professionalism in the field of home/hospital teaching and strongly recommended increased training for homebound and hospital school teachers. This need for further certification standards and training for the teacher specializing in homebound/hospital programs is further demonstrated when one looks at the changing nature of the populations served by home/hospital programs. Originally provided for those children who were physically handicapped or temporarily disabled by illness but were otherwise normal, homebound programs have gradually expanded to include children with a wide range of mental, emotional, cognitive, and physical handicaps. As Connor (1964) noted, even "from the scant survey data available, it is clear that no longer can the teacher depend upon his pupils' having a single disability or even similar educational problems. The age and ability ranges of pupils can be expected to be great, and the length of enrollment in the program will vary" (p. 4). Simches and Cicenia (1958) report that of 33 states responding to a survey, only 5 states required a special certificate for home teachers, and 4 others reported that special requirements were being drafted. In a follow-up study conducted by this author (1980), of 39 states reporting, 8 require either special certification or have established some form of competency standards. States reporting special standards are Florida, Georgia, Iowa, Maryland, Michigan, Nebraska, Utah, and West Virginia. A trend that is apparent in a few states is one toward the assignment of teachers to home/hospital populations based upon the child's preexisting needs. Thus, children previously receiving special education services would be provided with home/hospital teachers certified in that area, while teachers with general certifications would be assigned to those children who had been on regular school rolls prior to their accident or illness.

State departments of education nationwide are beginning to reexamine and modify their certification standards. Pressure for this trend comes from two sources: the least restrictive environment provisions of PL 94–142 and the use of competency-based standards to evaluate performance.

One consequence of the least restrictive environment provision has been the increased presence of mildly handicapped children in regular education classes. As a result, many states are beginning to require some minimal special educational training on a preservice or in-service level for regular educators holding general certificates, although this requirement is being hotly contested by teacher training institutions and teachers' unions. There are few national programs that provide teachers of the homebound or hospitalized population with the training necessary to develop educational strategies so that they can provide a comprehensive program for the chronically ill child. Unfortunately, home teachers are not adequately prepared for the difficult role they must perform (Wolinsky, 1970). They need training in (1) the development of IEPs, (2) understanding and dealing with the diverse emotional, medical, and cognitive problems of the children they encounter, and (3) the development of communication skills to deal with the parents and various health professionals involved with each child's care. Providing education for the chronically ill child can be rewarding, but it is often emotionally draining and lonely. Teachers of the homebound or hospitalized need support systems within their departments and among colleagues, as well as continual in-service education.

Competency-Based Standards

Certification of teachers specifically for the homebound/hospitalized population, considering the diverse ages and needs of that population, may not be a feasible solution to the problem of adequate teacher training. Competency-based standards could well provide an alternative option to school systems. Using these standards, home/hospital staffs could then be evaluated and recruited from the larger corps of trained educators. A primary goal of home/hospital programs should be the development of a core of dedicated, well-trained, full-time educators. In a discussion of educational programming for the short-term hospitalized child, P. Buerke (1966) recommends that teachers have a wide repertoire of experiences with children in a variety of settings. She points to the need for perception and flexibility as well as for empathy in dealing with the ill child and family. The resource manual of programs for the homebound/hospitalized in Florida suggests the following competencies for teachers:

1. Broad knowledge of curriculum
2. Individualized instruction
3. Evaluates the utility of various instructional strategies
4. Interprets task analysis
5. Evaluates the appropriateness of resources for programming use

6. Utilizes behavioral management strategies
7. Has knowledge and experience with exceptional students
8. Provides a humanly supportive environment
9. Works cooperatively with adults
10. Has perception and flexibility (Florida State Manual, 1979, pp. 22-24)

Competencies for the Child Life Specialist

The national child life study section of the Association for Care of Children's Health (ACCH) developed the following competencies for child life specialists, who perform a different yet overlapping role in hospitals.

Competencies are observable, acquired skills that can be behaviorally defined. The following are competencies necessary to function in the role of child life specialist.

General information, education, and programming competencies include:

- demonstrates knowledge of human growth and development across the life span

- demonstrates knowledge of how to modify or adapt activities, equipment, and/or facilities to meet specific individual and/or group needs

- demonstrates knowledge and ability to provide an appropriate educational, recreational, and therapeutic environment for individuals and groups (ages 0–21)

- demonstrates knowledge and ability to participate in the preparation of children for hospitalization and/or medical procedures

- demonstrates understanding of society's attitudes towards illness and disability

- demonstrates knowledge of the role and function of evaluation in the delivery of services and how to carry out such evaluations

Knowledge of psychosocial issues should include:

- demonstrates knowledge of the effects of stress and trauma on children's behavior and development, and of the basic therapeutic techniques for dealing with these

- demonstrates knowledge of the special needs of chronically ill and/or handicapped children

- demonstrates knowledge of the dynamics of the family system, including the impact illness has on the family

- demonstrates knowledge of the psychosocial needs of patients, family, and staff by dealing effectively with those of all educational, racial, religious, economic, and cultural backgrounds
- demonstrates knowledge and ability to respond appropriately to the death- and loss-related concerns of patients and family
- demonstrates understanding of group dynamics and process
- demonstrates knowledge of the basic principles of counseling

Knowledge of research and medical issues includes:

- demonstrates knowledge of basic medical procedures and terminology in relation to children's illnesses
- demonstrates familiarity with the research literature concerning children in health settings
- demonstrates understanding of the nature and etiology of illness and disability

Communication skills and administrative abilities include:

- demonstrates knowledge and ability to observe, assess, and record information regarding children's developmental skills and hospital adjustment
- demonstrates knowledge and ability to orient, supervise, and evaluate students and volunteers
- demonstrates knowledge and ability to represent child life issues/concerns/philosophy to others (e.g., in-services, public relations work)
- demonstrates knowledge and ability to perform administrative duties, such as budgeting, scheduling, and volunteer/student training
- demonstrates knowledge and ability to utilize communication skills in working with a variety of professionals within the hospital and community
- demonstrates knowledge of the function and interrelationships of various disciplines in health care and rehabilitation

Based on these and other suggested criteria, the following set of competency-based standards would be recommended for adoption nationally. Homebound/hospital teachers should:

- have a background in education curriculum development and program implementation

- have experience in a variety of settings with a variety of children

- have the ability to adapt programs, equipment, and material to suit the individual needs of children with a variety of disabilities

- have flexibility in scheduling

- have the ability to perform task analysis, develop behavioral objectives, and develop IEPs

- have the ability to communicate effectively with a wide variety of people, including parents and health professionals

- have a working knowledge of medical terminology and the ability to use resources to obtain information on specific diseases and their effects on children

- have an understanding of the effects of illness, physical disability, and hospitalization on children

- be able to understand and develop ways to alleviate stress in children

- have an understanding of the effects of terminal illness on children, their parents, and their teachers

FUNDING

Defining competency standards and providing in-service training for homebound/hospital teachers must be accomplished if the needs of the chronically ill child are to be met. Increasing the quantity and quality of home/hospital programs is costly, and while home/hospital services are generally available in most states (only Arkansas, New Hampshire, and Puerto Rico reported no statewide mandate for services [Kleinberg, 1980]), they still remain somewhat fragmented and poorly funded. There is a current debate centering on the appropriate administrative assignment of home/hospital programs, which may have an impact on funding availability. If homebound/hospital programs are administered under divisions of special education, they will have to compete with the other categories of exceptionalities for money and personnel. As the most fragmented of the special education services, they may well be caught in a fiscal squeeze, and their future viability may be threatened. Yet as a consequence of PL 94–142, more monies are available for funding special education programs than for funding general education programs. If home/hospital programs are administered under general education divisions, there may be even less money available, and the programs may well be further fragmented among the elementary, secondary, and vocational subdivisions of school systems.

A constituency of home/hospital personnel and parents may need to be developed in order to ensure that these issues are resolved without the loss of quality or quantity in homebound/hospital programs.

Limits on Instructional Time

Ideally, children excluded from school due to accident, illness, or other reasons should be provided with an education equal in terms of time and quality of instruction to that of children included in school programs. Realistically, shortages of funds and personnel limit the feasibility of this. Most states have established minimum and maximum hours per week for instructional time, which range from one to six hours per week. Within state guidelines, a great deal of flexibility is allowed in terms of the number of hours per day allotted to teaching, and the number of hours that are required varies depending upon the age of the child. The dilemma for the conscientious teacher is that these hours of instruction time often do not allow for the time involved in planning (paper work), obtaining books and other materials from home schools or other resources, and scheduling essential meetings with parents, health professionals, and regular school teachers. Often, these tasks must be accomplished for no reimbursement or at the expense of instructional time.

Matching hours of instructional time with actual credit hours can create additional problems, especially for secondary students. One solution to this problem could be the move toward competency standards for students rather than hour-by-hour matched credit. Thus, a student receives credit for work accomplished, rather than for time spent. Individualized teaching in home settings often allows the child to learn at a more rapid pace and may meet the child's special needs for adapted instructional techniques, allowing increased learning to take place.

A final problem presented by time limitations has major implications for the chronically ill. Most school systems require a period of from ten days to four weeks of extended school absence before a child can be enrolled in a homebound/hospitalized program. Students who are chronically ill and miss school periodically are not well served by these requirements. Only a few states have taken action to alleviate this problem.

One solution developed and operated by the Baltimore City public schools is the Chronic Health Impaired Program (CHIP). This program is designed to meet the educational and psychosocial needs of the chronically ill student. Home teaching is provided on those days when the child's illness prevents school attendance, and remedial instruction to compensate for previous periods of absence is also offered. Counseling is available to help students and their families cope with the problems related to childhood chronic illness. It would seem that in order for a school district to achieve full compliance under PL 94-142, it would need to offer a similar program. To date, only a few states have developed such provisions.

Service Models

Homebound/hospitalized instruction is a service delivery system designed to provide continuity of education for children with chronic illnesses, temporary disabilities, or short-term illnesses. It also provides services for children excluded from regular programs until appropriate screening and placement decisions can be made. It is the most restrictive form of educational programming, and its use is therefore considered temporary and short-term. The ultimate goal of any homebound/hospital program is to return all students to some form of grouped school placement. As noted by Wolinsky (1970), "exclusion from day school implies deviancy of behavior" (p. 673). The instructional pattern of one-to-one that exists in the homebound situation is atypical, and its long-term use may create socialization and attention problems for children. Additionally, the time and expense involved in home teaching and the need to provide individualized instruction create funding and staffing problems.

As a consequence, a variety of imaginative alternative delivery systems has emerged, some made possible by modern technology. Among the most innovative are teleteaching, closed circuit TV units, and computer programs. Hospital-based programs provide another alternative to the restrictive environment of one-to-one teaching, and the use of special resource people and materials provides a third supplementing model.

Technology-Assisted Systems

While there can be no replacement for the caring and sensitive human being in the educational system, computer programs that allow children to learn a great variety of material via home computer terminals may play an important part in future home teaching programs. Teachers need to be available as well to provide the human touch and to meet the equally essential psychosocial needs of the child.

Teleteaching is another approach that is being used more frequently today. Exemplary programs in Florida and Baltimore City provide telephone hookups in homes and hospitals so that students can converse with one another and with the teacher, thus allowing for group programming and interaction. It is most successful for the upper grade levels and for students who are functioning close to grade equivalency. It is a particularly good solution to the problem of excessive time spent traveling to students' homes in rural areas.

Inexpensive machines that allow a child to use a wide variety of packaged learning materials can be supplied by homebound teachers as an adjunct to regular instructional time. For children with physical handicaps, adapted equipment can be invaluable in helping them learn independently.

Hospital Schools

Unlike the one-to-one tutoring in homes or at bedside in hospitals, hospital schools can provide an opportunity for group interaction and a more normal setting for the hospitalized child. Children can attend school as a regular part of their day, allowing them to keep up with their academic work. Of equal importance, the school can provide a setting for socialization and can serve to help a child who has been too ill for school to slowly return to a group context in a safe setting. Education in hospital schools is provided in many pediatric hospitals and in a few general hospitals with pediatric wards. Of concern here is the lack of uniformity in providing guidelines for teachers in hospital settings. Coordination among school districts, teachers, and hospital personnel is often poor or nonexistent. Assignment of adequate space to the schoolteacher for classroom and supplies is a constant source of conflict in some hospitals. Often, the teacher is not informed of changes in the medical status of the children, and discharge planning usually occurs in the teacher's absence. The Association for the Care of Children's Health is attempting to address this problem by developing a directory of hospital schools and a set of guidelines for their operations. At Mt. Washington Pediatric Hospital, a contract between the child life department and the Baltimore City public schools home/hospital program was negotiated, and specific delineated responsibilities were outlined (see Exhibit 1-1). This has resulted in a smoothly coordinated program, one in which the patients hopefully receive optimal education and program planning.

Resource Help

Parents, siblings, and friends can be provided with supplementary activities to help the homebound or hospitalized child reinforce skills. Relatives and friends may feel awkward when visiting a chronically ill child, and resource materials can help make such visits pleasant and interesting. Newsletters from classmates, telephone calls, and special projects can help to maintain the social ties between chronically ill children and their peers. Special visitors such as librarians, zoo or aquarium staff, local television celebrities, and the like can be persuaded to stop by hospitals to share their talents and expertise with the patients.

Exhibit 1-1 Memorandum of Agreement

School (#352) based at Mt. Washington Pediatric Hospital, Inc. was established by the Baltimore City public schools home/hospital division as of September 1976. By joint signature of this letter, representatives of the two agencies agree to the following conditions and responsibilities.

Responsibilities of Baltimore City Public School Home/Hospital Division

The home/hospital department of the Baltimore City public schools will:
1. Interview, hire, discharge, and provide all employment benefits for teachers assigned to Mt. Washington Pediatric Hospital School #352.
2. Assume full insurance liability for all teachers assigned.
3. Provide orientation and in-service education for Baltimore City public schoolteachers assigned in relation to duties and responsibilities of hospital-based teachers.
4. Provide supplies and equipment for the program to the extent budgeted by their department.
5. Maintain regular contact with Baltimore City public schoolteachers assigned and with hospital child life director to ensure adequate communication.
6. Provide on-site periodic supervision of Baltimore City public schoolteachers.
7. Keep Director of Child Life and Education informed as to any changes in home/hospital regulations, assignments, and responsibilities.

Responsibilities of Mt. Washington Pediatric Hospital, Inc., Child Life and Education Department

The Mt. Washington Pediatric Hospital Child Life and Education Department will:
1. Interview teachers assigned to hospital school.
2. Retain the right to request transfer of a teacher, after consultation with home/hospital coordinator.
3. Provide adequate, appropriate space and equipment for Baltimore City public schoolteachers for programs and for storage of personal belongings.
4. Provide complete orientation of all Baltimore City public schoolteachers to hospital staff, policies, and procedures.

Exhibit 1-1 continued

> 5. Provide the opportunity for Baltimore City public school-teachers to attend all pertinent meetings and in-services.
> 6. Provide transportation for the students to and from the classrooms at the appropriate times.
>
> **Baltimore City Public Schoolteachers Will:**
>
> 1. Comply with all the policies and procedures of the Baltimore City public system.
> 2. Comply with all policies and procedures of Mt. Washington Pediatric Hospital, Inc. and its child life and education department.
> 3. Coordinate all individualized education programs with hospital teachers and with clinical staff of hospital.
> 4. Register and discharge patients on hospital rolls in accordance with Baltimore City public school procedures.
> 5. Attend all pertinent hospital meetings and in-services.
> 6. Make written evaluations and IEPs available to hospital staff through charts and school reports.
>
> **Mt. Washington Pediatric Hospital Will:**
>
> 1. Coordinate program with home/hospital teachers.
> 2. Keep Baltimore City public schoolteachers informed of all hospital meetings, procedures, and programs.

Generally, the goal for homebound/hospitalized programs should be to bring the world to the child until the child can join the world. Later chapters will provide detailed educational strategies for a variety of chronically ill children in a variety of settings. The need for special educational methods and materials for the chronically ill child is great; the legal mandate is clear. It is hoped that this handbook represents one step toward achieving the goal of providing appropriate, equal educational opportunities for children with chronic illness.

REFERENCES

Association for Care of Children's Health, Child Life Study Section. Competency-based standards, 1980.

Buerke, P. Educational programming for the short-term hospitalized child. *Exceptional children*, 1966, *32*, 559–563.

Commission on Chronic Illness. *Chronic illness in the U.S.* (Vol. 1), *Prevention of chronic illness.* Cambridge, MA. Harvard University Press, 1957.

Connor, F. *Education of the homebound/hospitalized child.* New York: Columbia University, Teachers College, 1964.

Education of handicapped children: Implementation of Part B of the Education of the Handicapped Act. *Federal Register,* 1977, *42,* 42474-42518.

Florida State Department of Education, Bureau of Education for Exceptional Students. *A resource manual for the development and evaluation of special programs for exceptional students* (Vol. 2-H), *Homebound/hospitalized,* 1979.

Green, M., & Haggerty, R. *Ambulatory pediatrics.* Philadelphia: W.B. Saunders, 1968.

Holt, K. The problem in the young. *Proceedings of the Royal Society of Medicine,* 1972, *65,* 4-5.

Kleinberg, S. Survey of home-hospital teaching provisions. Unpublished, 1980.

Mattsson, A. Long-term physical illness in childhood: A challenge to psychosocial adaptation. *Pediatrics,* 1972, *50,* 801-811.

Myers, B.R. The child with a chronic illness. In R.H. Haslam & P. Valletutti (Eds.), *Medical problems in the classroom.* Baltimore: University Park Press, 1975.

Newman, M.P. Education for the ill. *Occupations,* 1950, *28,* 381-382.

Plank, E., Archer, M., & Crocker, B. Living and learning in the hospital. *Childhood Education,* 1959, *35,* 219-222.

Pless, I., Satterwhite, B., & Van Vechten, D. Chronic illness in childhood: A regional survey of care. *Pediatrics,* 1976, *58,* 37-46.

Reichmeister, J.P. Seminar on chronic illness, presented by Mt. Washington Pediatric Hospital, Baltimore, Maryland, 1980.

Simches, R.R., & Cicenia, E.F. Home teaching provisions at the state level. *Exceptional Children,* 1958, *25*(1), 11-15.

Travis, G. *Chronic illness in children.* Stanford, CA: Stanford University Press, 1976.

Wolinsky, G. A special education problem. Home instruction: States, issues and recommendations. *Exceptional Children,* 1970, *36,* 674-677.

Chapter 2

Normal Growth and Development: A Psychosocial Overview

OVERVIEW

This chapter will present a psychosocial overview of development, from infancy through young adulthood. Such a focus is crucial, for a person's conception of human development can greatly influence how one relates to children, what expectations one has of children's abilities, and what behaviors one considers appropriate in varying circumstances.

SYNTHESIS: A WORKING MODEL OF DEVELOPMENT

This book takes the position that development is a complex, dynamic, multidimensional process. It is based upon a vision of the child as essentially competent, able to learn and use a variety of coping strategies. In this view, the individual is seen as, first, a physical organism with unique genetic potentials, temperament variations, and an inner striving for mastery and for interaction with the environment. The growing organism's interaction with its environment has the potential to enhance or impede the development of the individual, while he or she gradually develops the capacity to alter the environment, adapt to it, or withdraw from it.

As this process occurs, the child faces a variety of developmental tasks. These are determined by such factors as physical maturation, increasing cognitive and communicative capacities, and changing social and affective needs. For example, one of the 15-month-old child's central developmental tasks is to walk independently. The child's success in this task will depend first upon his motor skills and the lack of any serious motor impairment. His temperament will play a role as well. A passive child is less likely to attempt to walk early, while a child with strong drives toward exploration may rush headlong into a new world. Parental attitudes and responses also play a role

23

in the child's pursuits toward competency. An overanxious mother can hamper progress, while a neglectful one may precipitate unnecessary accidents, possibly creating a situation in which a fearful child refrains from further risk-taking, thus slowing development (see Figure 2-1).

The following pages will attempt to trace the child's psychosocial development, using this model. While later discussions may separate the physical, emotional, and environmental effects of chronic illness for the sake of clarity, it should be noted that the author's conception is that of the total child in the context of his or her individuality, family, and society.

INFANCY

At birth, the infant brings with him or her a wide repertoire of motor activities practiced in utero and a rich genetic potential for maturation. Current research into infant competencies by T.G.R. Bower (1977) and others has increased our awareness of the complex abilities that infants exhibit in the early weeks of life. Their visual and sensory perception and discrimination skills seem to be much more sophisticated than we previously believed. We know, for example, that infants as young as a few weeks prefer to look at complex shapes rather than simple ones and clearly show preference for shapes that resemble human faces. Physically and emotionally, infants remain totally dependent upon the adults in their environment for their very survival. They cannot sustain themselves without human contact. The healthy newborn must be fed by adults on a reasonably consistent basis and be held and comforted as well. When caretakers spend time with their infants meeting these essential physical and social needs, a gradual bonding or attachment forms between the caretaker and the infant. Out of this relationship, a growing sense of *trust* is established. E.H. Erikson (1963) suggests that the development of this basic trust lays the foundation for all future relationships.

Inconsistent parenting or parenting by too many caretakers thus may have serious implications for the psychosocial development of a child. Children born with serious birth defects or illnesses requiring hospital care in their early months of life can consequently be highly vulnerable to emotional dysfunction, the effects of which will be discussed in detail in a later chapter.

The first year of life is one of rapid growth. By the end of the first year, totally dependent neonates are able to move through space independently, make their basic needs known through both verbal and nonverbal communication, and react to people around them as unique social beings. Two threads of this development deserve special attention: the process of attachment and the growth of social interaction.

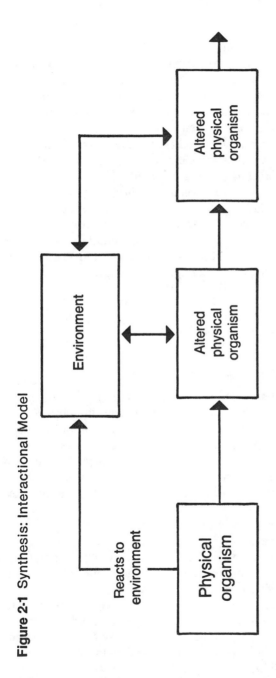

Figure 2-1 Synthesis: Interactional Model

Attachment

As noted earlier, attachment seems to occur as an outgrowth of consistent physical and social contact between parent and child. Studies by M.D.S. Ainsworth et al. (1978), J. Bowlby (1969), and others suggest that this developing attachment reaches its peak when the infant is between six and eight months old, and accounts for the distress seen in these children when separation from mother occurs. More recent studies by Lamb (1978) suggest that attachment exists between infants and their fathers as well, and most of the research seems to indicate that attachment is not solely dependent upon the frequency of interactions but upon their quality as well. Infants become attached to those caregivers who succeed in alleviating the infant's distress (Kagan, Kearsley, & Zelazo, 1979). As a consequence, separation from these familiar caregivers can be very traumatic for a young child. Ainsworth et al. (1978) vividly describe the various reactions of infants to separation. They will quietly stop play, change their vocalizations, and cry out—responses painfully familiar to all parents or caregivers who have placed young children with strangers or in strange surroundings.

Social Interaction

Infant-parent interactions always occur in a social context. Feeding a baby or changing an infant's diaper requires touching and movement in space. Additionally, caregivers talk to the infant and delight in noting the baby's responses, however slight. These are the first communications between infant and parent. As a consequence of these interactions, babies become increasingly more responsive. Gradually, their growing motor skills allow them to engage in more complex gesture games. In order to get attention and out of a need to interact, babies spend hours reaching for adults, playing peek-a-boo, dropping toys, and imitating sounds and body movements. One is always amazed at infants' persistence and lack of boredom.

This continual experience of social interaction acts in three ways. First, it establishes a pattern of interaction between parents and their children that is usually carried over into future parent-child interactions. For example, parents who are verbally responsive to their infant's early demands to play will tend to use language in later communications. Second, children often pattern future social interactions after those experienced and practiced at home in early relationships. Finally, children often identify with their parents' ways of responding in social interactions and may internalize and model these patterns in later relationships.

TODDLERHOOD

As children move toward and beyond the second birthday, they begin to show the first signs of increasing independence from their parents. This independence, however, is quite shaky, and, like their walking, toddlers teeter between independence and dependence, between needing the security and physical comforts of their parents and reaching out to explore their new world. Thus we see toddlers in a constant see-sawing pattern, with strong inner drives toward exploring their environment, reaching out, examining, touching, tasting, smelling, while at the same time continually checking on their parents to make sure they are available to them.

The phrase the "terrible two's," coined by A. Gesell (1948), is familiar to most parents. The child's urge toward exploration comes headlong into conflict with both the realities of the external world and the realities of the child's own limitations. Frustrated by these barriers, toddlers often lose control of their tenuously learned social behaviors, and temper tantrums result.

Around this period, the parents begin to more forcibly transmit society's rules to their children. They must use the appropriate silverware, they must not break things that are considered in the adult world to be important, and, most importantly, they must remove their daily bodily waste not in their diapers whenever they feel like it, but at a place and time demanded by the adults in their environment. This issue becomes a subtle test of wills in some families, creating unnecessary conflict and often setting up battle lines to be replayed with other focuses as the child matures. E.H. Erikson (1963) suggests that such battles often create feelings of incompetency on the part of the child.

During this time toddlers become effective verbal communicators, using the symbols of their culture, language, to begin to express their wants and needs and to expand their own reality. They begin to name things, categorize and identify objects, and discriminate between those things that are alike and those things that are different. During the end of this period they begin to expand their physical curiosity into verbal demands to know why. Why is the sky blue? Why do I hiccup? Why do I have to go to bed?

One can be fooled by toddlers' growing competency in language to assume that their understanding of the world is greater than it is. Toddlers have a very limited understanding of their world and often misinterpret things that happen, words that are spoken, and demands that are made upon them. For example, according to toddlers' perceptions of time and reality, parents who leave them for an evening out or, more traumatically, during a stay in the hospital are gone forever. This is because a toddler has no fixed concept of time.

Toddlers, as they move toward preschool and school age, have gained a great deal of confidence and knowledge about their environment, especially as compared with their first year of life. They are, however, still in need of a great deal of support, both physical and emotional, and continued guidance by their parents for many years to come.

PRESCHOOL YEARS

Preschoolers begin to both want and need more independence and control, which is usually expressed in their constantly testing limits. They slowly become more certain of their own abilities and have less need of their parents' constant supervision. My own daughter, at age three, expressed this best in her classic statement, "I'm the boss of me!" Armed with a primitive set of social rules of conduct, preschoolers expand their interactions with peers. Often, the play and communication of two three year olds seem to be occurring along parallel lines, with little true interaction, but the need for social contact is great at this age.

Play becomes an essential tool of childhood now. Preschoolers use play in a variety of ways to learn about their environment, about themselves, and about social relationships. They gradually develop a mastery of materials and can easily manipulate both tiny pegs and tricycles. They role-play endlessly, testing behaviors, trying on identities.

Self-Awareness

Preschoolers become increasingly aware of themselves as persons, separate from others. As expressed by L.J. Stone and J. Church (1975), "His awareness both of himself and of the environment increases as he becomes psychologically more differentiated from his surroundings, as he comes to distinguish between external events and internal ones, and as he learns to suspend action in favor of contemplation, thought, and feeling" (p. 285).

As a consequence of this increasing awareness, preschoolers become more conscious of their bodies and the body's sexuality and vulnerability to pain. Preschoolers are often beset with fears: of ghosts and witches, of the dark, and of death. They are often fearful of being mutilated, and medical treatment can often make these fears seem more realistic. For example, young children are often certain that blood tests will draw out *all* their blood, and they need a great deal of reassurance when treated.

Fears of death are quite pervasive. While preschoolers do not have the ability to think of death abstractly, they do understand that people and animals can die, and often they have had experience with a pet or older relative dying. Although the facts that they base their fears on are often confused and inconsistent, the fears are no less real. Joey, age five, had lost a grandfather recently. He died during surgery. A few weeks later, Joey's teacher told him that she was going to be out for a week, having surgery on her ankle. Joey burst into tears. "Don't die," he cried. "If you have surgery, you'll die." Joey needed much reassurance to overcome this fear.

As shall be detailed later, the separation from family during hospitalization and the need for frequent medical treatments that may entail pain or disfigurement can be particularly traumatic during the preschool years.

SCHOOL AGE YEARS

School age children are becoming more aware of the world around them. They are beginning to learn the rules of the world and gradually develop an internalized sense of what is right and what is wrong. One could say that the school age child begins to develop a conscience.

A number of important tasks confront the school age child. Although child development texts have often referred to this period as one of latency, or rest, school age children are in fact continuing to change in a complex interaction with their environment.

Friends play an increasingly important role in the life of a 5 to 12 year old. The rules they make and rigidly adhere to, the games they play, the clothes they wear, all have a great influence on school age children. They are moving farther away from the tight family circle. Other adults—teachers, community leaders, religious teachers—begin to play a prominent role in their lives. They begin to take responsibility for their physical care and spend increasingly less time at home and more time with friends and in school.

Being "normal," able to be competent in academic pursuits, social interactions, and physical sports is very important to the school age child. Equally important is the desire to be physically independent. Chronic illness and its effects can drastically interfere with these developmental tasks, as will be detailed later.

By the middle school years, the growing individual seems to possess the language and thought processes necessary to sustain logical abstract thinking and reasoning. Vocabulary may be quite extensive and precocious, and the school age child may be able to perform well in selected abstract academic subjects. This may be deceptive. As Stone and Church (1975) point out:

> The world of the middle-years child includes isolated domains or segments of experience which are logically organized and about which the child can reason in a mature fashion. However, the world as a whole has not yet come to be a coherent, integrated system, and clouds of magicalism surround and sometimes invade the more orderly realms of thought. (p. 399)

Information given to school age children in relation to their illness or required treatment needs to be disseminated carefully with an eye toward their still maturing but incomplete abstract abilities. A verbal, bright 11 year old was severely burned and required extensive surgery and rehabilitation. He often participated in discussions about the next treatment goals and was frequently present during medical rounds. At one point, he began to refuse all physical therapy services for range of motion—procrastinating, hiding from the therapist, and falling asleep immediately before scheduled therapy. After much questioning and discussion with the therapist, it was determined that Aaron had overheard that a simple surgical procedure could be done if physical therapy did not accomplish full range of motion. In a limited logical way, Aaron reasoned that he could avoid the long dreary hours of physical therapy and just have surgery later. He failed to remember, or take into account, the fact that even after surgery, he had to restart range of motion, and that surgery was vastly more painful than the physical therapy exercises.

The middle years of childhood, from 5 to 12, represent a crucial period in the life of an individual. Moving out of the security of the family, children must learn to create a place for themselves in the larger world of friends, school, and community. They bring with them their own inherent competencies, their experience with previous relationships, and their developing patterns of coping with frustration, failure, and success. And they continue to grow and change.

ADOLESCENCE

Adolescence is a time of changing demands and expectations. Adolescents are undergoing a period of rapid growth, hormonal changes, and changes in physical development. The boy's legs and arms seem suddenly longer and always in the way; the girl's face breaks out, she experiences her first menstrual cycle, and hair appears on legs, underarms, and in genital areas. As a result of these developments, adolescents are continually concerned about their bodies, their sexual identity, and their self-image.

At the same time, adolescents are facing new demands from society. They are seen as "adults-in-training" by society, which is all too anxious to mold them so that they conform. For adolescents in today's world, there are no simple rites of passage, no rituals of puberty. They are faced with a contradictory and confusing set of standards, one that often changes from country to country, from state to state. Society has no standard definitions of adulthood and no firm legal, biologic, or social guidelines (McCollum, 1975).

It is no wonder that the time of adolescence has been seen as a time of turmoil, of storm and stress. The adolescent is much like the preschooler—needing and deserving more physical and emotional independence from parents, yet ambivalent about breaking away from the security of home and family. Adolescents begin to move toward establishing an identity, defining themselves, their goals, their ambitions, and their future. They often use this time to try various roles, much like the dress-up play fantasies of the preschooler. They may become vegetarians, experiment with drugs, or perhaps turn toward religion or a "cause." Often, these roles are transitory and reflect a testing rather than a permanent choice of life style.

Adolescents begin to value the company, value judgments, and affection of their friends, often at the expense of their families' feelings. This movement toward emancipation, while painful to both parents and adolescents, is one of the primary developmental tasks of adolescence (Perkins, 1975).

A few issues, then, emerge as crucial in the life of the adolescent:

- accepting and adjusting to a changing body
- developing a sense of sexual identity and pleasurable sexual relationships
- achieving a measure of independence from family
- developing a sense of identity (Perkins, 1975)

YOUNG ADULTHOOD

In Erikson's model, young adults must confront the issues of intimacy versus isolation. They begin to develop meaningful affectional relationships with members of the opposite sex. They are also involved in planning or participating in vocational pursuits. They are attempting to define themselves as adults in the world of work and in the world of relationships. They continue to grow and change, to gain new insights into themselves and the world, and to effect change. This process, which is ongoing, allows individuals to continually alter their environment, or assimilate to it, in ways that are adaptive and productive.

COMPETENCY MODEL

The process of psychosocial growth described above is necessarily idealized, but it is one that clearly recognizes health and competency as ultimate goals in human development. While these goals are rarely actualized, such a model allows the educator or health professional to view the child in positive, humanistic ways. It represents a departure from the medical model, which often ignores the totality of the person, focusing on the pathology. It recognizes the strengths in people, their successful coping strategies, rather than their deficiencies. Most importantly, it sees growing children as central protagonists in their own development, rather than as passive recipients of either their hereditary makeup or environmental manipulation.

The next chapter will examine the ways that chronic illness can affect the growing child, as well as his or her family, and will review support systems that may be available in the community.

SUMMARY

The following chart delineates the crucial psychosocial issues and tasks that affect the developing individual.

Infancy (0–1)
   trust
   dependence
   attachment
   social interactions
Toddlerhood (1–2½)
   exploration
   bowel control
   autonomy
Preschool (2½–5)
   initiative
   limit-testing
   self-awareness
   play and fantasy
School Age (5–12)
   industry
   peer relationships
   competency in physical sports
Adolescence (12–18)
   body identity changes
   awareness of self as sexual being
   independence from family
Young Adulthood
   intimacy with others
   vocational pursuits
   choice of life styles

REFERENCES

Ainsworth, M.D.S., Blehar, M.C., Waters, E., & Wall, S. *Patterns of attachment: A psychological study of the strange situation.* Hillsdale, NJ: Lawrence Erlbaum, 1978.

Bower, T.G.R. *A primer of infant development.* San Francisco: W.H. Freemand & Company, 1977.

Bowlby, J. *Attachment and loss* (Vol. 1). New York: Basic Books, 1969.

Erikson, E.H. *Childhood and society.* New York: W.W. Norton, 1963.

Gesell, A. *Studies in child development.* New York: Harper & Brothers, 1948.

Kagan, J., Kearsley, R., & Zelazo, P. *Infancy: Its place in human development.* Cambridge, MA: Harvard University Press, 1979.

Lamb, M. The father's role in the infant's social world. In *Mother/child, father/child relationships.* J. Stevens and M. Mathews (eds.), Washington, D.C.: National Association for the Education of Young Children, 1978.

McCollum, A. *Coping with prolonged health impairment in your child.* Boston: Little, Brown, and Company, 1975.

Perkins, H. *Human development.* California: Wadsworth Publishing Company, 1975.

Stone, L.J., & Church, J. *Childhood and adolescence* (3rd ed.). New York: Random House, 1975.

BIBLIOGRAPHY

Bandura, A. *Principles of behavior modification.* New York: Holt, Rinehart and Winston, Inc., 1969.

Bee, H. *The developing child.* New York: Harper & Row, 1975.

Freud, A. *Studies in child development.* New York: International Universities Press, 1946.

Hall, C.S., & Lindzey, G. *Theories of personality* (3rd ed.). New York: John Wiley & Sons, 1978.

Ilg, F.L., & Ames, L.B. *Child behavior.* New York: Harper & Row, 1955.

Piaget, J. *The essential Piaget* (H.E. Gruber & J.J. Voneche, Eds. and trans.). New York: Basic Books, 1977.

Skinner, B.F. *Science and human behavior.* New York: Macmillan, 1953.

Chapter 3

The Impact of Chronic Illness

OVERVIEW

Chapter 2 attempted to provide a psychosocial framework within which the impact of chronic illness upon the developing child can be explored. But the child is not an isolated entity. He or she is a child within a family system, with a unique social and cultural heritage. Because chronic illness affects the family system as well, this chapter will review its impact upon the parents and siblings of the chronically ill child. Separating these factors will be necessary for the following discussion, although it should be understood that the child's perspective is intimately bound up within the reactions of the family and is, in fact, often altered by their responses to stress. For example, the excessive tensions in a family as they try to cope with a new diagnosis of asthma may create excessive fears of dying in the child. Alternatively, a family's ability to cope successfully with stress may enable the child with a terminal illness to come to terms with imminent death.

THE CHILD'S PERSPECTIVE

Each chronic illness brings with it unique effects; the age of onset, the severity of symptoms, the degree of pain or discomfort, and the life-threatening specter all differ from one diagnosis to another. The chapters that follow will provide the reader with information describing these specific effects for the most common chronic illnesses. This chapter will explore those elements common to most chronic illnesses as they affect the child and his or her family.

Children are vulnerable, and chronic illness increases this vulnerability. In all but the mildest conditions, chronic illness interrupts normal developmental continuity. Its effects are global. Many children experience pain or lack of

35

normal motor control. The very young child may be psychologically harmed by the lack of consistent mothering due to frequent hospitalizations. In addition, there are special stresses that accompany specific disorders, such as the fear of suffocation in asthma, the unpredictability of symptoms in seizures, and the fear of death in terminal illness. The child must grow up with a perpetual feeling of being different, unique. As Mary Robinson (1980) poignantly states, the child grows up with the sense that "your body can betray you." Often, the physical condition or necessary treatments limit the full range of motor abilities and interfere with the child's normal life experiences.

This is often the case when young children's activity levels need to be drastically curtailed, as in rheumatic heart conditions, or when children are repeatedly hospitalized and physically restrained by intravenous setups, dialysis units, or casting.

Ake Mattsson (1972) notes that the child is also stressed by the changes in the emotional climate of the family. Times of acute stress or crisis usually bring on support and care by the parents. As symptoms remiss, parents and children often develop an unrealistic expectation that they will return to normal. These stresses often affect the child's psychological growth. As Mattsson summarizes (1972):

> The final outcome of the child's attempts at mastering the continuous stress associated with his disability cannot be assessed until young adulthood. Each progressive step in his emotional, intellectual, and social development changes the psychologic impact of the illness on his personality and on his family, and usually equips him with better means to cope. Changes in disease process and in family circumstances will also affect the adaptational process. (p. 805)

The child's developmental stage and behavioral characteristics prior to the onset of illness will also have an effect upon his or her responses to the illness. The hyperactive child will have great difficulty when physically confined, the child who has had no structure or limit-setting at home may continually test the limits and the patience of medical staff, while the frightened, fearful child may withdraw and become lethargic and nonresponsive to staff or to treatments. Toddlers, just mastering ambulation, may be fearful of walking after repeated surgery. Adolescents, with strong needs to be accepted by peers as equals, may refuse to comply with medical treatments that alter their physical appearance, such as taking steroids or wearing jobst stockings.

H.A. Sultz, E.R. Schlesinger, J.G. Feldman, and W.E. Mosher (1972) report findings that indicate a correlation between emotional and behavioral deviations and the onset and episodic recurrence of certain chronic conditions that have strong psychophysiological components, such as ulcers, asthma, and eczema. Overdependence, insecurity, and unchanneled hostility were found in a number of studies (Dubo et al., 1961; Sultz et al., 1970).

Chapter 2 followed the child through a series of issues and tasks that were most relevant at each stage of development. The reader's attention will again be directed to these stages to assess the impact that chronic illness has upon them.

Infants

The reader will recall that the basic Eriksonian issue of infancy is the development of trust. Infants' lives revolve around establishing basic relationships, feeding and being fed, and beginning to explore the world through their senses and their growing motor abilities. How does the presence of a chronic illness interfere with these basic needs?

The diagnosis of chronic illness in infancy is often made within the first days or weeks of life, necessitating prolonged hospitalization after birth. The conditions that are most often diagnosed at birth are quite severe: heart defects, meningomyelocele, and some cases of cystic fibrosis. Hospitals, with their established routines and complicated medical procedures, often unwittingly discourage parents' participation in the care of a sick newborn. Parents may feel overwhelmed by the diagnosis and its implications and may be afraid to touch or hold their children for fear of hurting them. They may have been told that the prognosis for the child's recovery is quite poor and consequently may be afraid to become attached to a child they will soon lose. On occasion parents may actually begin to mourn for their child and accept his or her death. When such children survive, parents often find it difficult to become "reattached." Some parents find it difficult to accept a sick child, and a subtle rejection process begins to occur. They visit the hospital less often, they willingly abdicate their role of parent to the nurses and other professionals caring for their child, and they may even find excuses for postponing discharge to home.

These factors can all combine to create a sense of mistrust in the infant, which may interfere with future attempts to relate to others and to trust others. Sandy, born with meningomyelocele, underwent numerous painful surgical techniques during her first two years of life. Her family was chaotic and unsupportive, and Sandy spent those years in hospitals, treated by a succession of caretakers. As a young adult, still living in a chronic hospital setting, Sandy had never developed lasting relationships. She had, however, developed a coping strategy of "using" staff to meet her needs for affection by cajoling them into buying presents for her and bringing her special treats.

Food has special meaning for infants and for their parents. It is equated with love and attention and is the baby's main source of gratification. When infants need to be on special diets and parents must restrict their intake of certain foods, parents often feel guilty and confused. This anxiety is often felt by the infant. Infants with intestinal disorders may suffer great pain and discomfort from feeding. What kind of a message does this send to a young infant when food brings pain rather than pleasure?

Infants born with chronic disorders often need to undergo a series of painful surgical procedures and other treatments. As Georgia Travis (1976) expresses it, the infant "cannot distinguish whether the pain comes from outside or inside. He is completely vulnerable to the shock of pain and has no tools whatsoever to express distress except cries of rage" (p. 57). Such infants often spend many months immobilized in cribs or casts. Yet infants have strong inner drives toward movement and toward exploration of their environment. How can a four month old take pleasure in discovering his own toes and fingers if they are encased in plaster casts or restrained by I.V. setups? What effect does this have on later growth, both physical and psychological? Although there are no definitive studies to confirm this, clinical observation leads one to realize that for the infant, chronic illness can have lifelong consequences. Without the development of a framework of basic trust, the child may grow up to view the world and his or her place in it as fragmented and threatening.

Sensitive hospital policies can go a long way towards lessening this stress and the resulting trauma. Families should be encouraged to participate as much as possible in the care of their chronically ill infant. They should be allowed to provide as normal an environment as possible for their growing infant, both physically and emotionally.

On a visit to the infant intensive care unit of a city hospital, this author observed a scene that exemplifies this sensitivity. A premature infant, weighing only 2½ lbs, was surrounded by machines that monitored heartbeat, respiration, and urinary output. Every available body opening was attached by tube to a machine. The effect was inhuman. Yet in the crib was a soft, fuzzy teddy bear, placed so that the infant could see it, and next to the crib sat the infant's mother, gently singing a lullaby in a low voice.

Toddlers

As children move toward the second year of life, they begin to test their own capacities, to explore their world and their ability to control and manipulate it. Erikson (1963) sees this stage as one that concerns itself with the striving toward autonomy. The normal toddler brings to this task an energy level and curiosity that stagger the imagination and could exhaust the best-trained athlete. When toddlers are burdened by chronic illness, their energy levels are often affected, and they may be listless and tired, as in leukemia and cystic fibrosis, or suffer from pain when attempting to move independently. Issues of control are affected as well. Toddlers with meningomyelocele may have little or no bowel or bladder control. They may not be able to do for themselves those simple tasks that help to develop a feeling of competency and mastery, such as feeding oneself or climbing a flight of stairs, or even obtaining a toy out of reach.

Hospitalization and separation from family members is very traumatic for the toddler. The toddler's thrust toward independence is still tentative and depends upon the sense of security and trust that comes with the knowledge that someone special will be available in case of need. Descriptions by M.D.S. Ainsworth, M.C. Blehar, E. Waters, and S. Wall (1975) of children in strange surroundings vividly depict toddlers freely exploring their environment, then rushing back towards mother to touch base before returning to the strange toys they are offered. Toddlers separated from their parents often display extreme distress and often regress behaviorally to compensate for their loss. A sense of abandonment persists. Toddlers, having no clear concept of time, may view this as permanent. J. Bowlby's studies (1975) of reaction to separation describe three basic stages: protest, despair, and finally detachment or denial.

Hospitalization also takes away from toddlers their newly gained sense of control over their bodies. They may not be able to run and climb and explore if they are in bulky casts or attached to machines. They cannot refuse medicines as they refuse foods at home. Generally, they are pushed backwards into the infancy stage.

Again, sensitive hospital policies can go far in ameliorating most of these effects. Parents should be encouraged to room-in and care for their children, and programs should be offered to allow toddlers to continue to explore their environment in playrooms and at cribside. Whenever possible, as few caretakers as possible should be assigned to the child, to provide continuity of care. Normal functions and behaviors should be encouraged, such as self-feeding and exploration of the environment.

At home, parents need to allow their toddlers continual freedom to explore their environment and to act independently. This can be hampered when parents are fearful of the excessive bleeding that may result from a fall in a child suffering from hemophilia or when routines of care take up much of the time and energy of both parents and child, as in cystic fibrosis.

Preschoolers

Preschoolers begin to engage more with the world around them. They are becoming more aware of their bodies, of their abilities to interact with and master their environment. They have a rich fount of language and often use play and fantasy to explore their feelings and thoughts. Again, chronic illness affects these normal processes, interfering with developmental continuity and with their inner drives toward more independence. Their medical condition may require that their parents retain control and responsibility for bodily care beyond the age when normal preschoolers are assuming some of that control. Thus, children limited by meningomyelocele or muscular dystrophy may need physical assistance in dressing themselves or toileting. Food intake may need to be carefully monitored, and certain foods restricted or limited. Parents may be used to performing a variety of intrusive medical treatments such as daily insulin injections or frequent postural drainage. They may need to continue these treatments well into the school years, either because of the child's inability to take over such functions or the parents' inability to give up the control. In either event, the effect is often to infantilize the preschooler, thus postponing the attainment of physical independence and mastery.

The natural limit-testing behaviors of preschoolers conflict with parental needs to provide adequate medical care. Care needs to be taken to allow preschoolers opportunities to make choices, to have control over a part of their lives, and to occasionally say no.

Illness as Punishment

Preschoolers are becoming increasingly aware of their bodies at this time. Fears of mutilation and disfigurement often accompany this growing awareness. Armed with a primitive sense of cause and effect relationships, they often view their illness as punishment for real or imagined crimes. A vase or ashtray broken the morning of an acute asthmatic attack is often seen as the precipitating cause for the attack, and the pain from a sickle cell crisis may be viewed as just punishment for evil thoughts of retribution against an older brother. Parents frequently feed into these visions, either consciously or unconsciously. They may themselves have limited understanding of the causes of certain diseases or may use the fear of recurrent attacks as a weapon to force compliance. "If you run wild, you'll get an attack," and "If you're not good, you'll have to go back to the hospital for shots," are examples of threats often heard in doctors' waiting rooms.

Just as illness is seen by these children as a punishment, the treatments frequently administered may also be viewed as painful and punishing. Increasingly, medical technology has provided us with an arsenal of sophisticated medical procedures. A child with spina bifida may, by age five, have undergone three or more painful surgical operations, necessitating months of immobilization in casts. Bone marrow tests and transplants in cancer and range of motion exercises used to help children with rheumatoid arthritis can cause severe pain as well. Hospitalization is also viewed as punishment, and the preschooler often reacts with fear to such separations. The child's active imagination can frequently change neutral x-ray or dialysis machines into fearful monsters or dreaded extraterrestrial beings. These fantasies can also be used by parents and hospital staff to assist the child in relating to these machines. More than one child has embarked on fantastic voyages to other planets via an x-ray table. However, care must be taken to explain treatments as well as possible, in language and concepts appropriate to the child's developmental level, to allay fears of punishment and mutilation. Upon overhearing that a simple operation was to be performed on him to remove an "impacted stool," a bright four-year-old boy with spina bifida became petrified of sitting on small chairs. He couldn't understand how a "stool" had managed to get inside him, but he wasn't taking any more chances. Clearly, language must be adjusted to each child's understanding.

Play and Illness

Hospitalization is a time of great stress for a child. Illness changes the child's characteristic life patterns, and separation from familiar places, people, and routines can create great anxiety. Children must surrender to strange adults their freedom, privacy, and sense of control and submit to painful and frightening experiences (Adams, 1976). Play can be seen as a tool to help children master anxiety and explore and understand their feelings. Because a child remains a child while hospitalized, there must be recognition that play experiences that foster normal development are an essential component of hospital play. As Adams (1976) points out, "Play in the hospital setting allows a child to engage in an activity that is reminiscent of life outside the hospital" (p. 418).

The young child's normal life-style is daily involved with play, with social interaction, and with learning about his or her world. For the hospitalized child, these experiences need to be provided to assure continued growth. The developing child cannot afford an interruption of these experiences. Thus, according to N. Plank (1962),

> When a child is hospitalized, the hospital has to take on tasks beyond its healing function: Tasks which must be accomplished so the rhythm of life and growth can go on. The child's normal way of living involves relating to other children, to grownups, and to play and learning. They have to be skillfully fitted into a day filled with diagnostic and treatment procedures. The task is complicated by the threat of illness itself, of operations, and the possible nearness of death. (p. 1)

School Age Children

The school age child must deal with issues of competency, mastery, and peer relationships. According to Erikson, this is a period characterized by the striving for industrious habits. This goal is intimately bound up with developing a sense of self-worth and the need to achieve status academically, socially, and in games that require physical prowess and stamina.

School age children look toward peers and adults outside the family to measure their self-worth. It is an age that relies heavily on being like one of the gang. Children with chronic illness may, for the first time, come into contact with the stares and teasing of peers. Some conditions or the necessary treatments leave a child looking quite different from the normal school age child. The puffy moon face or short stature of a child on steroids, the hacking cough of a cystic child, lack of hair, protruding abdomen, or pallor can all act to isolate children before they have a chance to prove their ability. Such children often are shy socially, since they have had little opportunity for social contacts at home or in the hospital. Being different, being labeled as "baldy" or "stinky," can be devastating to such a child.

Chronically ill children often suffer from a lowered energy level and are likely to be unable to compete physically with their peer group. Often, academic pursuits are viewed as a natural outlet for such children, allowing them to compensate for their illness by pouring all their energies into schoolwork.

A number of chronically ill children are able to cope successfully by devoting themselves to academic studies and by psychologically dealing with the trauma of their illness through a process of intellectualization. By age eleven or twelve, many of these children exhibit a knowledge of their disease, its prognosis, and possible treatment modalities that may equal that of their medical caretakers. These children often seem supersophisticated, using technical jargon and occasionally providing support to newly diagnosed peers in hospital or outpatient clinics.

Unfortunately, this ability to compensate for the effects of chronic illness through academic pursuits is available to only a small percentage of children with chronic illness. For the great majority, especially those suffering from sickle cell anemia, leukemia, cystic fibrosis, spina bifida, hemophilia, arthritis, and other serious chronic conditions, recurrent crises and the need for periodic hospitalization seriously interfere with their schooling. In a study of children with long-term illness conducted in Erie County, Pennsylvania between 1946 and 1961, researchers found that at least 26 percent of the population studied were well below grade level (Sultz et al., 1972).

While the question of grade may be complicated by a number of other variables aside from the chronic illness, such as learning disabilities or mental retardation, such a statistic is nevertheless significant. A full quarter of their sample had missed at least six weeks of schooling per year (Sultz et al., 1972). As was noted in an earlier chapter, most programs for the homebound or hospitalized population in the United States fail to make allowances for the population of chronically ill children who may miss only a few days at a time during the school year, but who are absent overall for a considerable portion of the school year. Such inconsistent attendance, combined with the child's feeling of differentness, often leads to a sense of inferiority and consequent fear of the school setting. A child who is absent from school for a week while undergoing tests or recovering from a crisis may return to a classroom in which the children have formed tight cliques and in which the teacher is discussing a review of work covered during the child's absence. It may be easier for such a child to feign a headache or other symptom and return home to the safety and security of the family than to attempt to break through this barrier. The more extended the absence, the more difficult it becomes for the child to return to the classroom and become reintegrated into the academic and social mainstream. Children with invisible illnesses such as sickle cell anemia, asthma, and diabetes may find such integration more difficult then those with more visible signs of their differences. M. Debuskey (1970) notes that visible handicaps may be easier to explain and may engender feelings of samaritanism among peers. The more normal a child looks, the less his or her weaknesses or restrictions are taken into account by peers.

Fear of Dying

Finally, school age children, unlike preschoolers, gradually develop an understanding of their own vulnerability, their own mortality. As they approach adolescence, they begin to come face to face with the possibilities of death or the death of the healthy adult they will never become. They may become more dependent upon parents, avoiding even natural risks, overly fearful of precipitating a medical crisis. Fearful of bodily mutilation, increasingly uncertain of their own self-worth, school age children often retreat into themselves. How they react to their condition depends upon a combination of interwoven factors and, as B.R. Myers points out (1975), "one may observe varying combinations of denial, rebellion, immaturity, overdependence, excessive independence, depression, anxiety, passive resignation, or mature acceptance, depending upon the many influences on the attitudes of the affected child" (p. 104).

Adolescents

As chronically ill children move toward adolescence, the psychosocial stresses upon them increase dramatically. They are faced with the issue of identity, defining themselves in an increasingly complex world, striving for independence from their families and for control of their own lives. As Georgia Travis (1976) notes, "Adolescence is a period when the self-image coalesces. If it incorporates hundreds of negative perceptions of self elicited by bodily limitation and negative reactions from others, the youth feels different, and inferior" (p. 61).

Body Image

Those who have ever lived with a teenager or remember their own adolescence will recall the havoc a pimple or unruly hair can wreak upon the self-image. How much more devastating must a puffy face or baldness or the smell of urine from an ostomy bag be to the chronically ill adolescent? For adolescents who have had their disease for a number of years, reactions to the long-term use of drugs like steroids or Dilantin may begin to appear. There is often a retardation of growth and the subsequent delay of puberty in a number of conditions such as cystic fibrosis, sickle cell anemia, and renal failure. The adolescent's already damaged body may be assaulted by the continued need for daily injections, dialysis, blood transfusions, or postural drainage, thus further damaging an already fragile body image. For adolescents, body image is intimately tied up with their growing sexual awareness. Often, their real or perceived lack of attractiveness to the opposite sex begins to affect their social life. Even for those children who had been able to maintain a somewhat normal social life with same-sex peers, the onset of puberty may have the effect of thrusting them into the role of the social isolate. Frequently, social restrictions occur as the unfortunate byproduct of the condition or its treatment. The child on dialysis three times weekly cannot meet the gang for a special after-school outing, the leukemic child may be gradually losing energy and be unable to stay up late for parties, and the hemophiliac cannot go mountain climbing or skiing during the school holidays. Often, adolescents' sense of inferiority or social differentness leads them to use their illness to avoid social contacts. They may be ashamed of their disability; fearful of being exposed during a social event by a coughing fit or seizure; or fearful of marriage and future commitments, especially if their disease is inherited or degenerative. They may retreat into the world of home or hospital as a safe place, one in which they are accepted in spite of their disability. Many adolescents with chronic illness, especially those from families that have been unable to provide them with a nurturing, supportive environment, treat the staff at their local hospital as their social peers or parents. They often stop by the adolescent floor for a chat with nurses, social workers, or child life specialists after school and occasionally may precipitate a medical crisis through noncompliance so that they will be readmitted for a time in the hospital.

Randy's medical condition should have been well controlled by drugs and self-administered physical therapy. Yet she often was brought to the hospital in crisis, having failed to take her pills or perform her therapy. Each return to the adolescent ward was like a return home; she knew the staff and routines as well as the nurses on duty. She often precipitated a crisis during holidays, spending her Christmas and Easter vacations at the hospital. For Randy, whose family was nonsupportive and unable to cope with her continuing medical problems, the hospital environment provided an alternative family and social milieu, one that was safe from the critical stares of peers and one that provided her with the physical security she could not find at home.

For adolescents searching for identity, the opinions or reactions of others take on added significance. Wheelchair-bound by muscular dystrophy or spina bifida, bald or obese or with excessive facial hair, the chronically ill adolescent often becomes stigmatized (Goffman, 1963), and "shame becomes a central possibility, arising from the individual's perception of one of his own attributes as being a defiling thing to possess..." (p. 17). For such adolescents, the move from the relative security of their neighborhood primary school to the larger, less personal setting of junior or senior high school can be a devastating experience. Often, these children achieve a small measure of acceptance by teachers and peers in the lower grades, and the need to face the stares and teasing of strangers may precipitate a medical or psychological crisis. A similar process may occur for those children who suffer the visible aftereffects of a severe burn or accident. In such cases, the return to school after the relative safety and security of home and hospital should be done gradually, with professional staff helping the adolescent to develop the coping skills necessary to face the prospect of peer rejection.

Defenses

With or without such help, an adolescent's response to the social stresses resulting from chronic illness or injury will be individualized, although a few patterns are commonly observed. These psychological defense mechanisms, seen by Ake Mattsson (1980) as "unconscious means of making a threatening reality more bearable," are withdrawal, depression, denial, acting out, and regression.

Some adolescents *withdraw* from the possible effect of stigmatization, choosing instead to drop out of school or to return to a very restricted but more secure environment, such as a school for the orthopedically handicapped. Their affect may be poor, and they may seem to have little interest in anything and little energy to pursue even simple daily routines. Occasionally, such a child may become severely depressed. As Georgia Travis (1976) notes, mild depression is not uncommon in adolescence. Faced with the prospect of the loss of a normal future, adolescents suffering from chronic illness or the results of an accident may realistically need a time to grieve. A long-term depression, expressed by loss of interest in daily events or future plans, listlessness, resignation, and apathy, may require professional intervention. Occasionally, depressed adolescents may talk of suicide, of "giving it all up." G. Godene (personal communication) suggests that such threats should be taken seriously and responded to by professional therapeutic intervention. Pat phrases such as "it's not that bad," or "you'll get over it" are not helpful or realistic and often anger the adolescent. The severe scars of a burn or loss of abilities and paralysis are often permanent and need to be accepted.

Denial is often used as a protection against the devastating emotional effects of chronic illness or accident or the prospect of terminal illness. At times, adolescents may use this coping strategy to refuse further necessary treatments and thus precipitate a medical crisis. Many adolescents use denial in attempting to deal with the effects of spinal cord injury, refusing to believe that their condition is permanent and seeking external causes for their continued paralysis. Tommy was such a patient. Injured in an automobile accident at age 15 and totally paralyzed from the chest down, he talked often of the doctor's lack of faith in him, the physical therapist's unwillingness to take the trouble to order full leg braces as the reasons for his failure to walk again. He insisted that he needed more physical therapy than was offered, and yet often slept late, thereby missing scheduled outpatient appointments. It took a protracted inpatient stay in a rehabilitative center, with Tommy participating in setting therapy goals and schedules, for him to begin to accept the reality of his disability. Often, denial is helpful to adolescents as an escape against overwhelming fear of death or permanent disfigurement. Caution should be used in attempting to help a person accept reality. Denial may at times be an effective and necessary coping strategy.

Adolescence is a time for *testing limits*. Often, this is carried to an extreme, and the chronically ill adolescent may begin to disregard medical limitations to the point of risking death. This may also occur in a form of depression in which adolescents faced with the hopelessness of their condition, as in leukemia or inoperable heart or kidney disease, may refuse further treatment. The loneliness and boredom of social isolation may lead adolescents to abuse substances such as drugs and alcohol that allow them to escape their reality. Their familiarity with drugs and their use in the management of their illness or pain may make such abuses more frequent in this population and may give them a social advantage in peer groups.

Anger and rage at their plight may lead adolescents to *act out* physically, verbally abusing hospital staff, parents, peers, and siblings. Sarcasm and name-calling are frequently used by adolescents immobilized for long periods of time. J.E. Schowalter (1977) notes that for many teenagers, the fear of being unable to protect themselves from a threatening situation and the shame and embarrassment of being helpless combine to produce an overwhelming sense of rage, expressed verbally and physically toward others.

Pain, the forced dependency upon others in many forms of chronic illness, and the interference with normal developmental continuity all combine to make *regression* a common coping strategy for adolescents. Adolescents are attempting to move toward more independence and often feel ambivalent toward parental control. This normal ambivalence is exacerbated for the teenager with chronic illness. Often it may be easier to retreat backwards to an early stage, to be pampered and protected, rather than attempt to break away from parents. Weakened physically, with inadequate social skills, unused to risk-taking, the chronically ill adolescent may accept infantilization by parents or even demand to be cared for. This issue, dependency versus independence, is especially poignant for those adolescents suffering from progressively degenerating diseases, such as Friedreich's ataxia or muscular dystrophy. Just when normal children are beginning to achieve more physical and social independence, they are becoming less independent, gradually requiring the kind of total care and supervision given to infants, while remaining mentally alert and aware of their increasing dependency on others.

Parents can play a crucial role in helping chronically ill adolescents maintain a realistic, healthy balance between dependency and independence, between appropriate limit-testing and reckless risk-taking. The roots for creating a positive environment for optimal growth are founded in the earliest parent-child interactions and will be discussed later.

Fear of Death

By the time adolescence is reached, cognitively intact individuals are able to understand the abstract concepts of death and mortality. In Piagetian terms, they have attained the stage of formal operational thought and are capable of understanding the permanence and irreversability of death. For those adolescents suffering from leukemia or other cancers, hemophilia, or inoperable heart or kidney disease, such a realization is devastating. A sense of despair and hopelessness may persist, occasionally resulting in depression or refusals to comply with future treatments. A number of sensitive ethical issues arise out of this dilemma. Although they will be discussed in detail in Chapter 8, which deals with the special issues of the dying child, it should be noted that the right to consent to or refuse treatment exists for adult patients. The legal rights of minors is a complex issue and one that has been given great attention lately. According to A.R. Holder (1977), a minor who has been given the right to consent to treatment also has the legal right to refuse treatment. The parents and professionals dealing with a dying adolescent need to carefully evaluate the teenager's mental status, the prognosis for the disease, and their own feelings when counseling such a child. There are unfortunately no easy answers. One should always take seriously the concerns of adolescents who fear death and handle their questions openly and honestly. Occasionally, the fear of death may be unrealistic, based upon false or distorted information. Explanations should be given as often as necessary, handled with sensitivity and honesty.

Future Planning

Vocational planning for chronically ill adolescents will be affected by a number of factors. Choices may be limited by the nature and extent of their illness and the concomitant limitation of abilities. Life span may be shortened considerably, thus making careers that require extensive training periods unrealistic. The individual's own personality, interests, abilities, and talents, aside from the illness, clearly affect choice as well. Too often, vocational counselors will suggest a career goal well-suited to the disability rather than to the person. Sadly, the opportunities for job training, vocational habilitation and rehabilitation, and realistic job openings are scarce in the United States, with long waiting lists and often unrealistic prerequisites. Examples abound of bright wheelchair-bound young adults sitting at home or in rehabilitation facilities, watching T.V., unable to find the right combination of living quarters, job, and transportation. With unemployment figures high and chronic in both recessionary and nonrecessionary times, even those young adults with mild handicaps are at a disadvantage in the job market. Often, years of missed schooling adds to their handicap, making them particularly vulnerable to layoffs and unemployment. There is a need for careful, realistic vocational guidance, tied to educational programming and provided to chronically ill youngsters on an ongoing basis beginning in their early teens. Specific educational strategies will be discussed in later chapters.

As the adolescent reaches young adulthood, issues of career choices, marriage, and independent living become important. For some, independence will never be achieved, either because of the effects of the illness directly or as a result of the illness's intervention in developmental continuity. For most, coping with chronic illness and its stresses is life-long; the diabetic worries that she will have a difficult pregnancy and endanger the life of her infant; the job pressures for a young man or woman with asthma may precipitate an attack; ostomies and shunt sites begin to break down and need to be repaired; or a second kidney transplant may be rejected.

The way children cope with these stresses is dependent upon the complex interplay of forces mentioned earlier: the child's age, temperament, and personality; the severity of the condition; the family system and its reactions and strengths; and the presence of supportive professionals. The preceding section detailed some of the mediating variables from the perspective of the growing child. The family system will now be examined, with emphasis on those aspects that affect the child with a chronic illness and those that are affected by the presence of a chronically ill child in the family.

FAMILY SYSTEM

Family Functioning

In their study of child health, I.B. Pless and B.B. Satterwhite (1975) developed a family functioning index to examine the relationship between a family's ability to function and their child's psychological adjustment to chronic illness. They suggest that a full understanding of family dynamics is vital in understanding the effects a family has upon the chronically ill child. Among those dimensions examined were family size, relationships within the family, decision-making patterns, and the communication patterns established by families. Families can be assessed by investigating the degree to which they function along these dimensions in a stable, harmonious pattern. Each of us has had the experience of being in a family, as child and possibly as parent, and we have had the opportunity to know other families and observe their patterns of functioning both personally and professionally. Out of these observations, some common perceptions emerge. Family systems are unique; no two are truly alike. They are dynamic, changing over time and in reaction to external pressures such as death, marriage, divorce, and illness. Families develop and move through stages, much as the individual confronts and masters various tasks at various ages. Young families with preschool children have very different needs, and family members often play different roles within their system than families whose children have grown and established independent lives and families of their own.

Within the last decade, new alternative family patterns have developed; there are many more single-parent homes than previously; divorce and remarriage have created complex three- and four-parent family networks; some families are experimenting with multiple family living arrangements. The economy and changing life styles have also had a dramatic impact upon family functioning. Two-parent working families are becoming commonplace, with concomitant changes in child care patterns. All of these factors act upon the ability of families to function in a stable, organized fashion. The degree to which a family unit is functioning successfully prior to a major crisis such as the onset of chronic illness will play a major role in that family's reaction to the crisis, and ultimately in their ability to adjust to the change that such a situation produces in the family system. Studies of stress and its effects upon individuals and family systems are abundant in the literature. While it is generally noted that some stress can be constructive and act as a catalyst for growth and change, there are limits to the amount of stress a person or family can functionally manage. These limits depend upon a number of factors, such as the system's vulnerability, the suddenness of the stress, the family's capacity to endure stress, and the number or severity of other stressful conditions (Travis, 1976). When faced with the diagnosis of chronic illness, families who are functioning marginally are more likely to become disorganized and chaotic than those that are functioning more optimally. For all families, the diagnosis of chronic illness in a child is a traumatic event, one that is likely to be disintegrative rather than integrative at least in the short term (Magrab, 1978). J. Bruhn (1977) reports an increase in divorce rates following diagnosis of chronic illness.

Chronic illness represents a major loss for a family in that they must relinquish their hopes and expectations for the normal child, while anticipating changes in life patterns, routines, daily management, and finances. If this crisis occurs in families that exhibit serious disturbances either in the parent-child relationship or in the relationship between the parents, the family's ability to come to grips with the reality of the diagnosis and to begin to develop strategies to adjust to the crisis and learn to cope adequately may be hampered in a variety of ways. For example, a family for whom the child serves as an expression of their own goals and aspirations may be devastated by that child's illness and concomitant inability to fulfill their high role expectations. Thus, the future quarterback for the Colts may develop muscular dystrophy, or the future physician become the victim of cancer. In another circumstance, a mother who is unable to accept the growing independence and separateness of her child may use the occasion of that child's illness to provide her with the justification for overprotectiveness and the consequent stifling of her child's groping toward autonomy.

Family Structure

In examining family functioning and its relationship to chronic illness, another dimension deserves special consideration, that of the structure of the family unit. As Georgia Travis (1976) notes, when there is a chronically ill child in the family, the need for the presence of two adults is manifest. With greatly increased financial pressures, one parent at least must bring in a steady income. But the special care and attention needed by a sick child at home or in the hospital requires the parents to be available, often 24 hours a day. Two parents can spell each other at the hospital or the child's bedside during a painful or frightening crisis. Often, the young teenager with a physical disability requires the aid of two adults to be bathed or transferred from bed to wheelchair, from car to home. Added to these physical demands is the everpresent need for parents to provide emotional support to each other, to share the grief as well as the chores.

Imagine, then, the dilemma faced by a single parent, having to balance the needs of the child against the need to be a full-time wage earner; the need for love and support versus the everpresent burdens of caring for an ill child.

Parents may live together, but if their style of communication is maladaptive and they cannot function effectively as a team in times of crisis, the needed supports will be lacking, both for the parents and for the child.

The size of the family also has implications for the chronically ill child. As summarized by Travis (1976), only children may be excessively isolated, with no peer contacts, having parents who tend to devote an excessive amount of attention toward them, while large families present problems of excessive fatigue on the part of the parents and usually suffer from a lower financial base than smaller families. Siblings can, however, be sources of support for parents and chronically ill children, sharing the physical labor, bringing in the outside world to the child, and providing a measure of peer interaction.

Reaction to Crisis

Taking into account all of the various dimensions involved in an analysis of family functioning, it is readily apparent that, while some families function better than others, all need supports, personal and institutional, in times of crisis. As Ake Mattsson (1980) notes, there exists, for families of chronically ill children, a lifelong need for intervention in times of crisis, caused by either the situational context or other family problems. In reference to the above discussion of stress, it becomes clear that for families with chronically ill children, chronic stress becomes an integral part of the family's coping strategy. Thus, new stresses placed upon the family as they continue to grow occur against a background of a family more vulnerable to stress and its characteristic potential for family disorganization.

Professional intervention is vital for those families who, already plagued by disorganization and dysfunction, face the crisis of chronic illness.

Even for families whose lives are relatively stable, the onset of chronic illness in a child may necessitate short-term therapeutic intervention. When a child is born with or develops a serious, potentially life-threatening illness, the family system is thrown into a period of disorganization. Feelings of shock and anxiety predominate. Depending upon the severity of the illness and the prognosis, there may be a constant fear that the child will not survive. P.D. Steinhauer, M.B. Mushin, and Q. Rae-Grant (1974) suggest that "the more debilitating the illness and the poorer the prognosis, particularly in a previously healthy child, the greater the stress on the family" (p. 830). The age of onset and diagnosis also affect the degree of stress that families undergo. If the condition is diagnosed at birth, so that the child was never normal to the parents except in their idealized image, a process of mourning for the expected ideal may occur. Such parents often find it difficult to become attached to their child, especially if the infant requires extensive hospitalizations or frequent surgery. If, however, the child has been normal for a period of years, its place in the family may be established, and the parents may have complex expectations for the child. The loss of a healthy child needs also to be mourned, but this process is complicated by the relationships and goals that existed prior to the onset of the illness. As a general rule, the longer and the more the child was seen as normal, the less likely that the onset of illness will interfere permanently with the child's development and with preexisting family relationships.

Given time and sensitive supportive professionals and friends, families begin to come to grips with the reality of chronic illness in their lives. But the initial shock that accompanies the onset does not constitute a single situation; like a rock thrown into the water, its effects ripple outward, in overlapping patterns. Often, families become overwhelmed by crisis and find themselves unable to handle even everyday routine matters. Frequently, the diagnosis of chronic illness is made after a period of severe, acute illness. The child may have been near death or may have undergone surgery or a series of painful, intrusive diagnostic techniques. Parents spend hours in the unfamiliar, unfriendly halls of hospitals, anxiously awaiting the doctor's appearance, afraid to hear the verdict. Their eating habits, work routines, and sleeping patterns are disrupted. They cannot read or plan ahead. The children may be fearful and in pain, irritable and moody, seeking constant reassurance from their parents. If the disease suspected has a congenital etiology, parents may be feeling a sense of overwhelming guilt and may place blame on themselves and each other. Siblings are virtually ignored, although periodically parents may feel torn and guilty about abandoning them to friends or relatives, especially if the sick child is hospitalized for an extended period of time. Even when families previously had developed a relatively stable relationship, such major disruptions cannot help but cause temporary disorganization.

Against this background of anxiety and dysfunction, physicians often need to confer with parents as to possible diagnoses, potentially dangerous diagnostic tests, and future outcomes. It is no wonder that parents often appear dazed and uncertain after conferences, especially when physicians do not take the time or effort to patiently share such information with them. Often, physicians' overloaded schedules or their own discomfort with the diagnosis and with the need to impart painful messages to parents cause them to rush their conferences, meeting parents briefly in crowded hallways or with one hand on the elevator button.

Medical terminology is complex and often seems to be a foreign language to laypeople. How can the parents of a child with suspected leukemia make an intelligent, informed decision when asked, in passing, if they want to risk a course of treatment with chemotherapy in addition to immunosuppressive drugs, listed in endless medical jargon?

When an ill child is hospitalized, parents often feel a sense of loss of control; they are unable to comfort their child or make him or her better; others are meeting the child's physical needs. At the same time, parents are often forced to make decisions regarding treatment or therapy, decisions that may have life or death implications, the results of which are often uncertain or inconclusive. Toby, a pale, listless 27 month old, had spent most of his life in hospitals, suffering from congenital kidney obstruction and hydronephrosis. Although his parents visited only on weekends and had long since abdicated their responsibilities for day-to-day physical and emotional care to hospital staff, their physician met with them to discuss the possibilities of home management, kidney dialysis, and future kidney transplants. While nominally these parents had custody of their child, they felt helpless to make such decisions for a child that they had never become attached to, never parented in a literal sense.

Health professionals routinely expect parents to make such decisions as these. Legal issues of refusal to consent to treatment or surgery in such cases have occurred, issues that have serious ethical implications and that have been reviewed in depth in the current literature (Holder, 1977).

Physicians need to recognize the importance of providing parents the time, privacy, and acceptance they need in order to come to grips with the realities of their child's condition. In a discussion relating to the management of the parent in pediatric practice, V.B. Tisza (1962) exhorts other physicians to offer such guidance to parents of the chronically ill child. She suggests that parents need reassurance, realism, and repetition in order to begin to understand and deal with the ramifications of chronic illness, both long- and short-term.

When confronted with the diagnosis, even parents who have received sensitive reassurance may well be unable to accept the permanence of their child's condition. As the initial crisis passes, parents may feel a tremendous surge of relief that their child did not die. Often, remission of symptoms occurs after an initial hospitalization, even in terminal conditions such as the cancers or degenerative diseases. It is common for children to be discharged after relatively short hospital stays, often before children or their parents have fully understood the full ramifications of the disease and its prognosis. It is not uncommon for parents to view an early remission as an indication of possible misdiagnosis. Denial, coupled with anger at the physicians for needless anxiety, may surface. As Tisza (1962) notes, "hospitalization works in the service of denial. While the child was at home, he was healthy; now he is sick and in the hospital ... this situation permits the fantasy 'once he is discharged ... he will be healthy again'" (p. 57).

Much like the stages of mourning described by Elisabeth Kübler-Ross (1969), there are a variety of ways in which parents of chronically ill children can be seen to react. Denial usually occurs in the earliest stages of the illness for reasons described above. Often, this is followed by anger and rage—anger that the physician cannot cure the child, anger at the child for creating the problem in the first place, and rage at others who do not understand or will not help. Torn between such feelings of anger and the sense that it will be futile, parents begin to feel guilty and blame themselves for the illness. These various reactions usually occur in most parents, although their severity and duration vary greatly. Some parents may never be able to accept their child's illness, continually seeking alternative diagnoses or treatments, sure that the fault lies with the professionals making the diagnosis. Others remain angry at the world, spending countless hours recounting horror stories of mismanagement and malpractice on the part of the professionals caring for their child. How parents react depends upon a number of factors—their previous experience with illness, their individual personalities and coping strategies, other losses they may have endured, the extent of the child's future disability, the child's reaction, and the support they provide each other and receive from family and friends.

When a child suffers from an acute illness, routine family patterns change abruptly; the child needs more attention, the family is anxious about the outcome, the pain and fear on the part of the child require added family support. Although the anxiety surrounding such a crisis is high, the outlook for total recovery is usually excellent, the duration of the stress is brief, and the family soon returns to its normal patterns, relieved at the outcome (Steinhauer et al., 1974). Anyone who has lived in a family with a child who becomes ill with influenza, tonsillitis, or appendicitis will recognize this cycle. Unfortunately, for the family with a chronically ill child, feelings of relief and a return to normal patterns do not follow the initial crisis. The family must return home and pick up the pieces of their lives, still shocked by the traumatic experience, not fully understanding the complicated prescriptions and therapies that their child must endure, and grieving the loss of a normal child. New demands are placed upon this already fragile system; sleeping arrangements may need revision, so that parents can hear the cries of a sick child or administer medicine during the night without waking others; special diets may need to be established for the diabetic or cystic child; additional housekeeping chores may be added to the overburdened family of an asthmatic. If a child is limited in mobility, the family may need to build on an extra ground-level room or adapt their present home for wheelchair accessibility. Children may need hours each day of special physical therapy, as in cystic fibrosis. Virtually every aspect of life may need to be examined and reorganized: jobs, car pool arrangements, school needs, and meals. One need only imagine how such changes affect the marital relationship of the parents and the delicate network of interfamily relationships. Parents may feel a great sense of love and pity for their child, especially in the face of their helplessness. At the same time, a growing sense of anger, disappointment, and resentment toward the child is understandable and to some extent may be unavoidable (Tisza, 1962).

Added to these pressures are those resulting from the increased financial burdens that chronic illness places upon families. Even with the extensive medical insurance coverage available today, the costs can be exorbitant. Special diets; special medicines unavailable through regular pharmacies; transportation to clinics, therapy sessions, and hospitals; wheelchairs; braces; and jobst garments all add to the strain placed on the family's finances. Parents may have used up their available personal leave time, yet still need to take off work days to adequately meet the ongoing medical and emotional needs of their child. Mothers may need to return to work to help repay costs of medical care, which puts added pressure on the family.

A frequent byproduct of chronic illness is a family's gradual social isolation from friends and community resources. Decreased energy, decreased financial resources, embarrassment or shame about their child's condition, and anger that others were spared the pain of a chronically ill child can lead to a gradual lessening of social contacts outside the home.

For the family, as for the child, developmental continuity has been interrupted. The family's ability to come to terms with their changed expectations, goals, and needs and to become reintegrated as a stable family system will depend upon their previous experience with crisis, their past successes as a stable family unit, the nature of their child's illness, and the prognosis, among other factors. That families can successfully cope with tragedy has been amply demonstrated by Jerome Shulman (1976) and others. A mother of a 13-year-old leukemic girl poignantly expressed her perspective this way: "You take each day as it comes, enjoying each pain-free, symptom-free day as if it were a gift."

Family Adjustment

The way in which families make the necessary long-term adjustments to chronic illness will necessarily influence their child's adjustment to the illness (Figure 3-1). The factor of chronic illness may well interfere with normal child rearing patterns. The ambiguous feelings of love and resentment described above can produce guilt on the parents' part and a concomitant difficulty in setting realistic limits. Expectations for appropriate behavior may be inconsistent, depending upon whether the child is symptomatic or seemingly normal. Parents may disagree upon the severity or duration of discipline, thus exacerbating family friction. An overprotective mother may not allow her husband to use physical punishment with an asthmatic child, fearing the onset of symptoms; a father may be unwilling to stop a child from rough-housing, even when the child seems fatigued or flushed. Children may sense these inconsistencies and use them as a wedge to gain extra privileges from one or the other parent. A child's anger and resistance to treatments and medicines and frequent oppositional behaviors may be the occasion for daily battles, which lead to parental frustration and resentment.

Travis (1976) details common family distortions that can occur in the process of long-term adjustment to chronic illness. One familiar problem is the changing role of the father from head of household to absentee breadwinner. The need for a steady income and the possible sense of rejection a father feels toward a weakened son may lead him to abdicate the role of nurturer, leading to a mother-son relationship that may become excessively isolated and interdependent. This happens most frequently with children suffering from hemophilia or cystic fibrosis. The need for constant hands-on therapy in cystic fibrosis or ostomy care can exacerbate this malfunctioning relationship, with possible distortions in the son's sexual identity and body image.

Figure 3-1   Relationship of Family Functioning to Child's Adjustment to Chronic Illness

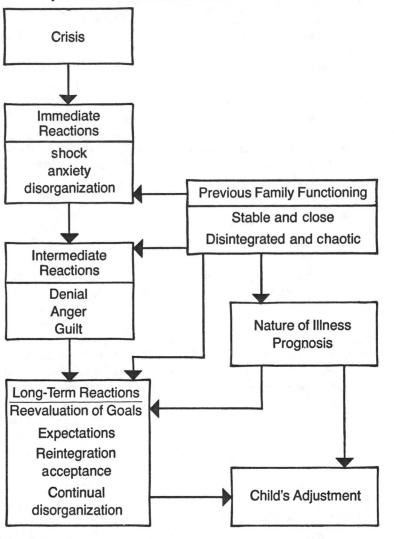

Neither parent may be able to relate appropriately to a child with congenital or acquired deformities. Prolonged separation from the child after birth, as in meningomyelocele, may hamper parental acceptance of a deformed child. The need to physically care for such a child in spite of rejection may lead to guilt and consequent infantilization or overprotection of the child. Frequently, such children are not permitted to experience even those normal developmental milestones that they are capable of, thus further handicapping them in their ability to become integrated into their community. Thus, a well-controlled diabetic or asthmatic child may be kept from engaging in outdoor neighborhood games, or a child with a degenerative disorder may be withdrawn from the school rolls years before the condition becomes debilitating. The balance between allowing a child to fully participate, thus increasing the risk of attack, and overprotection is quite fragile, and decisions affecting daily routines can often require the delicate judgment of a Solomon. What parent has not given in to the pleas of a ten year old to stay out one more hour or cross the main avenue or play one more inning of ball? Imagine the guilt if the result is a bleeding attack or the pain of an impending sickle cell crisis or a sudden dizzy spell or seizure at the busy intersection.

When death is imminent or possible, parental judgment may be even further tested. The extremes of concern evident in the parents of a child with a severe heart defect or end-stage renal disease lead to an image of the child as vulnerable (Travis, 1976).

The unexpected recurrence of symptoms may often create in parents a sense of hopelessness and loss of control. "I kept her in, and made sure she rested after school, and still she developed chest pains." In some conditions, especially those that are degenerative and progressive, nothing one does or fails to do seems to be of any avail. Occasionally, parents faced with such injustice may seek to place blame on themselves or others. Home teachers or neighbors are thus frequently placed in the uncomfortable position of listening to a mother's endless litany of the wrongs done to her child by doctors, therapists, and other health professionals.

Sensitive professional intervention can often assist families in whom such distortions of adjustment become apparent. The challenge of caring for a chronically ill child is enormous, and guidance and support by both professionals and parents with similar problems can be invaluable.

Siblings

When children become ill, all the family attention is directed toward them, often at the expense of their siblings. Young siblings may be confused about the origins of the disease and whether it is contagious. Older siblings may be ashamed to have their friends visit or fearful that they made themselves become victims of the disease. Imagine the panic of a five year old, who in a fit of resentment had wished his brother dead, when that brother contracts leukemia? Or the dread a young adolescent feels when his older brother begins to show the unmistakable symptoms of Friedreich's ataxia, an inherited disorder?

Young children may have little understanding of the long-term implications of their sibling's illness. Nevertheless, they often feel emotionally deprived and abandoned by parents who spend all their waking hours at the hospital or bedside of a sick child. Short tempers and uncertainty lead to the frequent dismissal of a sibling's constant questions, "Is she going to be alright?" "When will he come home?" "Can I have his room if he dies?" The innocent curiosity of childhood often shocks grief-stricken parents into excessive anger or resentment against the sibling. The need to "be nice to" a "monstrous" brother or sister often leads to resentment and unexpressible hostility. Many siblings react by acting out in school or home, suddenly performing poorly in their classes or withdrawing into themselves. They may wish that they had heart disease or dystrophy or even cancer in order to gain the attention of family members.

Older children may feel embarrassed by their sibling's distorted body or coughing fits or baldness. They may fear marriage or social contacts, especially if the condition is inherited. They may be expected to take on many added responsibilities just at a time when they had expected more freedom from family responsibilities. Some siblings react by taking on too much, being extra good or helpful, in hopes of gaining extra attention or alleviating guilt felt for not being the sick child.

For the child, the family, and the siblings, comprehensive care must be carefully orchestrated (Debuskey, 1970) to provide for optimal adjustment. For the child and siblings, the condition and its implications need to be fully explained, repeatedly, at the level appropriate to the child. Mysteries, whispered conferences, and hushed tones only serve to increase the anxiety of the child and siblings. Sensitive professionals can aid the family by carefully analyzing their various support systems to find the key to support for the child (Debuskey, 1970).

In the last analysis, it is only when families are able to successfully resolve the anxiety, depression, and resentment aroused by the illness that they are able to meet the physical and emotional needs of their chronically ill child (Steinhauer, 1974).

EFFECTS OF HOSPITALIZATION

Most chronically ill children spend the majority of their time at home, in school, and in the community. With modern technology and the increasing costs of hospitalization, hospital stays are usually relatively short. That same modern technology, however, often makes the stay especially painful and grim. Hospitalization usually occurs at times of increased stress: a dreaded diagnosis is being verified, a child has sustained a severe attack or injury, or the symptoms of cancer have reappeared. Pain and weakness often result from the illness or the necessary treatment, leaving the child even more vulnerable. For most children with chronic illness, periods of hospitalization are traumatic. The reasons for this are varied. Hospitalization causes separation between the child and family, a separation that is painful for all. The child is thrust into unfamiliar surroundings, bombarded by strange sounds, smells, and sights. The child is often confronted with a variety of caregivers, whose methods of child care and individual styles may be very different from those of the parents. Special cultural rituals or foods may be missing.

Added to these factors are the children's internal experiences. Their normal ability to function may be decreased by weakness, pain, or the forced immobility from casts or braces. They are never certain of the varying expectations placed upon them: "hold still," "be brave," "don't cry," and "this will only take a minute" are all exhortations that the child may be unable to obey. Hospital routines are often intrusive and unnecessarily disruptive of a child's normal routines: meals are served at odd hours, in odd trays; beds are large, high off the ground with crib sides and complicated buttons; needles or other painful treatments are given by strangers who often appear out of the blue, inflict pain, and leave a moment later. How appropriate, then, that children placed in such unnatural surroundings would be fearful and anxious. Depending upon their age, their fears may focus on issues of abandonment or punishment, disfigurement or death. Often, these fears are realized when parents fail to visit, needles are given, or body parts are surgically distorted or amputated. Asked how frightening a hospital is, a four-year-old patient who had been wheelchair-bound since age two and had undergone eight or nine surgical procedures for severe leg-length discrepancy replied, "It's real scary, but not as much as a haunted house." The lack of control over their lives and the lack of the right to make decisions regarding their daily schedules or treatment become other serious consequences of hospitalization. This is especially true for adolescents, who may have just begun to experience the freedom of autonomy from adult strictures at home. The normal behaviors and leisure activities engaged in by typical adolescents often run counter to hospital policies, creating a fertile battleground for patients and staff.

Families, as well, are vulnerable to the trauma of hospitalizing their sick child. Separation is painful for them, as is the increased anxiety that accompanies the necessity of hospitalization. They may have a guilty sense of having done or not done something that precipitated the admission and may place blame, real or imagined, on themselves or others. Their previous experience with hospitals, if this is a first admission for the child, may well affect their response. One parent, whose mother and father both had died shortly after being hospitalized, refused to admit her diabetic child to the hospital until he was comatose; another saw hospitals as havens of technologic miracles because his child had been successfully resuscitated after experiencing severe brain trauma as the result of an automobile accident. He welcomed the recommendation of a year-long hospital stay for rehabilitation, trusting the professional health team. Such experiences necessarily color a family's perception of hospitals and affect their outlook. Frequently, hospitalization of a child implies a loss of control by the parents over the child's safety and health, and often a sense of failure. "I was unable to keep her symptom-free at home," and "he's well when he's here, and has attacks at home" are comments by two parents of asthmatic children who had recurrent hospital admissions. Staff may unwittingly foster this feeling in parents by assuming total care of the child and by giving the impression of a supercompetency in managing the child with which parents cannot hope to compete. This loss of parental prerogatives in the daily care and decision making regarding their child is commonplace, yet avoidable. It comes out of the perspective that sees the professional as the expert, the parent as the clumsy novice. In a critical examination of the hospital as an institution, A. Beuf, in *Biting off the Bracelet* (1979), compares the hospital to other large-scale, impersonal institutions in this country such as schools and prisons. Following E. Goffman's (1961) description of the qualities of total institutions that assist in depersonalizing the patient or client, Beuf points out those similarities inherent in children's hospitals. Children's clothing and other personal belongings are removed, they are dressed identically, and they are given numbers on bracelets. Many children sleep in a single room, with resulting lack of privacy. All phases of the day are planned by others, prearranged and tightly scheduled. While the staff at many children's hospitals often provide individualized attention to children, aspects of this description are commonplace still in many hospitals. Change is slow, and the change toward a more humanistic and individualized view of hospitalization is occurring today against a background of three decades of research into the emotional and developmental needs of children in hospitals (Hardgrove & Dawson, 1972).

Historical Perspective and Current Research

Until the early 1950s, little research was done on the effects of hospitalization on children. Parents were often seen as intruders in the impersonal, highly routinized hospital. Visiting hours were restrictive and often nonexistent. In a large city hospital in 1964, parents admitting children for tonsillectomies were told to say goodby and return the next afternoon to pick up the child for discharge. In another city, patients with long-term illnesses, hospitalized for months or years, were allowed visitors every other Sunday. At the end of those days, staff often responded to the heartbroken cries of children forced to separate from their parents for another two weeks by noting that visits should be further restricted, for look how it upset the children, as well as the routine.

In the late 1940s, Spitz (1945) described children he had visited in hospitals and orphanages who were suffering from apathy and depression as a result of lack of human interaction. He termed this condition *hospitalism* and prescribed attachment to significant caretakers as the remedy. Later studies by D. Prugh et al. (1953), J. Robertson (1958), and J. Bowlby (1975) lent support to Spitz's research and described in great detail the deleterious effects that hospitalization can have on young children. Empirical research, reviewed by E. Mason in 1965, has consistently demonstrated the effect of hospitalization on children and families and has shown that the negative effects can be mediated considerably by the provision of hospital policies that are consonant with mental health principles (Shore & Goldston, 1978).

The advent of the child advocacy and consumers' rights movements in the 1960s has led to the development of a constituency to pressure for changes in hospital policies. Parents and professionals have bonded together for the rights of children. The Association for the Care of Children's Health (ACCH) (formerly Association for the Care of Children in Hospitals), an international multidisciplinary organization, has made great strides in the last 15 years in representing the psychosocial needs of children in health settings. Through its journals, conferences, guidebooks, bibliographies, and research, this organization advocates for change in health settings. Appendix B contains the text of a recent ACCH publication prepared by its metropolitan Washington affiliate and circulated to a national audience. The material represents a summary of the major policy issues of concern today and suggests specific steps needed to accomplish the goals of providing an optimal experience for children and families faced with hospitalization.

Although much positive change has occurred in hospitals over the last decade, there is still much work to be done. The earliest research concentrated on the theories of attachment and separation and provided a setting for major change in hospital nurseries and toddler units. The issues of adolescent care, outpatient services, and long-term care are just coming into focus in today's research perspective. Much work remains to be done.

SOCIAL SUPPORT SYSTEMS

Families of children with chronic illness often need the help of a variety of support systems—medical, financial, and social—to cope with the attendant stresses of chronic illness. Communities differ in the availability and effectiveness of these human services, and many agencies often appear for a year or more, only to lose funding or be reorganized and incorporated within other agencies. Some communities provide written directories or phone referral services, while in others one must rely on the telephone book for help. Federal policies and shifting trends toward self-help and peer group organizations also affect delivery models in various localities. The following, then, can provide only a brief generalized survey of the various types of support services available.

Anyone who has attempted to provide support systems to families of chronically ill children can attest to the delicacy and difficulty of the task. Of utmost importance is the realization that various agencies have overlapping functions and some operate under rigid, mandated regulations. Thus, both an outpatient clinic and a city department of social services may have social workers on staff, but the social service agency may be unable to pick up a case until a certain period of time has elapsed or until a family requires protective supervision, while the hospital or clinic may expect their social worker to transfer the family to the city's social service staff after an initial period of assessment. Problems such as this abound in practice and require the networking of a variety of agencies or professionals for optimal service. Part III will explore the roles of the various professionals in order to provide the reader with the necessary tools to serve as a coordinator of services.

Medical Systems

All children with chronic illness invariably come into contact with medical systems. At their best, hospitals, outpatient clinics, and neighborhood health clinics provide the kind of multidisciplinary care that Debuskey (1970) refers to as "well-orchestrated." Often the first agency that parents come into contact with, the medical system itself, can offer comprehensive evaluation and planning for the child's present and future needs. Too often, however, these systems provide fragmented, isolated services necessitating the seeking out of other programs for the child by families disorganized by the effects of the illness. Private physicians can assist the family at this juncture, but often the pressures of their work and their lack of knowledge about existing services hamper their efforts. Large-scale screening programs for Tay Sachs disease, lead poisoning, and sickle cell anemia point the way toward a preventive approach to chronic illness that can save countless lives and pain.

Social Service Agencies and Counseling Programs

Public agencies are funded under federal entitlement grants (Title XX) to provide a wide range of services to the nation's poor and needy. Most of these services vary from state to state, but usually they provide day-care services, protective services, homemaker services, foster care services, and other optional programs. They often provide essential supervision and support for families undergoing periods of crisis in their lives. Families living at or below the poverty line, whose daily lives may involve a series of overwhelming problems of management, may need the help of these agencies in providing a chronically ill child with basic medical care. New housing may need to be found for the asthmatic child, transportation for the child who needs to be seen weekly at the clinic, extra sources of support to provide funding for special diets or wheelchairs. The effectiveness of these agencies, which are plagued by lack of funds and the ills of a large bureaucracy, is too often questionable, but their intent and potential are apparent.

Private agencies can also be effective in providing families with necessary support networks. Many that are funded by United Way or that are affiliated with various religious organizations, such as Catholic Charities, Jewish Family and Children's Service, and Lutheran Social Services, provide nonsectarian services for families in areas of counseling, homemaker services, and the like. Various hospitals and clinics can also be explored for their counseling and parent support programs. Special counseling needs in the areas of genetic counseling or grief counseling may be met through university-based hospitals and clinics or pastoral counseling.

Financial Aid

The costs of chronic illness are staggering. Private insurance, widely available to blue- and white-collar workers through their employment, frequently has spending limitations or restrictions that affect the families of chronically ill children. While such policies cover basic medical and hospital expenses, they often restrict long convalescent stays and fail to cover extra costs such as wheelchair purchase and transportation. Health maintenance organizations (HMOs) are fast becoming an important alternative to provide insurance. Group prepaid programs, such as the Kaiser Permanente Plan, have been shown to reduce hospital costs markedly. Their emphasis on prevention is also cost-containing and hopefully points the way to a greater focus on prevention. Crippled Children's Services, funded federally under the original Social Security Act, has been a major source of supplementary income for medical expenses. Funding and administration of programs vary widely from state to state.

Also under the aegis of the Social Security Administration, Supplementary Security Income (SSI) funds are available for chronically ill children disabled by their disease. Disabled of all ages are eligible for these funds, regardless of a family's social security status. The child must qualify both financially and medically. Finally, Medicaid is available for low-income families unable to bear the excessive financial burdens of chronic illness. Beset by charges of fraud and by rising medical costs, eligibility requirements are often changed, and funds available fluctuate widely from year to year. To date, essential medical needs of low-income families are still met by Medicaid.

School and Rehabilitation Services

Essential to the developmental needs of the chronically ill child is the provision of adequate, appropriate, educational and rehabilitative programs.

Since this is the major focus of this book, little needs to be said here except to point to the need for continuing, cooperative efforts between health personnel and educational systems in the care of the chronically ill child.

Parent Groups and Voluntary Health Agencies

Aside from the necessarily crucial role that the medical system plays in chronic illness, parent groups and voluntary health agencies may well offer the families of chronically ill children the most consistent support. Appendix D lists some of those agencies, with national affiliations, for reference. These groups vary in their functions and membership. Some provide a listening ear to a frantic parent, some offer literature and special training programs, and some take on an advocacy role. Most provide a forum for parents to express their needs and fears in a supportive setting.

SUMMARY

This chapter examined the impact of chronic illness on children and their families. The various factors that affect the adjustment of child and family were explored, and a model was presented to depict the relationship between family functioning and the child's adjustment to chronic illness. The effects of hospitalization were reviewed, with a strong emphasis on policy issues relating to the need for humanistic approaches toward child care in health settings.

Finally, social support systems were described briefly as they affect chronic illness and its impact. Throughout this chapter are woven the issues of choice and change—choice between options that allow for growth as opposed to those that stunt developmental potential; choice between options that allow for adjustment and coping and those that lead to maladjustment and disorganization; and change in the prospect of prevention and humanistic caring models.

REFERENCES

Adams, M.A. A hospital play program: Helping children with serious illness. *American Journal of Orthopsychiatry*, 1976, *46*(3), 416–424.

Ainsworth, M.D.S., Blehar, M.C., Waters, E., & Wall, S. *Patterns of attachment: A psychological study of the strange situation*. Hillsdale, NJ: Lawrence Erlbaum, 1978.

Beuf, A. *Biting off the bracelet*. Philadelphia: University of Pennsylvania Press, 1979.

Bowlby, J. Attachment theory: Separation anxiety and mourning. In S. Arieti (Ed.), *American handbook of psychiatry* (2nd ed.), Vol. 6. New York: Basic Books, 1975, pp. 292–309.

Bruhn, J. Effects of chronic illness on the family. *Journal of Family Practice*, 1977, *4*, 1057-1060.

Debuskey, M. (Ed.). *The chronically ill child and his family*. Springfield, IL: Charles C Thomas, 1970.

Dubo, S. et al. A study of relationships between family situation, bronchial asthma and personal adjustment of children. *Journal of Pediatrics*, 1961, *59*(3), 402-414.

Erikson, E.H. *Childhood and society*. New York: W.W. Norton, 1963.

Godene, G. Personal communication.

Goffman, E. *Asylums: Essays on the social situation of mental patients and other inmates*. Gordon City, NY: Anchor Books, 1961.

Goffman, E. *Stigma: The management of spoiled identity*. Englewood Cliffs, NJ: Prentice Hall, 1963.

Hardgrove, C., & Dawson, R. *Parents and children in the hospital*. Boston: Little, Brown and Company, 1972.

Holder, A.R. *Legal issues in pediatrics and adolescent medicine*. New York: John Wiley & Sons, 1977.

Kübler-Ross, E. *On death and dying*. New York: Macmillan, 1969.

Magrab, P. *Psychological management of pediatric problems*. Baltimore: University Park Press, 1978.

Mason, E. The hospitalized child: His emotional needs. *New England Journal of Medicine*, 1965, *272*, 406-415.

Mattsson, A. Long-term physical illness in childhood: A challenge to psychosocial adaptation. *Pediatrics*, 1972, *50*, 803-805.

Mattsson, A. Chronic illness in adolescents. Talk given at Association for the Care of Children in Hospitals Conference, Dallas, 1980.

Myers, B.R. The child with a chronic illness. In R. Haslam & P. Valletutti (Eds.), *Medical problems in the classroom*. Baltimore: University Park Press, 1975.

Plank, N. *Working with children in hospitals*. Cleveland: The Press of Case-Western Reserve University, 1962.

Pless, I.B., & Satterwhite, B.B. Chronic illness. In R.J. Haggerty, K.J. Roghmann, & I.B. Pless (Eds.), *Child health and the community*. New York: John Wiley & Sons, 1975.

Prugh, D. et al. A study of the emotional reactions of children and their families to hospitalization. *American Journal of Orthopsychiatry*, 1953, *23*, 70-106.

Robertson, J. *Young children in hospitals*. New York: Basic Books, 1958.

Robinson, M. Chronically ill child: Needs and realities. Keynote Speech, Seminar on Chronic Illness, Mt. Washington Pediatric Hospital, May 1980.

Schowalter, J.E. Psychological reactions to physical illness and hospitalization in adolescence. *Journal of American Academy of Child Psychiatry*, 1977, *16*(3), 500-516.

Shulman, J. *Coping with tragedy: Successfully facing the problem of a seriously ill child*. Chicago: Follett Publishing Company, 1976.

Shore, M.F., & Goldston, S.E. Mental health aspects of pediatric care: Historical review and current status. In P. Magrab (Ed.), *Psychological management of pediatric problems*. Baltimore: University Park Press, 1978.

Spitz, R. Hospitalism. In *The Psychoanalytic Study of the Child*, 1945, *I*, 53-74.

Steinhauer, P.D., Mushin, M.B., & Rae-Grant, Q. Psychological aspects of chronic illness. *Pediatric Clinics of North America*, 1974, *21*, 825-840.

Sultz, H.A., Schlesinger, E.R., Feldman, J.G., & Mosher, W.E. The epidemiology of peptic ulcer in childhood. *American Journal of Physical Health,* 1970, *60,* 492-498.

Sultz, H., Schlesinger, E., Mosher, W., & Feldman, J. *Long-term childhood illness.* Pittsburgh: University of Pittsburgh Press, 1972.

Tisza, V.B. Management of the parents of the chronically ill child. *American Journal of Orthopsychiatry,* 1962, *32*(53), 53-59.

Travis, G. *Chronic illness in children.* Stanford, CA: Stanford University Press, 1976.

Chronic Illness: Educational Strategies

OVERVIEW

Part I attempted to lay the foundation for a study of the issues involved in educating the chronically ill child. Part II will describe a number of chronic illnesses from their medical management perspective and will examine the educational strategies available to mediate these conditions and provide developmental continuity in various settings for various age groups.

In providing a detailed summary of a variety of chronic illnesses, these chapters hopefully can serve the teacher as an atlas and source of reference. The educational strategies presented are meant to serve as guidelines in developing individual educational programs for each child.

The final chapters in this section relate to terminal illnesses and the special concerns that accompany them. The unique perspectives of the child, the family, and the caregivers are examined, and legal and ethical dilemmas are addressed as well.

Chapter 4

Educational Strategies: General Considerations

OVERVIEW

There is a need to develop policies and procedures designed to help home-bound/hospital teachers fulfill their special teaching role. It is a difficult role, one in which a number of unique problems arise that need to be resolved for optimal educational benefit to the child and for job satisfaction for the teacher. Major issues include:

- the need for continuity of programming

- the need for communication between teachers and medical professionals, teachers and parents, teachers and local school personnel

- the need for a supportive relationship among homebound/hospital teachers within a state or local educational agency

- the need to develop or to obtain and organize appropriate instructional materials

- the need to teach within a reasonable, stable schedule

Additionally, unique problems exist in both home settings and hospital environments that may affect the teaching-learning situation.

CONTINUITY OF PROGRAMMING

For the chronically ill child, educational continuity is of vital concern. Absences from class are often frequent and recurrent. While often short-term, these absences can add up to a substantial amount of missed school time. School districts can minimize the negative effects of such absences by assigning the same teacher to a child for the school year, at the least. This can save precious time for education and avoid repetitive assessment and planning time. Good communication among the teacher, parents, school personnel, health professionals, and child is also enhanced by such continuity. Assignments can be resumed with little delay and may even be long-term, if expected returns to the home or hospital are contemplated. Short hospitalizations and periods of home instruction can, at times, aid the child in catching up with schoolwork in a structured one-to-one setting.

A face sheet for each child's file can provide the teacher with the information necessary to do adequate planning for the child. Such a form is also valuable if the child is transferred to another teacher's rolls (see Exhibit 4-1).

Exhibit 4-1 Face Sheet

Name of Child _____ D.O.B. _____ Age ___

Address   _____

_____

Home phone no. _____

Parent's name(s) and addresses (if different)

_____

_____

_____

Referral contacts (such as doctor, social worker, psychiatrist, etc.)

Names   Phone Numbers

_____   _____

_____   _____

_____   _____

Medical diagnosis: _____

Home school and address: _____

_____

Phone no. _____ Grade placement _____

Special programs, if any: _____

_____

Special adaptations needed, or special programs required: __

_____

_____

Date form completed: _____ By: _____

_____

COMMUNICATION

Teachers need to be open and receptive to a number of people in developing the teacher-student relationship. Often, they must walk a thin line to meet their professional objectives while supporting the goals of the child, parents, and other health professionals. Vital therapeutic treatments may need to take precedence over school assignments; the child's depression or sense of futility may interfere with concentration and motivation; the parents may need to vent their feelings and may turn to the teacher for comfort and support. A later chapter will explore this vital issue in greater depth. For now, it is sufficient to note that effective communication skills can have a significant impact upon the outcome of homebound/hospital teaching.

SUPPORTIVE RELATIONSHIPS

Home/hospital teaching can be a lonely, unsupported job. Teachers spend much of their day in noneducational settings, the home or hospital, or alone in their cars traveling from one site to another. Often, support networks of other teachers are missing or tenuous. Many teachers work part-time as home/hospital staff after classroom duty or other tasks are completed. N. Milne (1980) and others highly recommend regular in-service training for the homebound/hospital teacher. Such programs serve two purposes: they provide essential training and upgrading of the skills of the teachers, while affording them an opportunity to meet other colleagues and share ideas, problems, and support.

DEVELOPMENT AND ORGANIZATION OF INSTRUCTIONAL MATERIALS

The homebound/hospital teacher is a nomad, traveling from one child to another, each of whom requires an individualized set of materials, books, lesson plans, and the like. Collecting all the various materials, keeping them all organized and available, is a task that is often nearly impossible to achieve. Many experienced teachers have made use of boxes with dividers (Milne, 1980) or expandable file folders and use their cars as combination office, file cabinet, and classroom storage area. Wipeable, reusable cards, game-boards, and other materials can increase versatility and decrease space consumption.

Visits to home schools to obtain the child's current workbooks and assignments allow for a sense of increased continuity and can make the transition back to the classroom easier. The curriculum should include all subjects, although each should be taught individually. The world needs to be brought to the child by means of seasonal projects, books and materials from libraries, museums, art supply stores, and so forth. In-service training sessions can provide a valuable opportunity for teachers to swap ideas and strategies that have worked. District offices that coordinate homebound/hospital programs can collect and make available ideas and suggestions from a variety of teachers, thus increasing each teacher's store of ideas and materials at substantial savings of time and energy. Specific ideas will be offered in later sections, as examples.

SCHEDULING

Home teachers can best serve the child by attempting to make daily, regularly scheduled visits and by providing the child and parent with a schedule. This helps the child develop a set to learn and avoids interfering with family routines, therapy, or special television or radio shows. In hospitals, schedules often need to be arranged around complex routines, treatments, and staffing patterns.

HOME SETTING: SPECIAL PROBLEMS

One-to-one instruction in the home has both positive and negative aspects. Positively, it allows the child to learn to establish relationships and to develop personal contacts and friendships without group pressures to conform. On the other hand, reliance on individual attention can make reintegration into the classroom difficult. Children often grow to depend upon the support and attention they receive from individual teachers. The risks of returning to the group and competing with others may be feared.

Family values and living patterns differ from one home to another (Connor, 1964). Teachers must move from one setting to another. The role of the teacher ranges from intruder to guest to parent's friend and confidant to authority figure. Occasionally pressures can be put upon teachers by parents: to force children to comply with medicine administration or diet; to pressure children to learn or study beyond their abilities; to babysit for them. The practice of teaching the child with no adult present is illegal, but often practiced, especially in long-term home settings. Teachers are often pressed into the role of confidant to parents, listening to their problems, acting as supports. While parents need an opportunity to share their feelings, and the parent-teacher relationship should be warm and supportive, it is not appropriate for the teacher to be expected to act as counselor to the parent.

In addition, there are special problems of the one-parent family with a working mother. For example, is home teaching provided? When?

Space may be at a premium. Children need a place of their own to learn and study, a private place to store books, projects, and so forth. In some families, the child may have a private room. In others, the teacher may need to help the family find a nightstand for the child's use and provide a padlock. It should be remembered that privacy and a sense of control are very important to the homebound child.

Cooperation between the parents and the teacher is essential in ensuring a positive learning experience. The child's basic physical needs, such as bathing, dressing, and toileting should be attended to prior to the teacher's arrival, and the parent and child should be helped to understand the importance of being ready and available when the scheduled teaching time approaches (Bureau of Education for Exceptional Children, 1978).

The home teacher is in a unique position in being able to alert the health team to noted changes in the child's physical or emotional state or in the family situation if it affects the child. For example, the continual financial strains on a family may lead to increased tensions and family discord. This can, in turn, affect the child, causing potential physical or psychological disturbances.

HOSPITAL SETTING: SPECIAL PROBLEMS

As in the home, teachers in hospitals also enter a noneducational setting. The business of medicine often intrudes on the teacher's role, and schedules, places to teach, and hospital staff's recognition of the teacher's role as essential to the care of sick child are all issues that face the hospital teacher.

When a child is hospitalized, medical or rehabilitative treatments necessarily take precedence over educational programming. Teachers may have to provide instruction at bedside or at the side of a whirlpool tub; in isolation units; or in a noisy, crowded ward. Flexibility and ingenuity often become more important teaching tools than reading texts.

Teachers need to adjust schedules to fit the child's needs; the child's energy level also plays a role in scheduling. As F.P. Connor (1964) notes, however, agreement must be reached between the hospital teacher and the hospital staff regarding the essential need for educational programming.

Hospital staff may not fully understand the value or importance of educational continuity and may view the teacher as an obstruction. Early communication in which the policies and procedures of both the hospital and the educational system are identified can help to make the relationship between the two more cooperative and the instruction more effective.

Schedules for instructional time should be planned cooperatively by teachers and the health care team and followed as regularly as possible. Posting the schedule over the child's bed or in the nursing care plan can help to alert new or rotating staff to the child's schedule, thus avoiding unnecessary interruptions. Often, medical routines can be revised to allow for an uninterrupted hour of school if nursing and medical staff are helped to understand the benefits to the child of such a shift in schedules. Here, tact often pays off, and a diplomatic teacher can often convince the staff of the benefits they will derive when the child is involved and enthusiastic about schoolwork. These may include less frequent calls to the nurse. In many settings, nursing aides or volunteers can be taught to help children reinforce academic skills by playing improvised games with them when time allows.

Hospital schools that allow for group teaching can provide less restrictive environments than home settings, offering the child a set of peers and the sense of working in a group.

At best, teachers are given a room to use in the hospital, and many hospitals can thus provide a one-room schoolhouse for the children on that unit or floor. As the year progresses, the room begins to take on the atmosphere of a regular school: work in progress is displayed; parents can visit their children in school and feel some sense of relief that the world has not totally stopped for them; and the children begin to feel part of a group. Hospital teachers may be assigned for the whole year to such institutions, thus providing continuity for frequent readmissions and aiding communication between teacher and hospital staff. Such communication between school and hospital staff can provide a degree of agreement as to scheduling and space, thus providing a climate that can aid learning for the sick child.

In hospitals that have a professional child life staff, cooperation between them and the hospital teacher can create an educational team approach that benefits both the teacher and the child. The hospital teacher is thus provided with colleagues in the institution, and they can share information about the child and family, the school and hospital, to the benefit of all concerned.

A detailed exploration of the role of child life in the hospital and its relationship to the hospital school will be provided in a later chapter.

AFFECTIVE EDUCATION

In order to provide maximum learning experiences for the chronically ill child, all curriculum areas should be included in homebound and hospital school programs. Especially important is the area of affective education. Chronically ill children are often confused by their illness and accompanying pain, and feelings of differentness, lowered self-esteem, and an overpowering sense of helplessness are common. The inclusion of affective education can help such children to express their feelings openly, to begin to adjust to the illness and its accompanying pain or limitations, and to adjust to society's reactions to them as different.

The addition of this aspect of educational curriculum can be accomplished directly or indirectly through other school assignments. There are commer-

cially prepared games (such as the Ungame, published by Ungame Corporation) or games that can be developed by teachers to allow individual children
or children in groups to identify feelings and to describe through charades,
puppets, or other means some of their inner thoughts or feelings. Role-play-
ing games can be used to help children take the place of others and begin to
recognize the effects of other illnesses. General discussion groups of adolescents can be used to identify fears and anxieties and provide peer support.
These programs should not be used as a substitute for psychiatric therapy,
but as an adjunct to ongoing counseling done by professional psychiatrists,
psychologists, or social workers.

Indirectly, assignments in writing may include open ended sentences such
as "I hate being sick because _____ _____," "The
things I like about hospitals are _____," and "When I grow up
_____." These can be interspersed with more neutral sentences,
to avoid undue anxiety. Reading assignments can include books by or about
others with illnesses, and an advanced class could investigate geographic or
ethnic patterns of certain diseases such as thalassemia or sickle cell anemia.
A listing of books for and about children with diseases or handicaps appears
at the end of this chapter.

Special projects can be prepared by chronically ill children to explain their
own disease to classmates in home schools, which can help to ease the transition back into regular school. These projects can be incorporated into traditional subject areas such as math (food exchange or measuring techniques in
diabetes), science (anatomy or chemistry of a disease), social studies (geographic or ethnic disease patterns), and reading (book reviews of special
books, such as *Journey,* by the Massies, 1975). Assignments such as these
can lead to a discussion of feelings that can help children master their experiences and use them productively.

THE DEVELOPMENTALLY DISABLED

For the vast majority of children with mental retardation or with mental illness superimposed upon an existing or new physically disabling chronic illness, special education in supervised settings is usually required. For these
children, the need to accurately assess their abilities and to make frequent reassessments is crucial. One must be aware of the child's deficits and how they
affect (1) the child's understanding of the condition, (2) the management of
the illness, and (3) the child's ability to assume responsibility for self-care.
Teachers can be helpful in adapting patient education programs to the developmental level of the child, thus preventing needless frustration as nurse or
dietitian attempts, for example, to teach a retarded adolescent complex meal
exchange units or insulin measurement. Teachers can provide essential infor-

mation to the health care team regarding issues such as the child's ability to learn new information, the rate of learning, the need for concrete cues and visual representations of medical information, and methods to help the child follow simple directions.

In developing educational placements, teachers should be careful to identify the child's primary handicap and to ensure that all the educational needs and related services are addressed in school placements. For example, a child with serious learning disabilities who is injured and wheelchair-bound needs both a barrier-free environment and a special class placement for the remediation of academic skills. In planning for such children's future, academically oriented programs may not be the most beneficial. The homebound or hospital teacher needs to identify what skills are important for the child to know and to develop a program aimed at providing essential functional skills. Teachers assigned to these children should be specially certified in special education techniques and should be included in planning for special education placements.

Children who are retarded will tend to be more frightened and confused by changes in routine than other children. They often need more support from their parents and more simplified explanations. The teacher with special education training can often assist the nursing staff in helping the child adjust to hospital routines, preparing the child for surgical procedures, and helping the child express feelings of fear, pain, and loneliness. A mentally retarded child who is confused and fearful may react impulsively and require physical restraints. A sensitive teacher can help to make the child comfortable and avoid such extreme management techniques. Parents' knowledge of the child's needs and ways of communicating should be shared with staff, especially if the child is to undergo surgery (Kaisling & Kalafatich, 1978).

Each retarded child is different, and each must be treated with dignity and respect. Although they should be given information, directions, and the like based upon their *developmental level,* rather than their chronologic age, care should be taken to avoid treating retarded children as if they did not understand anything or had no feelings.

Children not in control of their bodies often appear to be retarded, as in severe cases of cerebral palsy. Again, appearances can be deceiving, and too often these children are treated as if they were retarded.

Spending one's life immobile when one's peers are actively exploring their world can often make an orthopedically handicapped child less independent and more passive. Since hospitalization tends to increase these feelings, the child with physical handicaps may appear to regress behaviorally in such settings.

In some instances, especially in cases of severe head trauma, the child is severely retarded and can respond only to basic sensory stimulation. In such cases, specialized professionals, working with a team of speech, physical, and occupational therapists, need to develop an individualized educational program to assist the child in maintaining contact with the external world and to provide basic sensory stimulation. Such stimulation usually involves the use of music, through tape recorders, records, radios, or other auditory materials. Children who respond to sound but who have little motor capacity may be provided with devices to assist them in starting or stopping music by head or arm pressure or by blowing on a control panel. Adaptive equipment to allow for such control of one's environment can be purchased commercially or can be handmade. An excellent source for instructions in handmade equipment is *Homemade Battery-Powered Toys and Education Devices for Severely Handicapped Children* by Linda Burkhart (1980).

Children recovering from severe head trauma may be left with severe residual behavioral disabilities. They often exhibit poor short-term memory, poor impulse control, and emotional liability. Information must be given to them with concrete cues, and directions should be simple and short. Teachers must be alert to sudden changes in mood and must provide a great deal of structure and routine in class. In home situations, the teacher may need to request that the tutoring be done in an empty room, with a closed door. Distractions should be minimized. Repetition and physical clues need to be incorporated into any lesson plans.

Children with head trauma represent a challenge to the home/hospital teacher. Recovery is often slow, and behavioral manifestations such as impulsivity may make teaching quite difficult. Staff support and the sharing of concerns by the health team are especially crucial to avoid the inevitable feelings of frustration that can accompany the reeducation of a child with head trauma. Chapter 6 will focus on the effects of head trauma in greater detail.

THE GIFTED CHILD

The current ground swell of interest in educational programs for the gifted and talented child deserves attention as it relates to the child with a chronic illness.

While it is not within the scope of this section to review in depth the philosophical and educational approaches to teaching gifted and talented children, these issues will be addressed briefly. The following pages will present a definition of the population, discuss the problems inherent in identification, and finally look at ways in which gifted and talented chronically ill children can be educated to achieve their maximum potential.

Definition

While gifted and talented children have always existed, their identification as exceptional children and the concomitant legislation to provide them with special educational services are relatively recent. The educational amendments of 1974 (PL 93-380) contain the first federal authority for the support of special education for the gifted and talented (Ballard, 1975).

In 1975, the right to education law, PL 94-142, listed gifted as one of the subcategories to be provided with services under those regulations. In 1978, further legislation was enacted to provide continued support to educational programs for this population. That law (Title IV, Part A, PL 95-561) defines gifted and talented as:

> children, and where applicable, youth, who are identified at the preschool, elementary, or secondary level as possessing demonstrated or potential abilities that give evidence of high performance capability in areas such as intellectual, creative, specific academic, or leadership ability, or in the performing and visual arts, and who by reason thereof require services or activities not ordinarily provided by the school. (Sellin & Birch, 1980, p. 22)

Identification

A major difficulty has been that of identifying children who meet such a definition. Standardized testing, such as I.Q. tests and achievement tests, have been criticized for their cultural biases, as well as for their limitations in tapping the creative talents of children outside of the academic or problem-solving spheres (Baldwin, 1978). Researchers are currently experimenting with new assessment tools, and educators are attempting to develop ways to identify these children in their early years. The populations most frequently referred to in the literature as being difficult to identify are minority children, rural children, and children with handicapping conditions. The program at Chapel Hill, North Carolina's preschool for the gifted handicapped is an excellent example of early identification (Leonard, 1977).

Educational discontinuity is often a consequence of chronic illness. Such illnesses often isolate the child from regular academic programs, and occasionally the disease or its treatment adversely affects the child's academic abilities. Social isolation and the emotional effects of having a disabling illness further interfere with educational pursuits.

The identification of a chronically ill child as gifted or talented thus becomes more difficult. Individual assessments and the provision of early education can help to find and develop the potential of such children. Gifted and talented children who are chronically ill represent a unique challenge to the teacher and bring with them a whole range of coping strategies.

Educational Implications

In attempting to cope with a chronic illness, children bring to the experience their ability to understand the implications of the condition. A gifted child may be more able to understand these factors and may thus be able to develop more effective ways of dealing with the knowledge. Increased understanding may, however, lead to greater anxiety on the part of the child, since the full meaning of a poor prognosis is more readily apparent. Often, gifted children use their abilities in a sophisticated process of denial or intellectualization, thus avoiding the emotional impact of the situation. They may, for example, learn a great deal about their illness and hold frequent discussions with medical staff and other health professionals regarding the facts of the disease or its treatment. Often, they sound like physicians-in-training themselves. They may never discuss the traumatic effect the illness has on their self-concept or future plans, however, preferring to be objective and to protect themselves from the emotional impact of the disease. Gifted children can also, however, use their intellect to develop compensatory abilities to substitute intellectual prowess for physical weakness. This aspect should be encouraged by the home/hospital teacher. In one hospital, a gifted child who had just undergone kidney surgery and was going to be placed on a hemodialysis unit awaiting a kidney transplant asked her science teacher for permission to build a model of the machine and show its function. She used scraps of material from the hospital lab and, with the teacher's help, created a model dialysis unit. She brought it to school her first day back and was able to explain to the class what treatments she would be undergoing, as well as the implications of her condition. The child was thus able to share with her class a major part of her life and at the same time provide them with new knowledge and understanding.

Two key features in the education of gifted learners, identified by H.B. Robinson, W.C. Roedell, and N.E. Jackson (1979), seem especially pertinent for this population: variance and individualization. If the principle of variance is true for gifted children generally, it is even more relevant to the gifted child with a chronic disabling illness. In addition, each child is unique, and the educational program must reflect this and must consequently be individualized. Gifted children can be helped to fully develop their intellectual skills, thus affording them the chance to move into careers that require fewer physical skills. Educational programs should use the child's illness and knowledge of the illness to advantage.

Scientific projects on the effects of diseases on the body and the development of teaching tools that explain the body's processes to classmates can be exciting educational challenges for the gifted chronically ill child. Materials should be diverse and adequate for the intellectual abilities of the child.

There is nothing more frustrating for gifted children than to be given assignments that are simplistic and below their levels. Without adequate social contacts, these children may rely on the excitement and stimulation of their schoolwork to a greater extent than other children. This may work against them if they learn to avoid social contacts, using their intelligence as an excuse to avoid the anxiety and stress of peer interactions.

Other talents, such as those in art, music, or handcrafts, should be encouraged and supported. The chronically ill child often develops these for leisure time pursuits; talented children can be encouraged to pursue these interests as career goals.

For a detailed discussion of the issues involved in educating gifted and talented children, the reader is directed to the text, *Educating Gifted and Talented Learners* by D.F. Sellin and J.W. Birch (1980).

BOOKS FOR CHILDREN ABOUT CHILDREN WITH HANDICAPS

Any Handicap

Grealish, Mary Jane Von Brausberg, and Grealish, Charles A. *Amy Maura.* Human Policy Press, 1975. 32 pp. $1.75 (paper). (Ages 5-8).

Southall, Ivan. *Let the Balloon Go.* St. Martin's Press, 1968. 142 pp. (Out of print.) (Ages 9-14).

Stein, Sara Bonnett. *About Handicaps: An Open Family Book for Parents and Children Together.* Walker & Co., 1974. 47 pp. $5.95. (Ages 3-8).

Learning Disabilities

Lasker, Joe. *He's My Brother.* Albert Whitman & Co., 1974. 36 pp. $3.95. (Ages 3-8).

Mental Retardation

Brightman, Alan J. *Like Me.* Behavioral Education Projects, 1975. (Order from Behavioral Education Projects, Read House, Harvard University, Cambridge, MA 02138). 48 pp. $2.95 (paper). (Ages 5-8).

Byars, Betsy. *The Summer of the Swans.* Viking Press, 1970. 142 pp. $4.95. Avon Books, 1974. $.95 (paper). (Ages 9-14).

Carpelan, Bo. *Bow Island.* (Translated from the Swedish by Sheila La Farge.) Delacorte Press, 1971. 140 pp. $3.95. (Ages 9-14).

Cleaver, Vera, and Cleaver, Bill. *Me Too.* J.B. Lippincott, 1973. 158 pp. $6.95. New American Library, 1975. $1.25 (paper). (Ages 11-14).

Fassler, Joan. *One Little Girl.* Human Sciences Press, 1969. 19 pp. $5.95. (Ages 3-8).

Little, Jean. *Take Wing*. Little, Brown & Co., 1968. 176 pp. $5.95. (Ages 9–14).

Reynolds, Pamela. *A Different Kind of Sister*. Lothrop, Lee & Shepard, 1968. 193 pp. $4.75. (Ages 9–14).

Wrightson, Patricia. *A Racecourse for Andy*. Harcourt, Brace & World, 1968. 156 pp. $4.95. (Ages 9–14).

Autism

Gold, Phyllis. *Please Don't Say Hello*. Human Sciences Press, 1975. 47 pp. $6.95. (Ages 9–12).

Parker, Richard. *He Is Your Brother*. Brockhampton Press, 1974. 88 pp. $4.50. (Available from Musson Book Company, 30 Lesmill Road, Don Mills, Ontario, Canada M3B 2T6). (Ages 9–12).

Rook, David. *Run Wild, Run Free*. (Original Title: *The White Colt*). Scholastic Book Services, 1967. 205 pp. $.75 (paper). (Ages 11–14).

Emotional Disturbances

Rubin, Theodore Isaac. *Jordi/Lisa and David*. (Two stories in one volume). Ballantine Books, 1962. 144 pp. $1.25 (paper). (Ages 11–14).

Physical Handicaps

Fassler, Joan. *Howie Helps Himself*. Albert Whitman & Co., 1975. 32 pp. $3.95. (Ages 3–8).

Killilea, Marie. *Wren*. Dell Publishing Co., 1968. 122 pp. $.95 (paper). (Ages 8–12).

Little, Jean. *Mine for Keeps*. Little, Brown & Co., 1962. 186 pp. $5.95. (Ages 9–12).

Savitz, Harriet May. *Fly, Wheels, Fly*. John Day, 1970. 90 pp. $4.50. (Ages 9–14).

Wolf, Bernard. *Don't Feel Sorry for Paul*. J.B. Lippincott, 1974. 96 pp. $7.95. (Ages 5–8).

Visual Handicaps

Heide, Florence Parry. *Sound of Sunshine, Sound of Rain*. Parents' Magazine Press, 1970. 34 pp. $5.50. (Ages 5–8).

Little, Jean. *From Anna*. Harper & Row, 1972. 201 pp. $4.95. $1.95 (paper). (Ages 9–12).

Hearing Impairments

Levine, Edna S. *Lisa and Her Soundless World*. Human Sciences Press, 1974. 32 pp. $5.70. (Ages 5–8).

Ronnei, Eleanor C., and Porter, Joan. *Tim and His Hearing Aid.* Alexander Graham Bell Association, 1965 (Rev. ed.). 47 pp. $3.00 (paper). (Ages 5-8).

Speech Impairments

Cunningham, Julia. *Burnish Me Bright.* Pantheon Books, 1970. 80 pp. $3.95. (Ages 9-12).
Lee, Mildred. *The Skating Rink.* The Seabury Press, 1969. 126 pp. $6.50. Dell Publishing Co. $.95 (paper). (Ages 11-14).
White, E.B. *The Trumpet of the Swan.* Harper & Row, 1970. 210 pp. $4.95. $1.25 (paper). (All ages).

Multiple Handicaps

Hickok, Lorena A. *The Story of Helen Keller.* Scholastic Books Services, 1958. 156 pp. $.75 (paper). (Ages 9-12).
Hunter, Edith Fisher. *Child of the Silent Night.* Dell Publishing Co., 1963. 124 pp. $.75 (paper). (Ages 7-10).

SUMMARY

This chapter reviewed a variety of educational strategies for use with children with chronic illnesses. General considerations were presented for the home and hospital setting, as well as for specialized populations such as the developmentally disabled child and the gifted and talented learner. In the following chapters, more specific educational strategies will be identified for children with special needs.

A key thread that runs through this chapter concerns the use of adaptation in the educational model, so that the program can fit the needs of the child, thus affording maximum educational productivity.

REFERENCES

Baldwin, A. (Ed.). *Educational planning for the gifted: Overcoming cultural, geographic and socioeconomic barriers.* Reston, VA: Council for Exceptional Children, 1978.

Ballard, J. Federal legislation for the education of gifted and talented children. In F. Weintraub, A. Abeson, J. Ballard, & M. LaVor (Eds.), *Public policy and the education of exceptional children.* Reston, VA: Council for Exceptional children, 1975.

Bureau of Education for Exceptional Children, Division of Physically Handicapped, Kentucky State Department of Education. *Handbook for programs for home and/or hospital instruction.* Frankfort, Ky., 1978.

Burkhart, L.J. *Homemade battery-powered toys and educational devices for severely handicapped children.* Millville, PA: L. Burkhart Inc., 1980.

Connor, F.P. *Education of the homebound/hospitalized child.* New York: Columbia University, Teachers College, 1964.

Kaisling, P.M., & Kalafatich, A.J. Caring for the mentally handicapped child undergoing surgery. *Journal of the Association for the Care of Children in Hospitals,* 1978, *6*(3), 15–16.

Leonard, J. (Ed.). *Services to the gifted handicapped: A project summary.* Chapel Hill, NC: Chapel Hill Training Outreach Project, 1977.

Massie, R., & Massie, S. *Journey.* New York: A. Knopf Co., 1975.

Milne, N. *In-service training for the hospital/homebound teacher.* Unpublished paper, 1980.

Robinson, H.B., Roedell, W.C., & Jackson, N.E. Early identification and intervention. In A.H. Passow (Ed.), *The gifted and the talented: Their education and development. The seventy-eighth yearbook of the national society for the study of education, part I.* Chicago: University of Chicago Press, 1979.

Sellin, D.F., & Birch, J.W. *Educating gifted and talented learners.* Rockville, MD: Aspen Systems Corp., 1980.

Ungame. Ungame Corporation. Anaheim, California 92806.

Chapter 5

Invisible Illnesses

OVERVIEW

This chapter reviews several invisible chronic illnesses and describes a variety of educational strategies. The illnesses to be examined are asthma, diabetes, renal diseases, hemophilia, epilepsy, sickle cell anemia, cardiac diseases, and cystic fibrosis. The unique commonality among these disease entities is their virtual invisibility to the outside world. Children with these diseases often seem healthy to others, until their disease is overtly manifested in coughing or wheezing attacks, seizures, weakness, pain, or other symptoms typical of acute onset. This paradox often creates special problems for the children thus affected. They want to, and do, appear normal. However, they may be betrayed by their disease at any moment. The precarious nature of the balance between health and illness requires concomitant educational strategies designed to support the child's healthy side, while making allowances for the special needs and limitations imposed by the illness.

ASTHMA

Asthma is a condition of the bronchial tubes of the lungs. It occurs as intermittent episodes of wheezing and dyspnea (shortness of breath) generally associated with a hyperresponsive state of the bronchi (Aaronson, 1972). In order to understand the mechanism of an asthmatic attack, it is necessary to know how the bronchial tubes function.

The bronchial tubes are connected to the windpipe (trachea) and distribute air to the lungs (see Figures 5-1 and 5-2). They resemble the roots of a tree. During an asthmatic attack, the sensitive walls of the bronchi become partially closed. This may be due to swelling of the lining or mucous membrane, a spasm of the bronchial muscles, or mucus plugs caught in the tubes.

Figure 5-1 Bronchial Tree

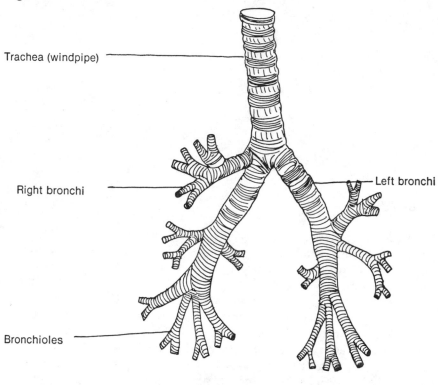

During an attack, breathing becomes difficult, and the child may have periods of dry coughing or may spit up mucus. Attacks may be mild and of relatively short duration, or they may last many hours. They may develop slowly over many hours or come on suddenly, often during the night. The attacks are generally episodic, with many symptom-free intervals. Recurrent attacks may result in permanent lung damage, causing the lung tissue to stretch and placing an extra burden on the heart as it works to force blood to the damaged lungs.

Some asthmatic attacks may be very severe, and children may feel that they are suffocating, able to breathe in but unable to release air. The panic that is felt on such occasions often exacerbates the attack. Children may begin to cough or vomit and may perspire. As fatigue and the lack of adequate oxygen increase, the child's lips and finger tips may become bluish, signaling a decrease in the level of oxygen. Emergency medical procedures are necessary at this point to prevent respiratory failure and damage from anoxia (Ellis, 1975). Severe episodes such as that described above are termed

Figure 5-2 Lungs

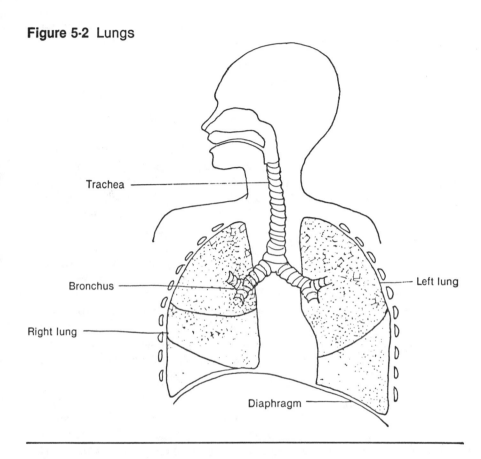

Trachea

Bronchus

Right lung

Left lung

Diaphragm

---

status asthmaticus and can be life-threatening if medical treatment is not prompt.

Prevalence

Asthma is the most common chronic disease of childhood. It is estimated that two to four percent of the population have asthma, and the American Lung Association (1980) reports that the U.S. Public Health Service has estimated that more than 2 million children under age 16 have asthma. It occurs in all races and countries and affects both males and females, although it is reported to be more prevalent in boys than in girls (American Lung Association, 1980).

Age of Onset

Asthmatic symptoms may be present during infancy, but the onset is most common between three and eight years of age. Often, chronic respiratory illnesses precede the onset of asthma in childhood. About 65 percent of children with asthma develop symptoms before age five (Fisher, 1980).

Etiology

There has been a great deal of discussion and disagreement over the question of the etiology of asthma. Medical research has focused on allergies and infections as the primary causal agents, while mental health professionals have explored the psychological aspects of the disease. Recent findings put these conflicting theories in perspective. As S.P. Bronheim (1978) summarizes, these approaches "have mistaken conditions correlated with exacerbation of symptoms with causative factors. Psychological stress, allergens and infections are all external agents" (p. 311). Conditions or situations that affect asthmatics do not trigger attacks in nonasthmatics. There thus seems to be an increased sensitivity in the bronchial tubes of asthmatics that allows for a variety of substances or situations to trigger attacks. Genetics are strongly implicated in asthma, and there is often a positive family history for asthma or other allergic reactions.

Thus it would seem that, through a complicated physiological process, the bronchial tubes' normal ability to react to a variety of irritants is in some way defective. Any number of factors, alone or in combination, such as allergens, psychological stress, infection, air pollution, cold, and exercise can precipitate an asthma attack.

Treatment Strategies

Treatment of asthma is aimed primarily at relaxing the bronchi so that attacks may be prevented and at removing triggering agents from the environment or minimizing their effects. A number of treatment strategies are commonly used in asthma. Among them are avoidance of allergens, allergy testing and desensitization, breathing exercises and relaxation techniques, psychological intervention, as well as a wide variety of drugs. Some of these methods are aimed at preventing attacks, while others are administered during an attack to minimize its effects.

Avoidance

Because of the complex nature of asthma and the difficulty encountered in identifying one or a few triggering allergens, avoidance is at best only a partial therapy. Parents may be asked to keep complex records of a child's food intake, activities, and behavior in an attempt to pinpoint causative agents. Houses may need to be thoroughly cleaned and kept dust-free, and pets may have to be given up or relegated to certain rooms. Air conditioning may need to be provided for a child's room. All these procedures may have the effect of draining the family's emotional or financial resources. Occasionally in severe cases, a move to another city or state is recommended, although this is not usual today.

While the family of an asthmatic child should make every effort to help the child avoid obvious allergens, the subtle nature of the disease may make avoidance all but impossible to achieve.

Allergy Testing and Desensitization

For children who exhibit clear-cut responses to certain foods or substances, testing and desensitization may provide a real measure of relief. After determination of a number of allergens that create a reaction in skin tests, a series of injections can be given that consists of an extract of the most allergenic substances. These desensitization injections can temporarily decrease a child's sensitivity to allergens and can thus decrease attacks for a season or year. The series needs to be repeated yearly for continued results.

Breathing Exercises and Postural Relaxation

Children can be trained to practice a series of breathing exercises designed to increase abdominal breathing and allow for a better exchange of air. The rationale behind such treatment is that children with asthma tend to develop faulty breathing habits and lose mobility of their lower chest. Their upper chest becomes overworked, and they need to learn to increase the movement of their lower chest. Breathing exercises need to be part of the treatment program so that the asthmatic child can do the following:

- increase abdominal breathing
- use exercises to stop an asthmatic episode early
- improve exercise tolerance and correct postural defects
- develop self-confidence

Special breathing during an asthmatic attack will reduce and even abort an attack. If the child learns how to use control at the time of an attack, the panic from breathlessness and hyperventilation can be avoided. Exhibit 5-1 outlines the steps in breathing exercises and lists blowing exercises that can be used for younger children to increase their ability to breathe in and out freely.

Medications

At home, asthmatics may be given a wide variety of medications to ingest or inhale, the aim of which is to increase the dilation of the bronchi. If home

Exhibit 5-1 Breathing Exercises for Asthmatics

A. Aim: To help patient get a better exchange of air.
B. Position: Be on back with hips and knees flexed (to relax abdominals); practice in sitting, standing, walking.
  1. Place one hand on mid chest, other on abdomen.
  2. Keep mouth closed and breathe in deeply through nose. Let abdomen rise, and chest should remain stationary.
  3. Breathe out slowly through pursed lips, making soft blowing "ssss" sound. Press abdomen inward and upward, and chest should still remain at rest. (Expiration through pursed lips prevents collapse of bronchial tubes.)
C. Blowing exercises
  1. Blow out candle at varying distances.
  2. Blow Ping-Pong balls.
  3. Blow bubbles through a straw.
  4. Blow musical instrument.
  5. Blow party horns, toys.

treatment using rest, forced liquids, breathing exercises, and medication all fail, emergency medical care must be given. Often, oxygen is needed, and corticosteroids are given, which can have serious side-effects if not monitored carefully. Children with asthma may need to be on maintenance doses of medication to prevent attacks or may need to take medication for a few days or weeks following a severe attack.

Psychological Interventions

There has been much controversy over the psychological component of asthma. Early studies seemed to implicate the mother-child relationship, pointing to a high proportion of overly dependent asthmatic children (Cohen, 1971), although the vast majority of controlled studies raise questions about the cause and effect relationship of asthma and dependency. L. Gordis (1973) suggests that the frequency of emotional disturbance seen in asthmatics may not be higher than the population of other groups with chronic illness and may be the result rather than the cause of the asthma. Stress and the fear of an attack may also increase the dependency of asthmatic children and may allow overprotective mothers the rationale for continued infantilization of their children. In some instances, such cyclical relationships develop between the fear of separation and the onset of an attack that environmental intervention may be necessary. The Children's Asthma Research Institute and Hospital in Denver removes children from their families for one or more years, on the assumption that such "parentectomy" (Peshkin, 1968) will drastically improve the severity of intractable asthma. As reported by Georgia Travis (1976), their latest research indicates the presence of two subgroups, those whose asthma improves dramatically after environmental change, and those who continue to suffer from severe asthma.

While the psychogenesis of asthma may be questionable, a number of factors are clearly related to the exacerbation of the condition. Anxiety and stress can indeed precipitate attacks, as can the family tensions that result from the presence of a chronically ill child. Additionally, a disorganized, chaotic family may not be able to provide the medical management and supervision necessary to protect the child from frequent, severe attacks. Standard psychotherapy techniques, as well as family therapy, can assist the child and family to better manage the condition. Occasionally, foster care or residential placement may be necessary to provide a safe environment for a child with severe asthma.

Prognosis

In many cases, asthma may be outgrown with time, although permanent lung damage may result. As the child grows, the bronchial passages also increase in size, allowing for a fuller airway. Children begin to recognize the foods or situations that can bring on an attack and may be more willing to cooperate in their own medical management. L. Fisher (1980) reports that even with good management, over half the children never outgrow asthma, although the frequency and severity of symptoms may decrease in time.

Special Considerations

Asthmatic children who are taking maintenance medication may appear listless or restless and irritable. They may have difficulty concentrating in school due to the effects of medications.

Children on large doses of steroids may be short-statured, and puberty may be delayed. Fear of attacks in school may lead an asthmatic child to appear inattentive or depressed or may account for frequent school absence.

School absence is a serious problem for asthmatics. Usually, only a few days are missed at any one time, making such children ineligible for home teaching in most states. Returning to the group and trying to catch up on missed work can add to the stress felt by school age children and can cause them to fall even further behind socially and academically.

Excessive exercise may increase the likelihood of an attack for some children. This presents a continuing dilemma for the teacher, who may not feel comfortable making the decision as to how much activity a child with asthma can engage in, and when to interfere in such a child's activity. The early warning symptoms of an attack may not be noticed by a teacher overwhelmed with work and other responsibilities, and children may not want to risk social isolation by placing limits on themselves in play.

DIABETES

"Juvenile diabetes mellitus is the most common endocrine abnormality of childhood. It is a chronic metabolic disorder of energy utilization" (Garner & Thompson, 1978, p. 222). The Islets of Langerhans, in the pancreas, fail to produce insulin. Insulin is necessary to break down carbohydrates so that they can be used for energy. The effect is that there is an increase of sugar in the blood (hyperglycemia) and in the urine (glycosuria). While there is no cure for diabetes, control can be achieved by the administration of insulin by injection. Juvenile diabetes typically develops suddenly and severely, and treatment must be prompt to prevent coma and death. The warning signals include frequent urination, abnormal thirst, unusual hunger, rapid weight loss, irritability, weakness, fatigue, and nausea or vomiting. Type I, or juvenile diabetes, is differentiated from type II, or adult diabetes, by age of onset and controllability of the condition. Usually, juvenile diabetes is the more difficult to control.

Prevalence and Onset

Children represent four to five percent of all diabetics. Knowles (1971) reports 1 child in 2,500 under age 15 with the condition. The symptoms appear most often in children aged 10 to 16, although they may appear at any age. The most prevalent time of onset is during the prepubertal growth spurt, at age 11 or 12. Once the disease is diagnosed, it is present for life. No cure or remission occurs, and in type I, juvenile onset, the pancreas usually ceases virtually all production of insulin within the first two years of the disease.

Etiology

Although the metabolic process is known, the cause for the malfunction of the pancreas remains a mystery. Genetics have been implicated in diabetes, although the exact mode of transmission has not yet been traced. Probably a multifactorial mode of transmission exists (Garner & Thompson, 1978) in which several genes are implicated, as well as viral and/or environmental predisposing factors. It seems that both parents need to have genetic manifestations of the disease, although they may not themselves have the clinical symptoms of diabetes.

Treatment

Diabetes is a life-threatening disease if not treated and controlled adequately. In fact, before the discovery of insulin in 1921, there was no effective treatment, and diabetics rarely survived more than a year or two after diagnosis (American Diabetes Association, 1977). Diagnosis is made through a test that measures the amount of sugar in the blood. Once the diagnosis has been made, hospitalization is usually required in order to determine the unique balance of insulin and diet that will be necessary to maintain control and to teach the child and family how to manage the disorder. For the diabetic child, control of the condition is the vital factor in treatment, a factor that is made complex by the nature of the condition and the methods necessary to maintain such control. Some juvenile diabetics are "brittle," which means that control is difficult to maintain regardless of how well they regulate their insulin and food intake. Infections, emotional stress, and exercise also affect this delicate balance, making the diabetic child at risk for either coma or insulin shock. The therapeutic goal is to maintain an equilibrium between insulin, food intake, and energy expenditure. Food intake and exercise must be carefully monitored, urine must be tested daily, and insulin must be injected on a regular, rigid schedule. The need to maintain such a constant monitoring and the basic processes that are affected can have a significant impact upon the child's developmental continuity. Food and eating are basic to life, and the emotional ties established between the provision of food and love have been well documented. The need to restrict certain foods, such as sugars, and limit others can interfere with this relationship, confusing both child and parent. The child may feel punished by the withholding of food, the parent guilty. Urine testing, which must be done four times daily, interferes with the child's developing sense of privacy and may make the school age child feel ashamed and embarrassed. The need for daily injections of insulin can add to the overall feeling of guilt and punishment for, after all, needles do hurt, even if daily shots become routine. The need to eat regularly, awaken early every day for food, urine testing, and injections, and watch the balance of food intake and exercise places additional burdens on children and their families. Parents, usually mothers, have to assume the responsibility for all these aspects of a diabetic child's care. As children mature, they can be taught to take over the responsibility for their own care. This should be done carefully, with the gradual transfer of responsibility from parent to child, to prevent crisis. Premature assumption of responsibility by a child may lead to confusion as to measurement of dosage or other mistakes that can result in coma or insulin reaction. Likewise, unnecessary delay in allowing the child to assume responsibility will result in abnormal dependence. By adolescence, the diabetic child should have control over daily therapeutic regimens to avoid battles over autonomy and control.

Urine must be tested for sugar levels and acetone, usually four times daily: after the first voiding in the morning, before lunch and dinner, and before bedtime. Regulations in food intake, exercise, or amount of insulin may be needed as a result of these tests. Insulin is administered by hypodermic syringe once or twice daily. The amount may vary as a result of urine tests, as well as the amount of exercise the child has had or contemplates. Insulin needs increase with age and decrease with exercise, since the body burns off excess sugar. Seasonal changes may affect the dosage, as well as infections and menstrual periods in girls. Parents, and later the children themselves, need to constantly weigh these factors in drawing up daily dosages.

Food exchange lists are used often to allow diabetic children some control in their diets, but they require training and experience (see Exhibit 5-2). Even with the best judgment and the most careful monitoring, the delicate balance may be lost.

Diabetic children, their parents, teachers, and peers need to be aware of the symptoms of ketoacidosis and insulin shock (hypoglycemia) and need to be prepared to deal with both events. Ketoacidosis can result if insufficient insulin is present. Symptoms vary somewhat from child to child, but they usually include excessive urination, thirst, hunger, weakness, drowsiness, vomiting, and finally unconsciousness. Ketoacidosis usually comes on slowly, the urine tests show large amounts of ketones, and the child after a time begins to recognize warning signals. The young child, or the child who may be too shy or embarrassed to tell anyone, may develop more severe signs. If untreated, ketoacidosis can lead to death.

Insulin shock, the reaction to an excess of insulin, is one of the everpresent threats of the disease. It can come on quickly and can cause permanent brain damage if untreated. Again, symptoms vary from child to child, but they usually involve trembling, dizziness, slurred speech, shaking, sweating, or emotional outbursts Convulsions and unconsciousness will follow if sugar is not administered quickly. Teachers, children, and parents need to keep lifesavers, chocolate, orange juice, or other forms of sugar available to prevent severe attacks. As A.M. Garner and C.W. Thompson (1978) note:

> The life-saving insulin therapy, then, is a mixed blessing. For this reason, recent experiments on transplants have been hailed with increasing enthusiasm ... (Ehrlich, 1974).
>
> In 1973, ... Lacy succeeded in transplanting the islets of Langerhans in inbred rats and thus in curing the diabetes (Kemp et al., 1973). Subsequent research confirmed the initial finding. The generalization of such research to human diabetic subjects would revolutionize the entire field of diabetes. (p. 228)

Treatment for diabetes needs to be coordinated by well-trained physicians, with the help of the children, their parents, and their teachers. One issue that

Exhibit 5-2 Food Exchange List for the Diabetic Child

The diabetic diet is broken down into six exchanges. By exchange we mean that we may trade or substitute one food within an exchange for another food within the same exchange group. The key is within the exchange group. You may not exchange one food for another food outside a particular exchange group.

For example, you may exchange an apple (from the fruit exchange) for an orange (also from the fruit exchange). You may not exchange an apple (from the fruit exchange) for a slice of bacon (from the fat exchange). The reason is that within each exchange, each food item has approximately the same amount of calories, carbohydrate, protein, and fat.

The six exchange groups include milk, fruit, vegetable, fat, meat, and bread exchanges.

The milk exchange contains 12 grams of carbohydrate and 8 grams of protein, for a total of approximately 80 calories.

	Amount
Skim milk	1 c.
Buttermilk	1 c.
Yogurt (made from skim milk, unflavored)	1 c.
Whole milk (omit 2 fats)	1 c.

The fat exchange contains 5 grams of fat and approximately 45 calories.

	Amount
Butter	1 tsp.
Margarine	1 tsp.
Bacon, crisp	1 tsp.
Cream, light	2 tbsp.
French dressing	1 tbsp.
Italian dressing	1 tbsp.
Mayonnaise	1 tsp.
Salad dressing	2 tsp.
Corn oil	1 tsp.
Olive oil	1 tsp.
Peanut oil	1 tsp.

Exhibit 5-2 continued

Almonds	10 whole
Pecans	2 large, whole
Peanuts	
Spanish	20 whole
Virginia	10 whole
Walnuts	6 small
Other nuts	6 small

The vegetable exchange contains 5 grams of carbohydrate and 2 grams of protein and approximately 25 calories. One exchange equals ½ cup of vegetable.

Asparagus
Beets
Broccoli
Carrots
Cauliflower
Celery
Kale
Mushrooms
Onions
Spinach
String beans
Tomatoes
Tomato juice
Zucchini

Raw vegetables as desired:
Endive
Escarole
Lettuce
Radishes
Romaine

The fruit exchange contains 10 grams of carbohydrate and approximately 40 calories.

	Amount
Apple	1
Apple juice	⅓ c.
Applesauce	½ c.
Banana	½
Berries	½ c.

Exhibit 5-2 continued

Cherries	10
Cranberry juice	½ c.
Fruit cocktail	½ c.
Grapefruit	½
Grapefruit juice	½ c.
Grapes	20
Melon:	
Cantaloupe	¼ melon
Honeydew	⅛ melon
Watermelon	1 c.
Nectarine	1
Orange	1
Orange juice	½ c.
Pear	1
Pineapple	½ c.
Raisins	2 tbsp.
Tangerine	1

Fruit may be fresh, cooked, canned, or frozen to which neither sugar nor syrup has been added. Use fruit packed in its own juice or unsweetened. You may not remove the sugar by washing or rinsing the fruit.

The meat exchange contains 7 grams of protein and approximately 3 grams of fat, to yield approximately 55 calories. Each exchange is equal to 1 ounce.

Beef	
Pork	
Lamb	
Veal	
Poultry	
Cheese (except cheddar)	
Creamed low-fat cottage cheese	¼ c.
Egg (1)	

High Fat Meat (omit one fat)
Capon
Duck
Goose
Cheddar cheese
Cold cuts

Exhibit 5-2 continued

Frankfurter
Peanut butter (omit 2 fats)   2 tbsp.

The bread exchange contains 15 grams of carbohydrate and 2 grams of protein, to yield approximately 70 calories.

Starchy vegetables

	Amount
Corn	⅓ c.
Lima beans	½ c.
Peas, green (canned or frozen)	½ c.
Potato	1 small or ½ c.
Sweet potato	¼ c.

Bread

White	1 sl.
Whole wheat	1 sl.
Rye	1 sl.
Bagel	½
English muffin	½
Hamburger bun	½
Hot dog bun	½
Angel food cake	1½″ sq.
Vanilla wafers	5

Cereal

Bran flakes	½ c.
Cereal (not sweetened)	¾ c.
Puffed cereal	1 c.
Cooked cereal	½ c.
Popcorn (no added fat)	3 c.
Pretzels	25 small

Crackers

Saltines	6
Soda, 2½″ sq.	4
Graham, 2½″ sq.	2
Biscuit, 2″ (omit 1 fat)	1
Corn muffin (omit 1 fat)	1
Pancake, 5″ × ½″ (omit 1 fat)	1

Exhibit 5-2 continued

Waffle, 5″ × ½″ (omit 1 fat)	1
French fried potato (omit 1 fat)	8
Potato chips (omit 2 fats)	15
Corn chips (omit 2 fats)	15
Ice cream (omit 2 fats)	½ c.

Free foods

Bouillon or consommé (fat-free)
Carbonated beverages without sugar
Soda water
Coffee (not Postum)
Garlic salt
Gelatin, unflavored or artificially sweetened
Horseradish, plain
Onion salt
Poppy seed
Salt
Spices
Tea
Vinegar

Use in small amounts

Catsup
Chili sauce
Chewing gum (sugarless)
Jam and jelly (artificially sweetened)
Lemon or lime juice
Worcestershire sauce
A-1 sauce
Soy sauce
Tabasco sauce

Avoid

Candy
Regular sweetened gum
Doughnuts
Soda
Jam
Jelly

Exhibit 5-2 continued

Marmalade
Honey
Molasses
Sugar-sweetened cereal
Sugar

The physician calculates the diet by using the patient's height, weight, age, and sex to determine the caloric requirements. Once these have been decided, the diet order is then picked up and verified by the dietitian, who divides the calories into three equal meals and usually two snacks, depending on the type of insulin the patient is using.

Source: Claudia R. Sick, Mt. Washington Pediatric Hospital. Unpublished material, 1981.

has aroused a great deal of controversy has to do with the degree of control that should be maintained. Some physicians recommend strict regimens, with no allowance for "cheating," while others argue that such rigidity has not been shown to decrease future complications and has the added risk of interfering with the normal emotional and social development of diabetic children. The agreed-upon goals of treatment are to protect such children from the damage of repeated ketoacidosis or insulin reaction while allowing them to engage in as normal a life experience as possible.

Prognosis

Except for the occasions of ketoacidosis or insulin reaction, diabetes is almost totally invisible. Neither the symptoms of the disease nor the medications affect the size, appearance, or growth of diabetic children. With good control, many diabetics can lead relatively normal lives. Unfortunately, with a metabolic disorder of such magnitude, complications in other body systems are not uncommon after a number of years. Three systems are particularly vulnerable: the vascular, or blood system; the retinal system, affecting vision; and the neural system, affecting the nerves. Small blood vessels may be affected over time, leading to retinal disease and possibly blindness, as well as kidney damage. It has been estimated that about 70 percent of diabetics develop some form of retinal dysfunction after 20 years (Paulsen & Colle, 1969). This requires frequent monitoring by eye specialists. Teachers need to be aware of this complication in order to request periodic vision screening of a diabetic child if school work seems to be affected.

The vascular complications inherent in diabetes are usually not seen until diabetes has been present for many years; hence, they are rarely seen in children. Such complications can affect the circulation of blood to the extremities. Infections must be treated promptly if circulation is impaired to avoid gangrene and possibly the loss of a limb. Again, careful monitoring can prevent serious complications.

Special Considerations

Most diabetic children, under good control, can attend school regularly. Teachers should be aware of their conditions and should have sugar or its equivalent available in case they exhibit symptoms of insulin shock. In such an event, a small amount of sugar should be given to the child (e.g., 4 ounces of juice or soda, 3 to 4 lifesavers), and the child should rest and be watched closely. According to Dr. P. Burgan, specialist in diabetic care (personal communication), if a person is in doubt over a symptom, the administration of sugar is the safest response, since the body's reaction to too much insulin is sudden and dangerous, while the reaction to an excess of sugar is much slower and can be corrected at the next urine testing. Patience is urged, since 15 to 20 minutes may pass before a behavioral change is noted. Teachers are also urged to be sensitive to mood swings or unusual behavioral manifestations because these may be signs of hypoglycemia.

Adolescents may express anger at having to be limited by diet and time constraints and may on occasion stop giving themselves insulin as a form of negativism. Symptoms of excess sugar often will be sufficient to cause them to restart the insulin, although frequent emergency hospital admissions during times of rebellion may be necessary. Counseling, either individually or in peer groups, may help such an adolescent to sort out feelings of anger, helplessness, and shame. At times, a well-controlled adolescent may stop the insulin in order to reconfirm the diagnosis; the onset of symptoms usually suffices to convince the adolescent to maintain the regimen.

Genetic counseling may be helpful for the diabetic child's family at onset and again as the child reaches adolescence and questions of sexual activity and marriage arise. Special summer camps for diabetic children can help the child overcome the early fears of peer reaction.

In class, the diabetic child may need to use the bathroom more frequently and may need special permission for snacks. The classroom teacher may be able to use the presence of a diabetic in the class as an educational tool. Sensitively handled, with the full permission of the child and family, the class can study endocrine function and energy and its relationship to sugar consumption and nutrition. Such classroom strategies can help make diabetic children accepted by peers, and children can share their special knowledge as class experts.

KIDNEY (RENAL) DISEASES

There are a number of renal diseases that can affect children and that vary in their severity, etiology, and age of onset. The kidneys are vital to life functioning. They consist of two bean-shaped organs that lie close to the backbone, below the rib cage. They have two outer layers, consisting of hundreds of thousands of nephrons, and an inner sac, or pouch. A large tube, called the ureter, connects the kidney with the bladder. The kidneys are a part of the cardiovascular renal system, receiving blood from the heart (see Figure 5-3). Their primary function is to maintain the body's chemical balance by filtering blood through the nephrons. From this filtrate, most of the essential chemicals are returned to the bloodstream. The wastes and excess water collect in the pouch as urine. The urine passes through the ureters and is stored in the bladder for later elimination. If these functions are interrupted, waste backup and toxic poisoning can result. There are a number of causes for such malfunction. There may be congenital abnormalities, affecting structure of the kidneys, ureter, and/or bladder. Some abnormalities may be treated surgically. Others may respond to medical management. Urinary tract infections, especially when poorly treated and recurrent, can eventually cause renal failure. Careful diagnosis and appropriate antibiotic therapy are necessary to prevent such a possibility.

Acute glomerulonephritis, the most common form of nephritis in children, appears to be caused by an allergic reaction to certain strains of streptococcus, not unlike rheumatic fever, and usually follows a sore throat. Although the acute stage of glomerulonephritis rarely leads to the chronic stage (Travis, 1976), careful medical management is necessary to avoid permanent kidney damage or death. Chronic glomerulonephritis is the disease that most often leads to kidney failure and is most common in older children and adolescents.

Children who develop nephrosis, a chronic, relapsing condition, exhibit signs of severe loss of protein in their urine. They are excessively fatigued and appear swollen, especially around their faces and extremities.

In all these diseases, renal failure represents the end result of an uncontrolled condition.

When the kidney is damaged to the extent that there are not sufficient nephrons to filter out the bodily wastes, excess water is not excreted either, and it collects in the body's tissues. This causes the swelling (edema). When kidneys thus cease to function, the toxic poisoning affects the brain and spinal fluid, which may result in lethargy, irritability, or mental confusion. Muscle weakness is also common, and patients may experience severe leg cramps or paralysis.

The kidneys also help to regulate blood pressure, and untreated kidney failure can lead to hypertension and severe headaches.

Figure 5-3 The Renal System

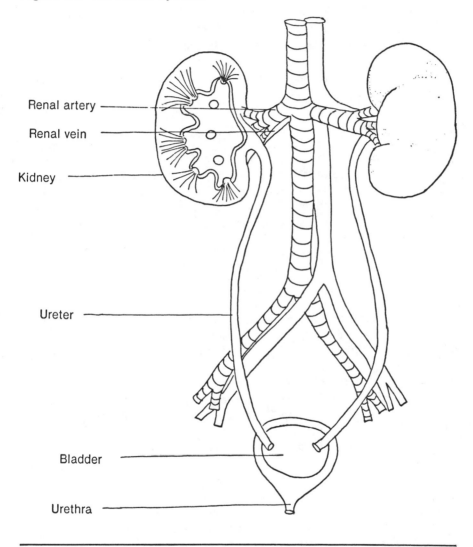

Renal artery

Renal vein

Kidney

Ureter

Bladder

Urethra

Early detection of the underlying pathology and prompt medical or surgical intervention may correct or arrest renal disease. Thus, it is estimated that 80 percent of all cases of nephrosis respond to therapy and do not end in renal failure (Magrab & Papadopoulou, 1978). In spite of this, the incidence of chronic kidney failure is 3.0 to 3.5 per million total population per year (MacGregor, Sheagren, Lipsett, & Woff, 1969).

Age of Onset

Onset varies with the condition and its etiology. In a table prepared by P.R. Magrab and Z.L. Papadopoulou (1978), 50 percent of renal failure in infants, toddlers, and school age children was attributed to congenital abnormalities or inherited disorders, while 66 percent of renal failure in adolescents was attributed to acquired conditions, with glomerulonephritis the most common cause.

Diagnostic Procedures

Tests of urine can indicate the presence of blood, pus, or albumin. Blood tests also can be used to test the kidney's efficiency in waste removal. Other tests are more intrusive and can be quite painful and feared by young children. Cystoscopy, which illuminates the structure of the ureters and bladder, usually requires an anesthetic and hospitalization. Pyelograms, performed by injecting dye into the bloodstream and taking x-rays of the kidneys, are also conducted periodically.

Treatment Strategies

Treatment strategies depend upon the nature of the underlying condition and the stage of the disease. In many congenital malformations, early and often repeated surgical operations are required to repair or reconstruct the renal system. These often are performed during the early months and years of a child's life and can create serious psychosocial trauma to the child and family. Rarely, surgery involves the external genitalia, which can interfere with normal psychosexual development and sexual identity (Freud, 1946). Repeated hospitalizations and the consequent separation of children from their parents can also affect long-term reactions to their illness. In addition, the painful and intrusive diagnostic tests continue to interfere with children's sense of bodily intactness and privacy and lead to a continual sense of betrayal and fears of punishment from adults.

Medications themselves that are given in the early stages of renal disease result in bodily changes that are traumatic and embarrassing. Long-term use of steroids results in delayed growth, moon-faced appearance, and severe acne.

Diet may be severely restricted, and the dietary limitations can make foods unpalatable for a young child. Loss of appetite due to general weakness and immobility during periods of treatment often add to the difficulty in helping children with renal disease maintain adequate nutrition. The diet requires low protein and low salt, with sufficient calories for normal metabolism. Special supplements are needed to make the diet palatable and high in calories.

As children grow, the need to maintain a strict diet and restrict fluids interferes with socialization and can tax the willpower of even the most compliant adolescent; french fries, pizza, soda, hot dogs, and potato chips are all prohibited.

Prognosis

Until the 1960s, chronic renal failure eventually resulted in death, as the kidneys ceased to function and dietary restrictions no longer controlled the buildup of unfiltered wastes. Two scientific breakthroughs have changed this picture. In the process, however, they have created awesome psychological, ethical, and legal issues.

The invention of artificial kidney machines has enabled the medical team to prolong life by hemodialysis, a process that involves connecting a person with end-stage renal disease to a machine that filters the wastes from the blood as it circulates through the machine and then back to the patient. The decision to place a child on hemodialysis is complex and must be made by parents with an awareness of all the complications and emotional and financial drain that dialysis entails. The process can take many hours and must be done two to three times weekly at a centrally located medical center. A shunt is usually prepared, often in the child's arm, by attaching a tube that connects an artery and vein, forming a loop so that a needle can be inserted and good access to the blood supply can be maintained. Shunts must be kept clean and dry, and children need to exercise extreme caution to avoid injury or infection to the shunt site. An alternative approach is to connect an artery and a vein and tie off an area above the juncture to provide a fistula, an enlarged area, for easy access.

The dialysis machine is large and noisy and can be frightening to a young child. In addition, the need to be dependent upon a machine for the sustenance of life creates major difficulties for preadolescents and adolescents and can be a source of fierce conflict between issues of dependence and independence, control and autonomy.

Dialysis is only a temporary, inefficient replacement for normal kidney function. The child must maintain a strict dietary regimen in between dialyses and often appears fatigued and bloated, especially the day before dialysis.

The ultimate goal of treatment then becomes kidney transplantation. This again is fraught with risk, both physical and psychological. Often, the damaged kidneys need to be removed by surgery first. As Magrab and Papadopoulou (1978) note:

> This procedure is very difficult for the child and his family to accept. The child views nephrectomy as a loss of part of himself and

the ultimate realization that his own kidneys have actually failed him and that now his life really must depend on the "kidney machine." From the parents' point of view it implies a negative verdict concerning the irreversibility of their child's kidney disease that they may be unwilling to accept, often questioning and arguing about the necessity of such a procedure. (pp. 275-276)

Kidney transplants are most successful when the donor is a relative. This raises issues of great importance to families: Who should offer their kidneys? Should siblings be "convinced" to give? Will a particular donor be unacceptable? The guilt and anxiety surrounding such decisions need to be dealt with by caring, sensitive professionals. Often, patients' blood and tissue samples are matched with anonymous donors through an intricate national computerized network, and the anxiety of waiting begins. Children in and out of school during this time need special considerations due to their anxiety, their fear of death, and periodic fatigue and reaction to medications.

After transplantation, the child receives massive doses of immunosuppressive drugs to prevent the body's rejection of the donor kidney. Reaction to the drugs, to the fear of rejection, and to the isolation needed due to increased risk of infection vary from child to child. Sensitive professionals need to be aware of children's reactions and need to develop techniques to help them adjust. Magrab and Papadopoulou (1978) cite the following typical problems in the first year after transplant: anxiety and fear of graft rejection, reactions to changes in physical appearance and their effects on self-image, and school adjustment difficulties. Occasionally, children who had expected to die and had adjusted to this possibility become confused and depressed by the change in outcome and need professional help in reevaluating future goals. Typically, young children return to school after transplantation with excessive amounts of energy and exuberance. In the years after successful transplantation, studies report a gradual restoration of family and personal equilibrium (Korsch et al., 1973).

The likelihood that children who have been ill and socially isolated for years will return to normal with no effects on social relationships is questioned by Georgia Travis (1976), as well as by this author. A great deal depends upon the duration of the disease prior to transplantation, the length of time the child was on dialysis, the family's functioning prior to the onset of illness, and the age of the child. Hopefully, with professional help during and after treatment, the effects can be minimized. On some occasions, positive growth and mastery may even result. In one such instance, a 15-year-old male admitted to Mt. Washington Pediatric Hospital for chronic end-stage renal failure entered with a history of a disorganized family system, poor school attendance, and periodic detentions for minor juvenile offenses. He was functionally illiterate, although he tested above the retarded range and had no significant learning disabilities.

After three years, during which he received dialysis and had social work counseling and intense academic and prevocational training, he received a successful kidney transplant. This was followed by vocational training, and he returned to his hometown to a future considerably brighter than when he left. He was able to read, drive, repair cars, and most importantly, relate to people more easily and recognize and deal with his feelings of anger, frustration, and hopelessness.

Special Considerations

Because kidney disease and the treatment modalities used to prolong life affect the behavior of children, their physical appearance, their energy level, and their school attendance, teachers need to be sensitive to all these areas and need to recognize early signs of kidney failure, such as extreme fatigue and swelling, in patients with chronic renal disease. Dialysis schedules must be obtained and, if possible, arranged to coincide with school schedules. Many school districts provide bedside tutoring for children on dialysis so that they can keep up their academic skills. Classroom teachers may want to prepare assignments that allow the child to do research or to complete study items in the hospital and may try to arrange class tests on days when the child is likely to be in school.

Occasionally, children in rural areas need to move closer to a hospital-based dialysis unit, and they must be transferred to other school districts. Good communication between districts can help, as can classroom teachers' sensitivity in keeping the children in touch with their classmates by letters, phone calls, or visits.

HEMOPHILIA

Hemophilia is a hemorrhagic, or bleeding, disease in which the child has periodic, unpredictable bleeding episodes.

Etiology

The classic and most common form of hemophilia (hemophilia A) is due to a deficiency of Factor VII, a protein required for normal clotting of blood. This disorder is transmitted by a mother to her male children via a recessive gene. The chances of inheriting hemophilia or carrying the disease follow classic sex-linked genetic patterns (see Figure 5-4). Daughters who inherit the gene are carriers, while sons develop the actual disease. If a female car-

Figure 5-4   Genetic Transmittal of Hemophilia (Sex-Linked)

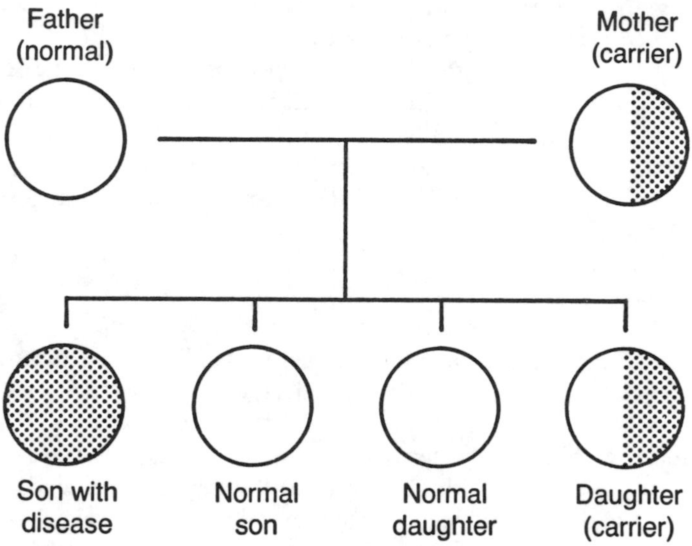

The chances of producing a hemophiliac son (one in four) or
a daughter who is a carrier (one in four), are the same for each pregnancy.

---

rier and a male with the disease have children, they could have a daughter
with the disorder. Hemophilia B, or Christmas disease, is also inherited as a
sex-linked recessive disorder. The protein that is missing, Factor IX, is different than the one missing in hemophilia A, but it, too, is required for blood
coagulation.

Prevalence

In their Erie County study, H. Sultz, E. Schlesinger, W. Mosher, and J.
Feldman, (1972) reported a prevalence of 14.6 cases of hemophilia A per
100,000 males.

Typically, hemophilia is recognized in the infancy and toddler periods, especially when the child begins to actively explore his environment—crawling,
walking, and consequently falling. Contrary to popular belief, internal bleeding is more common than bleeding from cuts and often occurs spontaneously
and without warning. There is often bleeding into joints, causing excessive
pain, swelling, and orthopedic problems. Bleeding into the throat or brain is
often a cause of death when untreated.

Prognosis

As in other chronic illnesses, prognosis for a lengthened life span has improved as medical technology has advanced. As Travis (1976) notes, 25 years ago only 25 percent of diagnosed hemophiliacs survived to age 16, while today almost all children are expected to reach adult life, given optimal medical care. Good medical care is often the key to survival, since access to sophisticated medical centers and ready supplies of vital blood or blood products may mean the difference between life and death for hemophiliacs.

Treatment

In the past, the only treatment for hemophilia consisted of massive, frequent blood transfusions, resulting in hospitalizations, painful reactions to transfusions, financial drains on the family, and the never-ending search for blood donors. New advances in technology have developed a method of concentrating the clotting factor and making it available as cryoprecipitate. This can be stored at home, with special refrigeration, and parents or children can be taught to administer the concentrate, thus preventing the needless delay and trauma of emergency trips to the hospital. Good supervision can prevent most hospitalizations.

Special Considerations

The costs of blood and its concentrates are high, and the need to provide a constant source of blood to blood banks through donors or financial reimbursement can create staggering financial and emotional burdens on the family. Choice of job or locality in which to live involve both the child and parents, distorting the family relationships and affecting the child's adjustment in school and at home. Parents of a hemophiliac child often develop characteristic patterns of maternal overprotection and paternal neglect, thus further emotionally disabling the child. This pattern, described more specifically in Chapter 3, often leads children to develop a fear of risk-taking and an overdependence upon their mothers. Maternal guilt, exacerbated by the knowledge of her role as genetic carrier of the disease, may make routine care and objective, balanced discipline difficult for the mother. Is overprotection inappropriate when a child may bleed after a game of ball or risk death from a head injury or fall? For the hemophiliac child, overprotection may well be normal, and parents must constantly temper their own fears with the knowledge of the consequences of risks allowed.

As a reaction to their disorder or to the overprotection of parents and others, some hemophiliacs may deliberately participate in high-risk activities such as motorcycle riding. In a poignant description of their lives as they were affected by their son's hemophilia, Robert and Suzanne Massie (1975) acknowledge the dramatic effects of the disease on their lives: "Everything that he is, everything that we are now, is because of hemophilia. Our life cannot be separated from it" (p. 409).

School adjustment is very difficult for hemophiliacs. This is due in part to the discontinuity of programming caused by the frequent attacks, by the changes in physical abilities and energy created by periodic bleeding and stiffness of the joints, and by the fears of the children that they may begin to bleed again if they engage in active games or join peers for a social outing. The teacher's attitude can also affect school adjustment. Many teachers or principals, fearful of a child "bleeding to death in class," have difficulty accepting the presence of a hemophiliac in their school even though their fears are based on misconceptions. Teachers may be concerned over the possibility that the child may fall in class or be hit or pushed by peers, thus precipitating a bleeding episode.

Children who are being maintained on home treatments, using the blood precipitant, and whose parents can provide good supervision and management, may be able to attend school with few absences for medical crises. Children with hemophilia, when managed well and with medical approval, are encouraged to become involved in noncompetitive activities such as swimming or fishing.

These activities allow them to maintain good physical health and help them to exercise joints and avoid prolonged disability; they also provide healthy social outlets. Sedentary sports and activities, especially those that involve two or more players such as checkers and chess, should be taught, for the hemophiliac will need to have leisure activities that can be pursued during times of immobility.

Vocational choices involve a number of factors, including academic abilities, severity of the condition and orthopedic complications, and the child's own interests and motivation. Jobs that entail heavy lifting or that are hazardous must be excluded, but a wide variety of career opportunities are available to hemophiliacs, providing they have not been limited by a lack of educational preparation. In a study of hemophiliacs, Katz (1970) reports that school achievement in this population was well below the average, with 34 percent of his study group failing to complete high school. Since job opportunities for non–high school graduates tend to rely heavily on manual labor, it seems that special efforts need to be made to provide the hemophiliac with the educational tools necessary to function in white-collar and technical jobs, which require fewer physical skills.

EPILEPSY*

The child with epilepsy has recurrent seizures. Seizures are sudden, brief attacks manifested by complete or partial loss of consciousness, involuntary motor activity, or cessation of body movement. They are caused by disturbances of cerebral function associated with temporary abnormal discharges of electrical impulses from the brain.

Etiology and Age of Onset

The etiologies of epilepsy are classified as idiopathic (cause unknown) or symptomatic. Eighty percent of cases of epilepsy are idiopathic and usually develop between the ages of 2 and 14. The remaining 20 percent are secondary to head trauma, infectious disease, anoxia at birth, and tumors. Symptomatic epilepsy usually begins before the age of two or in adulthood (Gadow, 1979).

The three major forms of seizures seen by school personnel are grand mal, petit mal, and psychomotor. Most children have only one type of seizure, with 30 percent having two or more types. About 80 percent experience grand mal alone or in combination with other seizures. Petit mal, primarily a disorder of childhood, affects 6 to 12 percent. Psychomotor seizures, which are found in 10 to 20 percent of older children, are rarely seen in children under six. Although prevalence statistics vary depending on population studied, it is commonly reported that 1 of each 100 persons has epilepsy (Epilepsy Foundation of America, 1975).

The grand mal seizure is what many people visualize when they hear the term epilepsy. Shortly before the seizure, about 50 percent experience an aura, or warning. This aura can be an unpleasant smell, a tingling sensation, or a strange noise. The person then loses consciousness and falls to the ground. The motor activity of the grand mal seizure usually includes tonic and clonic phases. In the tonic phase, the body becomes stiff and rigid with extremities positioned straight out and teeth clenched. A small number lose bladder and/or bowel control. During the clonic phase, the limbs of the body jerk repeatedly. After three to five minutes the seizure stops. In the postictal (after seizure) stage, the person may experience muscle aches, confusion, irritability, and fatigue. Some enter a deep sleep. The postictal stage may last from a few minutes to several days.

---

*The sections of this chapter on epilepsy, cardiac disease, sickle cell anemia, cystic fibrosis, and education of adolescents in homebound programs were written by Carol E. Rabin.

Treatment

Teacher Management

When a child has a grand mal seizure, the Epilepsy Foundation of America (1974) recommends the following first aid procedures:

1. Keep calm.
2. Ease child to the floor and loosen restrictive clothing.
3. Remove objects and furniture in the area that may injure the child.
4. Do not try to interfere with or impede movements.
5. Do not force anything between teeth.
6. Turn head to one side to release saliva, and place something soft under the head.
7. When the child regains consciousness, let him or her rest if necessary.

If the seizure lasts more than ten minutes or the child has one seizure after another (status epilepticus), call an ambulance or doctor. Status epilepticus is rare, but it should be treated as a true medical emergency.

Please note that the recommendations do not include trying to insert an object into the person's mouth to prevent tongue biting and/or swallowing. By the time a person enters the tonic phase, the teeth are so tightly clenched, it is virtually impossible to separate them without damaging them.

Petit mal seizures, found primarily in children, last 5 to 20 seconds. These are often described as "staring spells" or daydreaming. The staring is occasionally accompanied by twitching and rolling back of the eyes. Some children will experience up to 100 petit mal seizures a day. Although petit mal seizures disappear with the onset of adolescence, about 60 percent later develop other types of seizures. There is nothing a teacher can do during a petit mal seizure. Since children have no recollection of what transpired during the seizure, teachers are encouraged to repeat to them what was said or done during that time so that they can reorient themselves to the activity at hand.

Psychomotor (temporal lobe) epilepsy is characterized by automatic, stereotyped behavior. A person will cease activity, stare, and begin purposeful but inappropriate movements. Some common examples are repetitive lip smacking and picking at clothing. Usually children will exhibit the same repetitive movements during each seizure. They lose partial or total consciousness during the seizure and do not remember what has happened.

During a psychomotor seizure, the only thing a teacher can do is protect children from injury. Since they are not conscious of their behavior during this time, attempts to restrain may cause them to strike out to protect themselves. These actions do not mean that psychomotor seizures cause violence; rather, they are basically an instinctive response to possible danger.

Persons with psychomotor epilepsy are often mistaken for being intoxicated or insane because of the bizarre or inappropriate movements. The teacher should encourage these children to wear or carry some form of medical identification.

Medical Management

Eighty percent of all seizures can be partially or totally controlled through medication. Widely used anticonvulsants include phenobarbital, Dilantin, Depakene, and Tegretol. Some children experience side effects such as drowsiness and irritability (phenobarbital) and gum problems and hirsutism (Dilantin). These problems can often be somewhat alleviated by a change in dosage and/or by switching to another medication. A major reason for poor seizure control is medical noncompliance. To be effective, a certain level of the drug must be reached in the bloodstream. Reasons for noncompliance included denial of seizures, inability to pay for prescriptions, and inadequate information about administration of medicine.

Special Considerations

Problems related to epilepsy are not confined to concerns related to seizure control and medical compliance. It has been well documented that educational and psychosocial difficulties are experienced by a large segment of children with epilepsy. According to Rodin, Shapiro, and Lennox (1976), 48 percent experience intellectual problems and 54 percent, behavioral ones.

A teacher's questionnaire administered by Rutler, Graham, and Yule (1970) showed that children with epilepsy were rated twice as high as classmates in the areas of lack of concentration, irritability, and fidgeting. When 50 epileptic children were compared with a control group in the areas of academic and social skills, the children with epilepsy scored significantly below expected levels (Green & Hartlage, 1971). Bagley (1970) reported that reading and arithmetic abilities were significantly poorer for epileptic students. A survey of parents of children with epilepsy in Maryland conducted by the Comprehensive Care Clinic at Johns Hopkins Hospital in 1974 (Freeman et al. 1975), found that 50 percent of parents felt that their children had seizure-related behavior problems in school, and 90 percent felt that they had seizure-related learning problems.

The range of intelligence among children with epilepsy is the same as for the rest of the population. However, studies have shown that there are more children identified as having epilepsy in special education classes than there are in regular classes—6.6 percent versus 0.6 percent (U.S. Dept. of HEW, 1978). The poor academic achievement previously cited cannot be attributed to one specific cause. It appears that lowered parental expectations, undiagnosed subtle learning disabilities, teachers' attitudes, and epilepsy-related psychosocial problems all contribute to the lack of academic success of many children with epilepsy.

For many children, it is not the seizures but the psychosocial factors that cause the most adjustment problems. Recent studies have indicated that children with the best seizure control appear to have the most difficulty in coping with their epilepsy (Hodgman et al., 1979). Because of the widely held misconceptions and stigmas attached to epilepsy, many children experience rejection and exclusion.

When children are aware that their teacher is very uncomfortable with the prospect of a seizure in the classroom, they may use this information to avoid responsibility and manipulate unpleasant situations. For example, children may tell the teacher that they will have a seizure if punished for misbehaving.

It is important that teachers be familiar with basic medical information and first aid procedures so that they are able to deal with the child with epilepsy in a professional, matter-of-fact manner. This approach will be reassuring to children and serve as a role model for their classmates. Teachers need to remember that epilepsy does not affect intelligence and that, except when they are having a seizure, they should be treated like normal, healthy children.

Persons with epilepsy have great difficulty in securing employment. Teenagers with epilepsy should be provided with appropriate career and vocational guidance and training to facilitate transition into the job market. Areas to be stressed include:

- preemployment skills—good attendance, interpersonal relations, and attitudes toward work
- medical compliance to ensure optimal seizure control
- work experience
- epilepsy education so that the student can explain accurately his seizure disorder to an employer

In summary, teachers of children with epilepsy must foster attitudes of independence and normality. They should be aware that medication occasionally affects school performance, but that more frequently poor achievement is the result of lowered expectations and stigmatization.

SICKLE CELL ANEMIA

Sickle cell anemia (SCA) is an inherited hemolytic disorder characterized by sickle-shaped red blood cells. Chronic anemia occurs because the sickled cells are more fragile than normal red blood cells, and therefore are destroyed more quickly. As compared with nondisease populations, persons with SCA have one third to one half as many red blood cells. Iron supplements will not improve anemia caused by SCA.

Clinical symptoms of SCA related to the increased destruction of red cells include jaundiced eyes, pale skin, fatigue, and poor appetite. Frequent infections of lungs and bone are common. Many persons with SCA are small in stature, with short trunks and long extremities, and delayed in physical and/or sexual development. Complications of this disease, which result from lowered oxygen and red blood cell levels, affect the spleen, heart, and liver. The spleen gradually disappears as sickle cells block blood vessels.

When the sickled cells become jammed in the blood vessels and less oxygen and blood are able to reach tissues and organs, the person experiences an aplastic crisis or pain attack. An aplastic crisis occurs when the bone marrow stops making new red cells. As old cells are destroyed, severe anemia results, often accompanied by heart failure. Heart enlargement can also lead to heart failure and/or liver enlargement. Ankle ulcers, due to blocked blood vessels, are another common complication. Symptoms of the sickle cell crisis are localized pain, swelling of joints, loss of appetite, fatigue, jaundice, and dehydration. Treatment during periods of crisis is limited to bed rest, antibiotics to prevent infections, nonaspirin pain relievers, and fluids. In serious cases, blood transfusions may be required.

Eight to ten crises a year is the average for children under the age of ten, with the number diminishing as they move toward adulthood. Severity and frequency of crises are dependent on the form of sickle cell disease. Hemoglobin S disease is the most severe and causes frequent crisis and life-threatening complications. Hemoglobin C disease, a disease of the blood but not one of the sickling diseases, takes a milder course, with no crises and symptoms limited to abdominal pain and jaundice. Hemoglobin S-C disease results in milder, less frequent crises and retinal hemorrhages. Infants do not suffer from crises because fetal hemoglobin inhibits sickling (Mullins, 1979).

Etiology and Prevalence

Although SCA is predominantly found in blacks, the disease and its variant forms are also known in southern Indian, Mediterranean, and Latin American populations. In the United States, it is estimated that 1 in 400 blacks suffers from SCA and 1 in 10 is a carrier of sickle cell trait (Peterson & Cleveland, 1975).

To be born with SCA, the child must inherit a gene for sickle cell trait from each parent (see Figure 5-5). Carriers of sickle cell trait are asymptomatic. The trait is believed to have originated as a genetic mutation in Africa as a defense against malaria. Since malaria does not enter sickled cells, persons with sickle cell trait were protected from this previously widespread and fatal disease (Mullins, 1979). When both parents are carriers of sickle cell trait, there is a one in four chance that each offspring will have the disease state. Screening for sickle cell trait is a relatively simple procedure in which a blood sample is subjected to electrophoresis. If a set of prospective parents are both identified to be carriers of sickle cell trait, genetic counseling, focusing on probability statistics of producing a child with SCA and the ways in which the disease would affect a child, can be made available.

Diagnosis of the disease state is made by electrophoresic and microscopic study of the red blood cells. Laboratory analysis is made to determine if the levels of red blood cells and hemoglobin are decreased. Original diagnosis is usually made between the ages of two and six. Since 1972, a fairly reliable screening test for newborn infants has been available.

Prognosis

Until recently, SCA has meant a significantly shortened life expectancy for its victims, with an average mortality age of 40. It is felt in some circles that this prognosis is related not only to the complications of the disease, but to the failure of the medical community to recognize SCA (Allesberry et al., 1977). Frequently, it is not recognized or diagnosed until the child is suffering from a serious crisis. Hopefully, early diagnosis and better preventive health care will increase the life expectancy and quality of life of persons with SCA.

Special Considerations

SCA does not affect intelligence. Children with SCA should be able to function as well as their classmates. Ways of making up school work missed during periods of absence must be developed so that children can continue their educational progress. Since lack of physical stamina prohibits the child from entering occupations that require manual strength, it is vital for the child to acquire the academic skills needed for more sedentary jobs.

In physical education class, children should be allowed to participate as much as they are physically able, unless the physicians' recommendations are different. They should be allowed to stop when they need to rest without continually being reminded of their "limitations." If too much attention is paid, children may try to overexert themselves so that they are not singled out as being different from their peers.

Teachers should be aware that SCA causes frequent urination. Therefore, requests to use the bathroom need to be seen as a medical problem, rather

Figure 5-5 Genetic Transmittal of Sickle Cell Anemia and Cystic Fibrosis

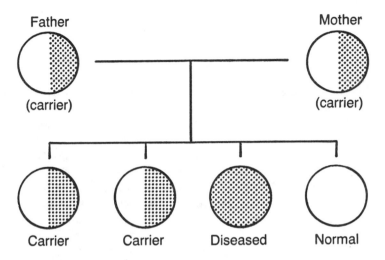

The chances of producing a child with the disease, one in four, are the same with each pregnancy.

than as an attempt to avoid classwork. Teachers must also recognize that although children with SCA may look younger than they are, they should be treated the same as their chronologic peers.

The problems of delayed maturation and low stamina are especially difficult in adolescence. Poor social skills resulting from frequent school absences and slow physical development adversely affect relationships with the opposite sex. Lack of stamina precludes these teenagers from participating in competitive sports. It is important to encourage junior and senior high school students to become involved in nonphysical extracurricular activities. These activities can provide opportunities for the student to improve social skills, gain recognition, and explore possible career areas.

CYSTIC FIBROSIS

Cystic fibrosis is an hereditary disorder of the exocrine glands that affects the respiratory and digestive systems. It is the most lethal of all genetically transmitted diseases of children.

Etiology and Prevalence

Although cystic fibrosis is most common in Caucasian populations, with an estimated incidence of 1 in 1,600 white births, children of other races can be afflicted. Both parents must be carriers of the cystic fibrosis gene for the child to acquire the disease (see Figure 5-5). With each pregnancy, there is a one-in-four chance that the child will have cystic fibrosis. New research may soon permit the identification of carriers by means of a skin test.

Although the basic defect is unknown, it is known that children with cystic fibrosis do not produce the enzymes necessary to break down certain substances within the body. A thick mucus therefore accumulates that clogs the ducts and linings of various vital organs. The cell linings of the lungs create a thick mucus that causes chronic respiratory infections and residual scarring of the lungs. Frequent coughing to expectorate the mucus occurs. Lung damage causes the child to be barrel-chested and may lead to heart failure. The ducts of the pancreas are blocked by thick secretions, and the enzymes required for food absorption cannot reach the intestines. Eventually, the cellular tissue of the pancreas is replaced by fibrous scar tissue, and then enzyme production is no longer possible. The liver can also be damaged if mucus plugs form in ducts. Liver complications include cirrhosis and portal hypertension. Thick, claylike, foul-smelling stools, excessive sweating, and heat sensitivity are other common symptoms caused by gastrointestinal tract and sweat gland involvement.

Observable symptoms of cystic fibrosis include wheezing, lack of physical stamina, excessive sweating, and poor weight gain accompanied by increased appetite. Children with cystic fibrosis are usually of small stature with barrel chests and thin extremities.

Cystic fibrosis is usually diagnosed during the infancy or toddler period. Very often the cystic fibrosis child has a history of repeated respiratory infections such as pneumonia and bronchitis. Clinical diagnosis is made by a combination of symptomatology and laboratory tests. Fingernail clippings are analyzed for certain body chemicals, and a sweat test, the most common test, which measures the salt content of perspiration, may also be done.

Treatment

Medical Management

Medical management focuses on lung and digestion problems. To prevent recurring respiratory infections, especially pneumonia, the following management methods are used:

- mist tents to decrease thickness of mucus in lungs
- postural drainage to drain the lungs of mucus

- breathing exercises to increase lung capacity

- antibiotics to combat infection

To compensate for the improper functioning of the pancreas, vitamins and enzymes are prescribed to aid in food absorption. A dietary regimen of high protein and decreased fat is often used in combination with frequent meals to facilitate digestion.

Teacher Management

It is important that the child with cystic fibrosis adhere to the "doctor's orders" even during the school day. The teacher should encourage and help the student to be medically compliant. The following guidelines can be helpful in class management:

- Suppressing a cough can be damaging to the lungs of children with cystic fibrosis, but out of embarrassment they may try not to cough. The teacher should let children leave the room, if necessary, and should not try to make them stop coughing. It might be worthwhile to allow such students to come to class five minutes late so that they can expectorate mucus in private. Also, it is important to reassure the other children in the class that the cough is not contagious.

- Some children may need postural drainage during school hours. Usually, parents will come to school during lunch to administer this therapy. When planning a field trip, the teacher should keep in mind the postural drainage schedule.

- With every meal, the child will need to take enzymes and vitamins to aid digestion. Some children will need to take up to 40 pills a day. If children are hesitant to let their classmates see them take these pills, arrangements should be made for them to go to the bathroom or nurse's suite to take the prescribed medication.

- Children with cystic fibrosis need more food than their healthy peers. Provisions for them to have a snack time during the day may be necessary. When planning the menu for class/school parties, the teacher needs to remember that the child's intake of fatty foods must be restricted.

- Moderate exercise, as approved by the doctor, is good for children with cystic fibrosis because it helps dislodge the mucus. They should be allowed to participate in approved physical activities. For those activities that are too strenuous, they can be involved as scorekeeper, coach, or referee so they don't feel excluded.

- Since children with cystic fibrosis are susceptible to infections, cold/flu season and inclement weather may cause them to be absent more frequently. It is a good idea to notify the parents if an outbreak of influenza or childhood illness occurs at school so that appropriate precautions can be taken.

Special Considerations

Some children and their families cope remarkably well with the stresses and responsibilities of this illness. However, many adjustment problems are common. As the result of small stature, inability to participate in sports, and barrel chest, the cystic fibrotic child may feel inadequate. Teenagers with cystic fibrosis are often troubled by their slow maturation as compared with that of their peers. These feelings of physical inadequacy are compounded by the lack of social skills due to frequent hospitalizations. In adolescents, fear of dying often causes poor school performance and isolation. The teenager with cystic fibrosis may have little motivation towards academics and vocational training, since the statistics indicate a severely shortened life span.

Family relations are often strained. The time, cost, and availability of medical treatment can limit the family's mobility. The mother is usually the parent most involved in the child's care, while the father works a second job to pay for medical expenses (Burton, 1975). Siblings may resort to inappropriate behavior to get some of the attention given to the child with cystic fibrosis. Anxiety is high, especially in those families in which one child has already died of cystic fibrosis and the family is watching another child duplicate the course.

Prognosis

Since respiratory and pulmonary infections can be better treated and controlled now than in the past, children with cystic fibrosis are living until their mid-teens, with 15 the mean age of death. As a result of earlier diagnosis and improved medical care, a fair number of children with cystic fibrosis are surviving into young adulthood (Cystic Fibrosis Foundation, 1977).

CARDIAC DISORDERS

The numerous types of cardiac problems found in children are best classified under two major headings: congenital heart defects and acquired heart disease. Congenital problems are those with which the child is born. Acquired heart disease is developed at some point later in life.

Etiology and Prevalence

Congenital heart defects are caused by genetic and environmental factors. Single mutant genes are the cause of congenital heart block and supravalvular aortic stenosis. Heart disease associated with Down's and Turner's syndromes is the result of chromosomal aberrations. Environmental etiologies include drugs ingested during pregnancy, rubella, and radiation. At birth, the incidence of cardiac disorder is 8:1,000. If a member of the immediate family has heart disease, the risk increases to 1:20 to 1:30. Women with diabetes have a 1:39 chance of producing a child with heart disease. One third of the children born with heart defects die during the first month, and 60 percent die during the first year (Berkow, 1977).

The majority of congenital defects are the result of structural abnormalities of the heart and great vessels. These abnormalities cause excessive cardiac workload and inadequate cardiac output. Symptoms may include fatigue and shortness of breath. Cyanosis, which makes the child's skin look bluish, is the result of decreased oxygen in the blood because some blood from the veins goes to the left side of the heart and then to the body without ever reaching the lungs to get oxygen (see Figure 5-6). The diagnosis of congenital defects is based on cyanotic appearance, heart murmur, abnormal heart rate, and heart failure.

Treatment

Of the 35 types of congenital heart malformations, most can be corrected or alleviated by surgery. New surgical techniques and equipment, such as valve replacements, have greatly increased the survival rate. Although corrective surgery is not always possible, those children who do benefit from it are able to do much more physically than they could prior to their operations.

Bacterial endocarditis, an infection of the lining of the heart, most commonly at the heart valves, is a serious problem for children with heart disease. Since the most frequent entry of infection into the blood is through infected teeth and gums, it is critical that good dental hygiene be maintained. Antibiotics such as penicillin are administered before tooth extractions and surgery as a prophylactic measure.

Rheumatic Heart Disease

The major cause of acquired heart disease is rheumatic fever. When it results in permanent heart damage, it is referred to as *rheumatic heart disease*. Rheumatic fever begins with a streptococcal infection manifested by a strep throat, scarlet fever, and/or a middle ear infection, followed by a two- to three-week dormancy period. The active period, which can last from weeks

Figure 5-6 Structure of the Heart

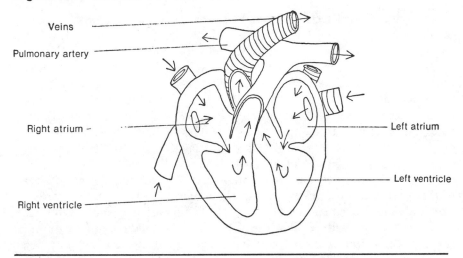

to eight months, is characterized by inflammatory complications including arthritis, chorea, or carditis. Some children experience hot and swollen joints while others just feel restless and tired. Once children have an attack of rheumatic fever, they are much more susceptible to recurring attacks.

If carditis is present, inflammation of the heart valves may occur. When this inflammation heals, it leaves scar tissue that prevents the valve from opening and closing properly. Symptoms of the residual valve damage include stenosis and regurgitation, and surgery may be required to open the damaged valve.

In ten percent of children with rheumatic fever, inflammation of the brain causes involuntary, purposeless movements or chorea (St. Vitus' dance). These movements, which include facial grimacing, clumsiness, and flailing limbs, may not occur until months after the rheumatic fever episode and are self-limiting in duration (Berkow, 1977).

In 1978, 851 cases of rheumatic fever were reported in the United States, with most cases being originally diagnosed in children 4 to 18. The incidence is falling dramatically, due partly to the increased use of throat cultures to detect strep throat. Malnutrition and overcrowding seem to predispose children to streptococcal infections and recurring attacks. Early treatment should be at the stage of the strep throat. Because of the prevalence in school age populations, teachers need to be familiar with the previously discussed symptoms so that early medical treatment can be received before the active stage is reached.

Usually, children with rheumatic fever return to normal school activities after a period of bedrest. Long-term antibiotics are usually prescribed to prevent further attacks. If heart damage has occurred, some alterations in the school routine may be necessary to accommodate the child's limitations. Some children may require a shortened day combined with home teaching, a modified physical education program, a daily rest period, and/or special meals or snacks.

Special Considerations

In both congenital and acquired heart disease, the limitations on physical activity are dependent on the type of problem and the severity of heart damage. Therefore, the number of restrictions to be placed on a child with a cardiac disorder must be decided on an individual basis.

Of all the chronic conditions, it seems that heart disease causes the most restrictions and overprotectiveness. Many teachers and parents unconsciously fear that if children become excited, are physically active, or are put in stressful situations, they will have a heart attack. Usually the worst consequences of overexertion are fatigue and shortness of breath. Children who are constantly prohibited from taking part in normal activity may react by rebelling to prove that they are "as strong" or "as healthy" as their peers or by continuing to be unnecessarily dependent on adults. It is important that the parents and teachers help the children to become independent by encouraging them to take responsibility for their daily medical management, limits on activity, diet, and medication (American Heart Association, 1971).

EDUCATIONAL STRATEGIES

Preschool

Chronic illness in young children brings with it a number of potential problems: frequent hospitalizations can lead to feelings of abandonment; painful treatments are often viewed as punishment; fatigue and the need for immobilization often interfere with the preschool child's natural exploration of the environment.

Educational intervention can prevent or minimize these problems and can provide essential developmental continuity for children with chronic illnesses diagnosed in the early years.

Hospital Setting

There is a need to provide a safe place to work through feelings and to provide developmentally appropriate experiences. Playrooms should be staffed by competent professionals, such as child life specialists, who usually perform these tasks in pediatric hospitals or hospitals with pediatric populations.

P.L. 94–142 includes the birth through age five population in its 1980–1981 regulations. School districts need to examine this law in light of the special needs of the chronically ill population of preschoolers.

Preparation for surgical techniques or painful treatments has been recognized as an essential component in the care of the hospitalized child (Prugh et al., 1953; Glaser, 1974). Such programs have been found to help the child cope with the unfamiliar and frightening experiences that are likely to occur (Vardaro, 1978; Wolfer & Visintainer, 1975).

Preparation for surgical techniques and treatments can be accomplished through puppets or commercial preparation programs such as the Family Communications videotape of a special Mr. Rogers' Neighborhood show entitled "Going to the Hospital" (Family Communications, 1976). Information needs to be given to preschoolers in language understandable to them and repeated often in a variety of contexts. Doctor play in the playroom allows the child to work through feelings of helplessness and loss of control. Children often respond to treatments with less fear when they have the opportunity to act out procedures that involve needles, thermometers, or plaster casts on dolls, puppets, or staff. Playrooms should also contain unstructured materials, such as sand, water, and clay, since these less threatening materials allow children to express their feelings, as well as provide satisfying sensory experiences. Further examples of the uses of hospital playrooms can be found in a variety of publications, such as Emma Plank's now classic book *Working with Children in Hospitals* (1962), M. Petrillo and S. Sanger's *Emotional Care of Hospitalized Children* (1972), and P. Azernoff and S. Flegal's *Pediatric Play Programs* (1975).

Home and School

Because of the likelihood of frequent school absences throughout their early years, the need for chronically ill preschoolers to be enrolled in developmental programs such as Head Start is great. Such programs can increase the child's opportunities for socialization and for interaction with developmental materials and allow for early identification and remediation of learning problems, sensory loss, or other developmental delays.

School Age

Hospital Setting*

The best way for teachers to begin working with children is to introduce themselves and explain what their role with the children is. This is best done on the first day, but after the children are settled in and the admission proce-

---

*The section on the hospitalized school age child was contributed by Celeste Klima, hospital school teacher.

dures are complete. The first few sessions with children should be used to gain information. This can often help them relax. A question such as "What grade are you in?" can give necessary information as well as serve to help a child adjust. The teacher can follow the child's reply with, "Oh, I have some books on that level. Would you like to see if they are like yours?" This allows children the excuse they need to enter the schoolroom and helps to emphasize the continuing process of education. This is an excellent informal way of gaining information.

Another way to gain information both formally and informally is to call the child's previous school placement and speak to teachers, counselors, principals, or the secretary, if necessary. Much information can often be gained from the phone conversation to help the teacher channel into the child's ability and functioning level as well as interest areas. Formal enrollment is important, but so is contact between the two systems. The school teachers feel better if they know where the child is and what is happening, and the hospital teacher can always benefit from the direction. The children benefit the most because they will recognize familiar work and like knowing that their class is not getting ahead of them.

School itself represents stress to many children and even more stress than usual to chronically ill children, since they usually miss more time than healthy children. Another stress factor is hospitalization. When this is combined with school, the teacher needs to exercise tact and sensitivity. One helpful element within the environment itself is that all the children within the hospital class have a problem. They are all coping, healing, and progressing together. This is often a reinforcing element to be used to the benefit of all concerned. The hospital school is also less risky, for the child needn't compete with a large class of healthy peers.

The next area to explore is the family. Many families view hospitals as threats. Once they are aware of the school program and the way it functions, it is often easier for them to accept and support the program. If children use their family as a support system, they will probably react favorably if the family has accepted the program. Needless to say, children can use the family's reactions (both consciously and unconsciously) to undermine their learning potential. The family is also a prime source of information. It may come in the form of cooperation or refusal to cooperate, denials, or distorted versions or aspects of past history, but all of these forms are providers of some information. The family interview should be conducted with an open mind, and teachers should verify any facts that seem to need substantiation. They must be observant and keep within the bounds of the teaching discipline. Signs given through family interaction should be used as constructive material when assessing and planning for the child.

During this time, children have been making their own adjustment to the program. They should be allowed to relax and enjoy the program for a few days. Once all of the above is accomplished and within a reasonable amount of time, the teacher should begin assessment and individualized instruction.

The assessment tests used in the programs at Mt. Washington Pediatric Hospital are of several types: individualized standardized tests and informal batteries. Most often the Woodcock Reading Mastery Test, the Key Math Diagnostic Arithmetic Tests, and the Woodcock-Johnson Psycho-Educational Battery are used. At times more specific testing is required either for another system and/or to help with placement decisions. When this is the case, some or all of the following can be given: individual word recognition tests, informal reading inventories, phonics mastery tests, spelling inventories, auditory discrimination tests, readiness profiles, and interest inventories. These tests can be obtained from teachers with expertise in reading and local federal Title I resource reading teachers.

Testing should begin only after the child has been prepared for it. Two points that need to be stressed are:

1. The child should understand that the test will be used for placement and instruction, not for grades.
2. The child will reach a point when he/she will not be able to successfully answer some of the questions on many of the tests.

Several things the tester should do include:

- Test in the least distractible environment possible.
- Be sure not to give clues with eyes, lips, or in any other way.
- Make sure the child always gets noncommittal types of answers when seeking an indicator of correctness.
- Be familiar with the test and the directions and procedures.

The test should be scored properly and immediately. All scores should be written on the test form, and all charts and graphs completed. When all this information is properly placed in the appropriate format, it is much easier to make educational placement and program decisions that will be effective and appropriate.

All of the newly gained information should be completed with previous test scores and the other information gained since admission and formally written up in an admission note and placed in the child's medical record. This information should also be shared and discussed informally with other disciplines. Each discipline has specific information to share with others, and this helps each one understand the others' program intent, progress, scheduling, goals, and problems. This should all bring into focus the final recommendations for a plan to be followed by the educational personnel during the hospitalization of the patient.

At this point an individualized educational program (IEP) should be developed according to the state guidelines. The IEP can direct the teacher in working out daily plans on a weekly basis, stressing short-term goals, which should be written in behavioral objective form. (Teacher training courses and workshops should instruct in the above.) These should be continually checked and revised to ensure the child's success.

At this point teachers should use their experienced judgment to choose the appropriate materials. Generally, this type of child responds to introductory and basic work from prepared materials (i.e., textbooks, workbooks, manipulable learning, tools, kits, and games). At times such materials also serve as excellent determiners of sequential progression, as skill builders and as reinforcement activities. Unfortunately, however, these materials are not always available or are not appropriate: at times they cannot be adapted, the lower levels necessary are too childish, or someone else needs them, and so forth. It is difficult to have all material for all grades in a small hospital school. This is when teacher-made materials can save the day.

Teacher-made materials can be an excellent instruction tool because they can be made specifically to meet the needs of that particular child and can then become the personal belonging of the child once they are no longer needed or upon discharge. They are usually inexpensive, reusable, and replaceable. Any subject area can be covered, and games can be individualized and named for each child, for example, "John's jumping consonants," or "Sally's silly rhymes." Many children enjoy sharing their learning experiences through these games and showing off their abilities when others join in. Many games can be extended to include new materials or redeveloped to fit another child with similar needs. Most often the quickest, easiest to store, least bulky, most inexpensive games are made of paper (various kinds—Manila, white, construction, tag-board, paper plates, newspaper, etc.), magic markers or crayons, and tape. The following are examples:

Multiplication Game

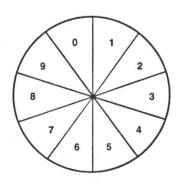

You spin to make up the problem:
1st spin—multiplicand: 4
2nd spin—multiplier: ×2
your answer: 8

Or you can make two spinners; each one gives you a number to multiply. Larger problems can be made by having little cards with directions: e.g., spin three times to get three numerals in the multiplicand, spin two times to get two numerals in the multiplier.

Word Matching Game

—word red on back

—word green on back

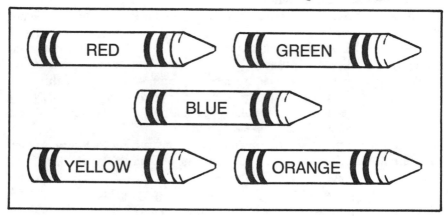

The object is to match the proper color crayon wrapper to the crayon. When the word is printed on the back it makes the activity self-checking. This games serves two purposes: it teaches colors and color word identification.

Numeral Identification

Toss a penny and identify the numeral it lands on or the numeral it tells you to identify.

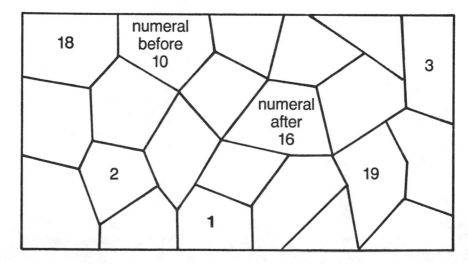

Other responsibilities of the hospital teacher include keeping abreast of recent developments in other disciplines and keeping the hospital staff up to date with the children's progress in school, maintaining medical charts, and preparing for successful discharge. This last may either be notifying the former school that the child will be returning or making necessary adjustment for a proper new placement.

Using educational programs to teach children information about disease and its management is another vital aspect of hospital school programs. For example, mathematics concepts and conversions can be taught so that a diabetic child can learn to measure insulin in centimeters, as marked on a syringe; caloric limit food substitutions can be taught for the diabetic child, as well.

Often affective education can be used to help children gain acceptance of hospitalization and illness, while reinforcing language arts. Examples would be asking children to complete open-ended sentences or to write compositions on topics of personal concern. "The thing about the hospital I hate most is _____," or "When I feel sick, it makes me _____ _____." Such assignments also allow teachers to identify unvoiced confusions or fears and can allow them to correct misperceptions or distortions.

Upon discharge, all reports should be finalized and placed in charts and files. It may be necessary to follow up with phone calls, written reports, meetings, screenings, or home visits to make sure the best possible plans are being carried out. Letting the classroom teacher know of a child's return will provide the teacher with the opportunity to prepare the class for the return of their peer. Welcome back signs or the assignment of a special friend to help the child catch up on missed work can ease the transition from hospital to school.

Often children are readmitted to the hospital. A few helpful hints include:

- Keep files available.
- Develop a system for updating and comparing reports, scores, and so forth.
- Recognize the children and welcome them.
- Continue with expected program.
- Recognize differences in abilities and alter expectancies.
- Realize that new goals may need to be set.
- Help others make necessary adjustments to the child.

Home Setting

Coming into people's homes presents unique problems. Teachers are used to working on their own "turf," and while control of the environment is possible in schools or hospital schools, it is not so possible in homes. The child has knowledge of the environment and can use it to manipulate the situation. But the child can also be used by the teacher as an ally. If the teacher can acknowledge that the child has control of the environment and ask for help, it allows the child control, and cooperation can be increased.

A place to work should be arranged. It should be quiet, separate, "special" for the child. Even in a crowded house, this is necessary. The teacher must be aware of the family's resources and their ability to provide privacy and protection of the child's belongings, especially school books. Frustration can result if the teacher gives the child expensive items such as a calculator or a teaching machine without assessing the child's and/or parent's ability to protect the property.

The parents' degree of cooperation needs to be assessed and used. Parents can do a great deal of informal teaching through games that reinforce skills.

The illness and its effects have a role in the success of home teaching. The teacher should assess the degree of pain, discomfort, and fatigue and its effects on performance and the time of teaching. The child's emotional reactions are also crucial. The child may be depressed or exhibit a lack of concentration. Children may refuse to work or may express anger and frustration, and this can tax a teacher's patience. Some children may be using the illness and the home stay for secondary gains and may enjoy the attention given by adults. They may thus manipulate adults, and this also needs to be assessed.

There is a need to coordinate the program. The teacher must obtain books, records, information from the school, the child's teacher, and other health professionals. The teacher can also obtain social information from the school and pass notes from the class to the child. Get well cards, class projects, and newspaper items can be used to maintain contact with the class.

Academic performance should be assessed informally and abilities checked periodically. The effects of illness and treatments must be considered in assessing the child's attention span, set to learn, motivational level, and other factors that directly affect learning.

Individualized work is most helpful. Children will be more motivated if work is presented in a meaningful way, keyed to their interest and motivational level. For example, if a child is reading at fifth grade level and is interested in stamp collecting, the teacher may have the child read newspaper sections on stamp collecting and circle new words, write definitions for new words, or summarize the article or story. Games or other materials can be made for children to reinforce skills. Games should be able to be played alone or with siblings or visiting friends. This can encourage peer interaction.

Bringing in the outside world is vital. The teacher needs to recognize the isolation of the child at home and try to correct for this. Seasonal items can be brought in and used for teaching: leaves, acorns, snow, and holiday ornaments. Stories can be written about seasons and holidays.

Often a common complaint of the teacher and parents is that the child doesn't want to turn off the T.V. for school. The television can be used constructively. A variety of assignments can be given in all subject areas, keyed to T.V. For example, students can be asked to write story plots or themes of soap operas or T.V. movies or to analyze the logic used in commercials. What do they promise? What do they leave out? Such assignments can often serve to break the ice between child and teacher. They also recognize the child's interests and show respect for the child's choices of leisure activities.

School

The classroom teacher should recognize the symptoms that indicate the onset of an attack and be prepared to take necessary action.

Chronically ill children spend most of their time in school with peers. There should be a plan to allow them to take medication, or rest, or report to the health suite, if necessary. If children are able, the responsibility to do these should be given to them.

Teachers should recognize when the child is manipulating them and the situation, such as using an attack as an excuse for failing to complete a lesson or requesting permission to leave the room. This requires tact and sensitivity. If illness is being used frequently as an excuse, a conference with the parents, child, involved health professionals, and school personnel may clarify the realities. Teachers should not, however, assume that all excuses are manipulative; chronic illness or treatments can result in inconsistent and variable symptoms, and ignoring them may present a danger to the child's health.

Children sent to the health suite may delay their return to the class; hence, a schedule or call-back arrangement can help make them more accountable. Often, the child feels safer in the health suite and may use it as a place to hide from the academic or social pressures of the classroom. Frequent school absences may also be related to such fears. Continuity in education is crucial during the school years, and such fears need to be addressed to prevent unnecessary absences. Warm, supportive teachers who can provide individual attention to their students, at least on occasion, can help ease the pressures on chronically ill children in the classroom.

Adolescence

Hospitalized

Group programming can be most effective with secondary students, but it is often difficult to accomplish. Tutors are often assigned for different subjects, on different days, for different children. Coordination of assignments for long-term patients can often increase motivation and peer contact and can increase learning, as well.

Persistent life situations are important components of the curriculum of hospital secondary programs. Learning to tell others about one's disability by writing essays, news articles, poems, or plays can help an adolescent overcome fears of social isolation or stigma. In the same way, older patients can be taught self-management and disease control. Reading newspaper ads for jobs and identifying different career requirements can also help in moving the adolescent toward realistic planning for the future. The use of home catalogs to buy clothes, furniture, and so forth is an important skill to learn and may be essential for the chronically ill child who will be essentially homebound as an adult.

In group programs, school newspapers, performances such as plays, variety shows, and puppet shows, and group projects help to support the peer interaction vital for adolescents, while essential academic skills are reinforced.

Homebound

The home teacher must develop instructional strategies that are individually tailored. Motivational level, severity of physical impairment, and resources in the home should be considered in designing the educational program. Some suggestions include:

- Development of long-term assignments to increase retention and foster independent learning. Since the secondary school student may have a different teacher for each subject, assignments should be scheduled so that the student is exposed to each subject for a short period each day. For example, for English composition a journal might be assigned in which the student must write everyday. If a project requires specific references and materials, the teacher must make sure that everything is available ahead of time.

- Utilization of resources in the home. Constructive use of television is an excellent technique. If the student is taking a literature course, certain plays and movies can become required watching. Assignments based on news programs can focus on current events, geography skills, or social studies (elections, economic issues). Having the student write a review of a television program is an excellent way to work on composition and critical thinking skills. The kitchen holds many possibilities for interesting lessons for the ambulatory student. Home economics units related to cooking and nutrition become real when kitchen resources are utilized. Math activities such as measuring, counting, and fractions are more interesting when the lesson revolves around a recipe for cookies. Science lessons on buoyancy become fun when experiments are done in the kitchen sink.

- Involve the family. Parent participation should not be limited to making sure the child is ready for instruction when the teacher arrives. Sharing ideas with parents on what they can do to help the child learn not only benefits the child, but makes the parents feel more useful. Assignments that require children to interview family members on current topics also remind parents that their children are capable of performing academically even if they are sick.

- Involve students in school-related activities. To maintain contact with their regular schools during an extended illness, students might write articles or draw cartoons for the school newspaper. By keeping in touch with regular school personnel, home teachers can find out about poster and essay contests in which their students might be interested in participating.

For many secondary students, home teaching may be the first time they have ever received one-to-one instruction. The teacher has a rare opportunity to discover academic problems that may have previously gone undiagnosed. This allows for time for intensive remedial work as well as time to arrange a more appropriate regular school placement if it is warranted.

One important area for the secondary student with a chronic or physical impairment is vocational planning. Since many of these students lack physical stamina, require possible additional periods of hospitalization and convalescence, and have not been exposed to the world of work, it is crucial that vocational preparation be included in their home teaching curriculum. The home teacher can administer or arrange for the student to take career interest inventories. It is also possible to do vocational assessment in the home. Assessment tools such as Jastak and the Talent Assessment Program (TAPS) are portable. The tests included in both assessment kits focus on skills such as manual dexterity, fine/gross motor skills, accuracy, speed, and mechanical abilities. Teacher-made work samples that simulate real tasks (filing, mail sorting, and typing) are also valuable in assisting the student to make career/vocational choices. Information gathered from vocational assessment can be used to help determine if students should be placed in a vocational education program, if they might be appropriate candidates for state vocational rehabilitation programs, or if they would benefit from postsecondary specialized training. For severely disabled teenagers, vocational assessment may be the first step in developing a "cottage trade or skill" that would allow them to earn money at home. It is also very important for the home teacher to assist students in understanding their illness or disability as it relates to employability. A thorough understanding of their medical condition will facilitate students' ability to choose an appropriate career. Lack of information causes students to be unrealistic. Some deny that any restrictions are necessary—"I can do anything"—while others perceive themselves as permanent invalids.

Being homebound is especially difficult for teenagers. During their period of development when peer relations and approval are of the utmost concern, it is hard for them to adjust to social isolation. This isolation can make them feel different and uncomfortable around their peers and create much anxiety about returning to school. Adolescence is the time when children are trying desperately to become independent, and it may be very difficult for them to cope with this forced dependency on their family. Different reactions ranging from withdrawal to angry outbursts may result. It is important for the home teacher to recognize these psychosocial problems, to help the child and family cope with these behaviors and feelings, and to assist the family in finding the appropriate counseling resources if they are necessary.

SUMMARY

The preceding sections have reviewed the medical realities of a number of disease entities. In discussions of asthma, diabetes, renal diseases, hemophilia, heart diseases, sickle cell anemia, cystic fibrosis, and epilepsy, an attempt was made to give the reader a valuable reference tool in educating chronically ill children. The strategies presented for providing an educational context for these children represent guidelines for the teacher. An important consideration in providing a comprehensive education to chronically ill children is the recognition of their movement through a number of educational systems, from home to hospital to school. Continuity and communication among the systems is essential in order to prevent fragmentation of services.

REFERENCES

Aaronson, D. Asthma: General concepts. In R. Patterson (Ed.), *Allergic disease: Diagnosis and management.* Philadelphia: J.B. Lippincott, 1972.

Allesberry, D. et al. *Assessment of vocational potential of sickle cell anemics.* Harrisburg, PA: Pennsylvania Bureau of Vocational Rehabilitation, 1977.

American Diabetes Association. Pamphlet, 1977.

American Heart Association. *A guide for teachers: Children with heart disease.* Dallas, 1971.

American Lung Association. Bulletin, 1980.

Azernoff, P., & Flegal, S. *A Pediatric Play Program.* Springfield, IL: Charles C Thomas, 1975.

Bagley, C.R. The educational performance of children with epilepsy. British Journal of Educational Psychology, 1970, *40,* 82.

Berkow, R. (Ed.). *The Merck manual of diagnosis and therapy* (13th ed.). Rahway, NJ: Merck & Co., Inc., 1977.

Bronheim, S.P. Pulmonary disorders: Asthma and cystic fibrosis. In P. Magrab (Ed.), *Psychological management of pediatric problems* (Vol. 1). Baltimore: University Park Press, 1978.

Burgan. Personal communication.

Burton, L. *The family life of sick children.* Boston: Routledge & K. Paul, 1975.

Cohen, S.I. Psychological factors in asthma: A review of their etiological and therapeutic significance. *Postgraduate Medical Journal,* 1971, *47,* 533-540.

Cystic Fibrosis Foundation. *A teachers' guide to cystic fibrosis.* Atlanta, 1977.

Debuskey, M. (Ed.). *The chronically ill child and his family.* Springfield, IL: Charles C Thomas, 1970.

Ehrlich, R.M. Diabetes mellitus in childhood. In H.W. Bain (Ed.), *Pediatric Clinics of North America: Symposium on Chronic Disease in Children. Volume 21.* Philadelphia: W.B. Saunders Co., 1974.

Ellis, E.F. Allergic disorders. In U. Vaugh & R.J. McKay (Eds.), *Nelson textbook of pediatrics.* Philadelphia: W.B. Saunders Co., 1975, pp. 492-521.

Epilepsy Foundation of America. *Basic statistics on the epilepsies.* Philadelphia: F.A. Davis Co., 1975.

Epilepsy Foundation of America. *Epilepsy school alert.* Washington, DC, 1974.

Family Communications, Inc. Going to the hospital (videotape). Pittsburgh: Family Communications, Inc., 1977.

Fisher, L. American Lung Association, Bulletin, 1980.

Freeman, J. et al. *Epilepsy in Maryland: An assessment of services and gaps in services.* Baltimore: The Johns Hopkins Hospital, Pediatric Seizure Clinic, 1975.

Freud, A. *The psychoanalytic treatment of children.* New York: International Universities Press, 1946.

Gadow, K. *Children on medication: A primer for school personnel.* Reston, VA: The Council for Exceptional Children, 1979.

Garner, A.M., & Thompson, C.W. Juvenile diabetes. In P. Magrab (Ed.), *Psychological management of pediatric problems.* Baltimore: University Park Press, 1978.

Glaser, H. The hospital as an environment. *Journal of the Association for the Care of Children in Hospitals,* 1974, *3*(1).

Gordis, L. *Epidemiology of chronic lung disease in children.* Baltimore: Johns Hopkins Press, 1973.

Green, J.B., and Hartlage, L.C. Comparative performance of epileptic and non-epileptic children and adolescents. *Disorders of the Nervous System,* 1971, *32,* 418.

Hodgman, C.H. et al. Emotional complications of adolescent grand mal epilepsy. *Journal of Pediatrics,* August 1979.

Katz, A. *Hemophilia: A study in hope and reality.* Springfield, IL: Charles C Thomas, 1970.

Kemp, C.B., Knight, M.J., Scharp, D.W., Lacy, P.E., & Ballinger, W.F. Transplantation of isolated pancreatic islets into the portal view of diabetic rats. *Nature,* 1973, *244,* 447.

Knowles, H.C., Jr. Diabetes mellitus in childhood and adolescence. In P. Felig and P.K. Bondy (Eds.), Symposium on Diabetes Mellitus. *The Medical Clinics of North America.* Philadelphia: W.B. Saunders, Co., 1971.

Korsch, B.M., Negrete, V.F., Gardner, J.E., Weinstock, C., Mercer, A., Grushkin, C.M., & Fine, R.N. Kidney transplantation in children: Psychosocial follow-up study on child and family. *Journal of Pediatrics,* 1973, *83,* 399-408.

MacGregor, R.R., Sheagren, J.N., Lipsett, M.B., & Woff, S.M. Alternate day prednisone therapy. *New England Journal of Medicine,* 1969, *280,* 1427-1431.

Magrab, P.R., & Papadopoulou, Z.L. Renal disease. In P.R. Magrab (Ed.), *Psychological management of pediatric problems* (Vol. 1). Baltimore: University Park Press, 1978.

Massie, R., & Massie, S. *Journey.* New York: A. Knopf Co., 1975.

Mullins, J.B. *A teacher's guide to management of physically handicapped students.* Springfield, IL: Charles C Thomas, 1979.

Paulsen, E.P., & Colle, E. Diabetes mellitus. In L.E. Gardner (Ed.), *Endocrine and genetic diseases of childhood.* Philadelphia: W.B. Saunders Co., 1969.

Peshkin, M. Analysis of the role of residential asthma centers for children with intractable asthma. *Journal of Asthma Research,* 1968, *6,* 59-92.

Peterson, R.M., & Cleveland, J.O. (Eds.). *Medical problems in the classroom.* Springfield, IL: Charles C Thomas, 1975.

Petrillo, M., & Sanger, S. *Emotional care of hospitalized children.* Philadephia: J.P. Lippincott, 1972.

Plank, N. *Working with children in hospitals.* Cleveland: The Press of Case-Western Reserve University, 1962.

Prugh, D. et al. A study of the emotional reactions of children and their families to hospitalization. *American Journal of Orthopsychiatry,* 1953, *23,* 70-106.

Rodin, E.A., Shapiro, H.L., & Lennox, K. *Epilepsy and life performance.* Detroit: Lafayette Clinic, 1976.

Rutler, M., Graham, P., & Yule, W. Neuropsychiatric study in childhood. *Clinics in developmental medicine, 35-36,* Philadelphia: J.P. Lippincott, 1970.

Sultz, H., Schlesinger, E., Mosher, W., & Feldman, J. *Long-term childhood illness.* Pittsburgh: University of Pittsburgh Press, 1972.

Travis, G. *Chronic illness in children.* Stanford, CA: Stanford University Press, 1976.

U.S. Department of Health, Education and Welfare. *Nationwide plan for nationwide action on epilepsy* (Vol. 1). Bethesda, MD: National Institutes of Health, 1978.

Vardaro, J.A. Pre-admission anxiety and mother-child relationships. *Journal of the Association for the Care of Children in Hospitals,* 1978, *7*(2), 8-15.

Wolfer, J.A., & Visintainer, M. Pediatric surgical patients' stress responses and adjustments. *Nursing Research,* 1975, *24,* 244-255.

Chapter 6

Visible Illnesses

OVERVIEW

This chapter will review the medical aspects of spinal cord injury, meningomyelocele, burns, juvenile arthritis, orthopedic diseases, and head trauma. The distinguishing characteristic of these entities is that they are visible to others, thus setting these children apart from their peers to a greater or lesser extent, depending upon the disease and degree of severity. These conditions also have in common the need for special educational strategies to address the physical limitations they impose upon children. The discussion of educational strategies will focus on the impact that such visibility and movement restriction have upon children's educational and vocational needs, as well as strategies to enhance the concept of the least restrictive environment philosophy. It should be noted that many of the methods described in Chapters 4 and 5 for general strategies and educational intervention in invisible chronic illnesses apply equally to those children with more visible conditions.

SPINAL CORD INJURY

The most common cause of death among children age 5 to 14 years is accidents (American Public Health Association, 1961). Yet a significant number of children survive accidents and are left with residual damage. Automobile accidents, surfing and diving accidents, and gunshot wounds are the most common causes of spinal cord injuries (Travis, 1976). With this fact in mind, it is not surprising that spinal cord injuries are most common among risk-taking children, especially adolescent boys and young men.

Damage to the spinal cord occurs most often from fractures of the spine. While the spinal cord is rarely totally severed, the bruising, hemorrhage, twisting, or pinching of the cord causes nerve pathways to die as a result of the damage inflicted. The damage is permanent, since nerve cells do not regenerate. The degree of damage is dependent upon the level of the injury and its severity. In order to fully understand the effects of spinal cord injury, an understanding of the function of the spinal cord is necessary.

The Spinal Cord

The spinal cord is a flexible column made up of a series of bones called vertebrae, encasing a cable of millions of nerve fibers. These vertebrae are numbered in three series, beginning at the neck and working down. The first 7 are cervical vertebrae, followed by 12 thoracic vertebrae, and 5 lumbar vertebrae. Spinal nerves from each of these areas affect varying areas of the body and are numbered consecutively. Cervical vertebrae affect the upper portion of the body, so that C4 affects the neck muscles, C5 the shoulders, and so forth. Likewise, the thoracic nerves affect the upper torso and trunk areas, and the lumbar nerves affect the lower trunk and legs. Thus, the higher the injury, the more severe the loss of functioning. All functioning below the level of the injury is affected (see Figure 6-1).

The nerve cells transmit sensory information and control both voluntary and automatic motor impulses. Thus, injury affects sensations of pain, pressure, cold, voluntary movement, and the functions of respiration, bowel, and bladder control.

Treatment

In the early weeks after a spinal cord injury, the cord may be in shock, and after initial recovery, some of the paralysis may improve. Early rehabilitation after the patient's condition is stabilized is essential to prevent further disability and to allow for optimal recovery. Total care and rehabilitation from a multidisciplinary team is crucial, for the residual effects of spinal cord injury are complex.

Foremost among these is the traumatic emotional impact such an injury has upon a previously normal child or adolescent. Sensitive counseling and psychological assessment is needed, as well as the services of highly trained physical therapists, occupational therapists, neurologists, orthopedic specialists, urologists, and vocational counselors. The goal in rehabilitation is to assess the patient's remaining functioning, optimize that functioning, and attempt to make each person as independent as possible, physically and socially.

Figure 6-1 The Spinal Cord

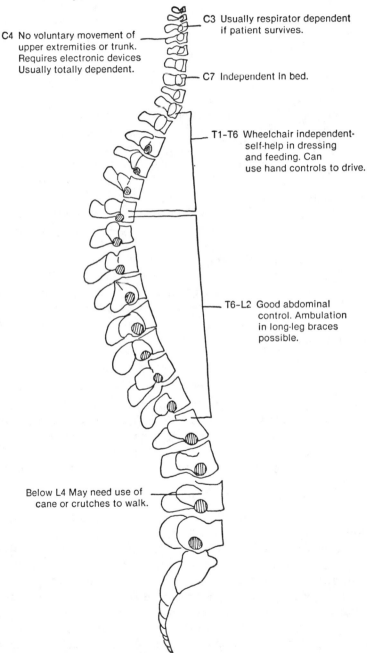

C3 Usually respirator dependent if patient survives.

C4 No voluntary movement of upper extremities or trunk. Requires electronic devices Usually totally dependent.

C7 Independent in bed.

T1–T6 Wheelchair independent-self-help in dressing and feeding. Can use hand controls to drive.

T6–L2 Good abdominal control. Ambulation in long-leg braces possible.

Below L4 May need use of cane or crutches to walk.

Physical Independence

When the injury is low enough for the patient to have upper extremity functioning but the lower extremities are paralyzed (paraplegia), arm and shoulder strengthening exercises are prescribed to teach the patient to lift his or her own weight, thus reducing dependence upon others. The ultimate goal is to attain independence in transfers from bed to wheelchair or from floor to wheelchair (in the event of accidental falls). The accomplishment of this takes enormous physical and psychological strength and months of arduous work by patient and therapist. If the injury is low enough for trunk control, independent ambulation without wheelchair assistance, with the help of braces and crutches, may be a therapy goal. This decision is often a difficult one for the patient and professional staff. While walking may seem to be a less restrictive mode of ambulation than a wheelchair, the energy and pain involved in dragging the dead weight of paralyzed legs and braces through space may be excessive, making walking unrealistic except for short distances. Wheelchairs must be ordered and adapted to the special needs of each patient. In some cases of high neck injury, electric wheelchairs that allow for minimal physical effort are necessary to achieve a modicum of independence. When all four limbs are affected (quadriplegia), rehabilitation focuses on basic self-help skills such as feeding. Equipment adaptations or the use of motorized devices may allow for independence in at least some areas for the person with a high neck injury.

Complications

Skin care is a vital part of the rehabilitation management plan and a goal for long-term maintenance. Because they have no sensation of pressure or pain, patients with spinal cord injury are prone to skin breakdowns, which lead to severe ulcers or pressure sores that often become infected. Skin must be inspected often, and patients or their families are taught how to change positions frequently to prevent breakdown.

Bladder problems are considered the leading cause of death in spinal injuries (Travis, 1976). Bladder control enhances social acceptance by peers. As a result of spinal cord injury, the bladder becomes neurogenic, out of control of the brain. Patients are taught a variety of methods by which they can prevent kidney infections by keeping the bladder emptied, thus avoiding a backup of urine into the kidneys. The goals are to prevent progressive renal damage and to control urinary incontinence. Among the methods used are catheterization, performed by the patient or caretakers to periodically empty the bladder, or Credé's method, in which patients use hand pressure to force the bladder to discharge. Permanent catheters are sometimes implanted, especially if the injury is high or if self-care may be a problem. All of these methods impose some dangers, and care must be given to help the patient and family learn the techniques and use them appropriately. Motivation and family intactness play a role in good management, and supports are needed at times to encourage patients to stick to the established regimen. Urinary diversion operations, in which urine is excreted into a bag external to the body along the stomach wall, is the treatment of last choice. As noted by Kathleen Hanrigan (1980), clinical nurse specialist, "Intermittent catheterization has emerged during the 70's as the treatment of choice and the alternative to surgical urinary diversion in the initial and long-term management of neurogenic bladder complications." S.J. Myers (1974) reports that patients have been complication-free for many years using the catheterization technique carefully.

In classroom settings, teachers should be aware of children's methods of urinary management and should make arrangements for them to visit the health suite or bathroom in privacy to allow them to follow through on their bladder program. Often, embarrassment over the need to perform self-catheterization leads a child to neglect self-care and can precipitate recurrent infections and school absence.

Bowel control is another essential task for the post–spinal cord injury patient to master. Without good management, constipation and/or bowel incontinence can be recurrent problems. Food intake needs to be monitored to provide high fiber and increased fluid. Early management can prevent bowel distention from chronic constipation. Patients are usually taught to manage their bowels with the aid of suppositories or stool softeners. A key to good management, regularity and consistency, may be difficult for an angry, rebellious adolescent or a disorganized family. Again, support systems are needed to prevent long-term complications.

Special Considerations

The effect of spinal cord injury is traumatic. Patients consistently report a sense of shock, disbelief, and depersonalization. They change overnight from ambulatory, independent beings, capable of controlling their environment and their bodily functions, to helpless people, dependent on others for their very existence. Denial of the permanence of the condition is frequently seen, and adolescents may begin to expect miracles from the medical staff and from themselves. When told of the permanence of the paralysis, many adolescents respond with anger and rejection. "I'll show them," "They can't keep me down"—such comments are frequently heard after the initial shock of the injury and the acute phase ends. Denial and anger take a good deal of energy, energy needed to begin the early stages of rehabilitation. Yet the psychological shock to the system may be too great to allow for the realities to be handled, and respect for the adolescent's needs to react individually must be maintained by health professionals. Rehabilitation goals must be realistic, based upon the child's physical and emotional abilities. As the child begins to accept the reality, a period of grieving for the death of a normal body needs to follow. Spinal cord injury represents a major life change for the child and family, and the process of grief and readjustment may take years.

Some researchers point to the personality of the spinal cord–injured adolescent, suggesting that a significant number exhibit premorbid tendencies toward high-risk, impulsive behaviors (Rigoni, 1977), resulting in gunshot wounds and motorcycle or automobile accidents. For this group, adjustment may be even more difficult, with attempts at risk-taking in the hospital or rehabilitation unit a frequent pattern. Psychotherapeutic intervention needs to address the underlying dynamics as well as the patient's reaction to the accident, a process that may involve years of counseling.

Angry at the unfairness of life, resistant to the demands of physical therapy, yet required to comply, injured adolescents may release their frustration in the hospital school or at the home teacher. Feelings of hopelessness and despair over a future destroyed by accident may lead them to refuse to attempt to participate in educational testing or programs. Teachers need to constantly balance their own sense of anger and frustration with these adolescents, while attempting to provide consistent support and realistic limits.

A primary focus for the teacher is to identify motivating circumstances for their students and use these to encourage them to set individual realistic goals that can be achieved successfully.

A 14-year-old black male with a T6 fracture refused to attend the hospital school and often wheeled in after class had started, cursing, throwing things, and disrupting the entire class. His anger and frustration were apparent. He was also refusing to learn bowel and bladder management. In a conference held after he had regained some control, the teacher explained her need to mark him absent and discussed at length the kind of school he wanted to return to after discharge. He expressed the desire to go back to a "regular" junior high school with his friends. After a few conferences, the teacher explained that he could return to such a school only if he was promoted at the end of the present year and if he could have adequate bowel and bladder control. Otherwise he would have to attend a special school for the handicapped, with active nursing, medical, and physical therapy involvement. This was not presented as a threat, but as a choice. His anger was also recognized by the teacher and acknowledged. After a period of purposeful resistance, his attempt to retain control, he agreed to sign a contract stating that he would comply with basic rules of school attendance and learn methods of bowel and bladder management. He was not expected to achieve 100 percent compliance, and he was able to succeed in fulfilling the contract.

The emotional effects of spinal cord injury should never be taken lightly. Added to the frustration of being wheelchair-bound and helpless is the effect such injury has upon the sexual function of the paraplegic adolescent. Individual reactions vary depending upon the location of the injury and the totality of the spinal cord fracture. Total severance of the spinal cord results in loss of all sensation and motor reactions. Males can occasionally be stimulated by reflex, although most often they must rely on alternate forms of sexual stimulation to satisfy a partner. Females, even with loss of sensation, can become pregnant and deliver infants normally. Sensitive counseling is needed to help such adolescents accept their disability and learn alternate ways of expressing love to a partner. Some males may never be able to accept this impotency, and it has been suggested that this "symbolic destruction of manhood" may be a possible cause for the high suicide rate among spinal cord-injured young adults (Travis, 1976, p. 491).

Rehabilitation and educational and vocational training need to focus on realistic goals for the future. As noted by S.J. Myers (1974), hospitalized patients often respond well in a rehabilitation setting; however, the goal of true rehabilitation is for the individual to function independently once outside the hospital. Homes need to be adapted to allow free movement for the wheelchair-bound, and family and neighborhood supports need to be developed so that they can reenter the social and educational milieu. A primary goal for the home teacher or school administration is to help the patient return to a neighborhood school as quickly as possible. It becomes too easy for the wheelchair-bound child or adolescent to remain at home all day, avoiding the stares of strangers; avoiding the difficulties encountered by high curbs, narrow doorways, or inaccessible buildings; locked into an increasingly limited world. Local community organizations providing wheelchair athletics and sports, recreational programs, and alternate transportation should be explored. Often, this can be done by the homebound or hospital teacher with the injured child or adolescent as part of an educational program. The home or hospital teacher can function as a guide to the child in exploring alternative opportunities and should encourage trips outside the home and hospital setting.

HEAD TRAUMA

Accidental injury to the head is very common in childhood and is one of the leading causes of death in children under 18 (Epstein, 1980). An estimated 200,000 children are hospitalized for head injury annually, and five to ten percent have residual impairments (Mealey, 1968). The majority of these serious injuries occur as a result of automobile and bicycle accidents.

The degree of brain damage resulting from head trauma is variable and depends upon a number of factors, such as the age of the child, the nature of the fall or blow to the head, the presence or absence of protective head gear, and whether the injury results in a closed or open skull wound (Haslam, 1975). In order to understand the full effects of head trauma, one needs to have knowledge of the structure of the brain and its functions. A brief summary, highlighting only the basic functions, follows. For more detailed information, there are a number of readable textbooks on the brain and its functions. (*The Conscious Brain* by S. Rose, 1976, is highly recommended.)

The Brain

The brain is a complex structure made up of nerve cells. The process of brain function involves receiving information from the outside world and the body, storing information, communicating information, and regulating the body's temperature, respiration, and all other life functions. The brain consists of a cerebrum, divided into two hemispheres and connected by the corpus callosum. The cerebrum contains an outer surface, known as the cortex, which is divided into four areas or lobes in each hemisphere. These lobes generally are involved with different functions in the control of bodily activity, although it should be recognized that the brain functions are intricately interrelated and not fully understood. The occipital lobe is related to the visual area, the parietal contains those areas responsible for coordination and control of sensory input and motor output, while the frontal and temporal lobes "have much more diffuse and less understood functions relating to speech, learning, memory, intelligence and performance" (Rose, 1976, p. 53).

The cerebellum lies behind the cerebral hemispheres and controls fine motor movements and purposeful motor action. The brain stem, which is continuous with the spinal cord, contains the areas that control vital functions, such as sleeping and waking, respiration, heartbeat, eating, and sexual activities. It consists of the medulla and pons, the pituitary gland, which produces many important hormones, and the thalamus, which is involved with the emotions.

The brain is covered with protective layers of membrane, the meninges. The entire brain is encased in bone, the skull, for further protection.

The central nervous system is not fully developed at birth, and a protective layer of fatty tissue, called myelin, covers the nerve fibers. The soft spots noted on a baby's skull at birth, the fontanels, mark the intersections of the sutures, the spaces between the bones of the skull. The sutures are open to allow space for brain growth and slowly close as the child matures. See Figure 6-2 for an illustration of the parts of the brain.

Not all head traumas are severe, nor do they involve loss of function or permanent damage. Forty percent cause nothing more than a mild concussion, which is a temporary loss of brain function without detectable structural damage. There is usually a brief alteration in the level of consciousness and

Figure 6-2 The Brain

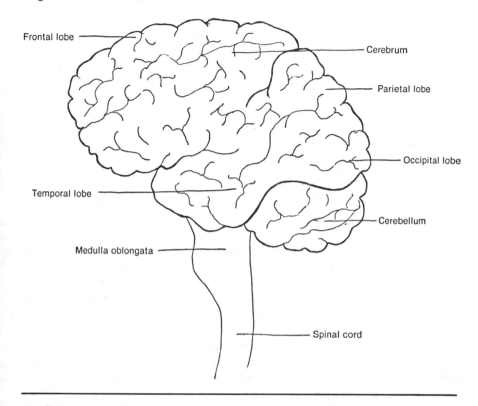

Frontal lobe

Cerebrum

Parietal lobe

Occipital lobe

Temporal lobe

Cerebellum

Medulla oblongata

Spinal cord

amnesia for the events directly associated with the injury. Lethargy, confusion, headache, and dizziness may accompany a concussion (Haslam, 1975).

Another 40 percent of head traumas result in skull fractures (Epstein, 1980). This does not necessarily imply injury to the underlying brain. The most common fractures are linear ones, which usually are self-healing and do not interfere with brain function. More serious are depressed fractures, in which an area of bone is dislodged and driven down into brain tissue. If such a fracture is open, there is an increased possibility of infection.

Most serious head traumas involve bleeding within the head. Subdural hemorrhage, which is bleeding between the brain and its membranes, is potentially fatal unless early diagnosis and treatment occur. Blood accumulating between the brain membranes or skull may push these structures apart, tear the blood vessels running in between, and produce more bleeding and further damage. Sometimes, bleeding occurs between the skull and the dura mater, the outer membranes covering the brain. This type of injury is completely curable if detected, but it is very difficult to detect (Epstein, 1980).

Diagnosis

A child who presents with a visible bruise or damage to the skull should be carefully evaluated for signs of impaired brain function, such as paresis or abnormal neurologic signs. If no hemorrhage or structural damage is detected and the family is reliable, the child can be sent home. The family must be given *proper* instructions to return if any of the following symptoms occur:

- vomiting
- decreased consciousness
- fluid from nose or ears
- unequal pupils

Until recently, ways of diagnosing head injury were either very limited in the information they provided, as in the case of skull x-rays, or were hazardous, as in the case of angiography. Today, with the use of computer-assisted tomography (CAT scanner), one can get a very clear anatomic picture of the brain, and damage can be pinpointed much more safely and accurately without intrusive techniques.

The amount of damage and the speed and success of intervention often affect the eventual outcome. No two injuries are alike. Emergency surgery may be necessary to release the pressure of a hemorrhage or to remove a blood clot. If bone is pressing on the brain, it must be lifted up or removed. Severe damage to the brain stem invariably causes massive irreversible damage (Epstein, 1980). Coma after injury results from brain stem damage, since this area affects the waking and sleeping states. If the damage to this area is severe, respiration and heartbeat are affected.

When there is no function in the brain for 48 hours, brain death is diagnosed. This condition is identified by the absence of all reflexes, the absence of eye movement, and the absence of electrical activity as measured by an electroencephalogram (a flat EEG). In such cases, the current ethical and legal practice in many states is, with the family's informed consent, to remove patients from all artificial means of breathing. Death usually follows.

If a child remains in a coma for more than a few days, feeding is usually aided by insertion of a nasogastric tube. Occasionally, a tracheotomy is performed to assist respiratory function.

It is very difficult to predict the degree of recovery on the basis of the injury. The amount of hemorrhage in the brain stem determines if and when the child will awaken. Occasionally, severe damage results in a state of permanent semicoma.

Minimal injury may require no special rehabilitation. The rule of thumb is usually that one year postaccident reveals the bulk of recovery that will occur naturally. Early rehabilitation ensures that function returns as rapidly as possible and, if return is not complete, teaches the person how best to compensate for lost function.

Removal of upper brain tissue, if it is destroyed by injury, is sometimes necessary. The effects vary depending upon the area of the brain removed and the amount of tissue removed. Usually, the need for removal indicates serious injury.

The scale in Exhibit 6-1, prepared by the Division of Neurological Services at Rancho Los Amigos Hospital in Downey, California, delineates the various levels of cognitive functioning in head trauma patients.

Exhibit 6-1 Levels of Cognitive Functioning

I. No Response
   Patient appears to be in a deep sleep and is completely unresponsive to any stimuli presented to him. Deep coma.
II. Generalized Response
   Patient reacts inconsistently and non-purposefully to stimuli in a non-specific manner. Responses are limited in nature and are often the same regardless of stimulus presented. Responses may be physiological changes, gross body movements, and/or vocalization. Often the earliest response is to deep pain. Responses are likely to be delayed.
III. Localized Response
   Patient reacts specifically but inconsistently to stimuli. Responses are directly related to the type of stimulus presented as in turning head toward a sound, focusing on an object presented. The patient may withdraw an extremity and/or vocalize when presented with a painful stimulus. He may follow simple commands in an inconsistent, delayed manner, such as closing his eyes, squeezing or extending an extremity. Once external stimulus is removed, he may lie quietly. He may also show a vague awareness of self and body by responding to discomfort by pulling at nasogastric tube or catheter or resisting restraints. He may show a bias by responding to some persons (especially family, friends) but not to others.
IV. Confused—Agitated
   Patient is in a heightened state of activity with severely decreased ability to process information. He is detached from

Exhibit 6-1 continued

the present and responds primarily to his own internal confusion. Behavior is frequently bizarre and non-purposeful relative to his immediate environment. He may cry out or scream out of proportion to stimuli and, even after removal, may show aggressive behavior, attempt to remove restraints or tubes, or crawl out of bed in a purposeful manner. He does not, however, discriminate among persons or objects and is unable to cooperate directly with treatment efforts. Verbalization is frequently incoherent and/or inappropriate to the environment. Confabulation may be present; he may be euphoric or hostile. Thus gross attention to environment is very short, and selective attention is often non-existent. Being unaware of present events, patient lacks short-term recall and may be reacting to events. He is unable to perform self-care (feeding, dressing) without maximum assistance. If not disabled physically, he may perform motor activities as in sitting, reaching, and ambulating, but as a result of his agitated state and not necessarily as a purposeful act or on request.

V. Confused, Inappropriate Non-Agitated

Patient appears alert and is able to respond to simple commands fairly consistently. However, with increased complexity of commands or lack of any external structure, responses are non-purposeful, random, or at best fragmented toward any desired goal. He may show agitated behavior not on an internal basis (as in Level IV), but rather as a result of external stimuli, and usually out of proportion to the stimulus. He has gross attention to the environment, but is highly distractible and lacks ability to focus attention to a specific task without frequent redirection back to it. With structure, he may be able to converse on a social, automatic level for short periods of time. Verbalization is often inappropriate; confabulation may be triggered by present events. His memory is severely impaired, with confusion of past and present in his reaction to ongoing activity. Patient lacks initiation of functional tasks and often shows inappropriate use of objects without external direction. He may be able to perform previously learned tasks when structured for him, but is unable to learn new information. He responds best to self, body, comfort, and family members. The patient can usually perform self-care activities with assistance and may accomplish feeding with maximum supervision. Management on the ward is often a problem if the patient is

Exhibit 6-1 continued

physically mobile, as he may wander either randomly or with vague intention of "going home."

VI. Confused-Appropriate

Patient shows goal-directed behavior, but is dependent on external input for direction. Response to discomfort is appropriate, and he is able to tolerate unpleasant stimuli (as NG tube) when need is explained. He follows simple directions consistently and shows carry-over for tasks he has relearned (as self-care). He is at least supervised with old learning; unable to maximally assist for new learning with little or no carry-over. Responses may be incorrect due to memory problems, but they are appropriate to the situation. They may be delayed to immediate, and he shows decreased ability to process information, with little or no anticipation or prediction of events. Past memories show more depth and detail than recent memory. The patient may show beginning immediate awareness of his situation by realizing he doesn't know an answer. He no longer wanders and is inconsistently oriented to time and place. Selective attention to tasks may be impaired, especially with difficult tasks and in unstructured settings, but is now functional for common daily activities (30 minutes with structure). He shows at least vague recognition of some states, has increased awareness of self, family, and basic needs (as food), again in an appropriate manner as in contrast to Level V.

VII. Automatic-Appropriate

Patient appears appropriate and oriented within hospital and home settings, goes through daily routine automatically, but frequently robot-like with minimal to absent confusion, but has shallow recall of what he has been doing. He shows increased awareness of self, body, family, foods, people, and interaction in the environment. He has superficial awareness of, but lacks insight into, his condition; he demonstrates decreased judgment and problem solving and lacks realistic planning for his future. He shows carry-over for new learning, but at a decreased rate. He requires at least minimal supervision for learning and for safety purposes. He is independent in self-care activities and supervised in home and community skills for safety. With structure he is able to initiate tasks as social or recreational activities in which he now has interest. His judgment remains impaired, such that he is unable to drive

Exhibit 6-1 continued

a car. Pre-vocational or avocational evaluation and counseling may be indicated.

VIII. Purposive and Appropriate

Patient is alert and purposive and is able to recall and integrate past and recent events and is aware of and responsive to his culture. He shows carry-over for new learning if acceptable to him and his life role, and needs no supervision once activities are learned. Within his physical capabilities, he is independent in home and community skills, including driving. Vocational rehabilitation to determine ability to return as a contributor to society (perhaps in a new capacity) is indicated. He may continue to show a decreased ability, relative to premorbid abilities, in reasoning, tolerance for stress, and judgment in emergencies or unusual circumstances. His social, emotional, and intellectual capacities may continue to be at a decreased level for him but are functional for society.

Source: Reprinted with permission from the Professional Staff Association of Rancho Los Amigos Hospital, Los Angeles, California, 1981.

The posttraumatic syndrome in children usually includes hyperactivity, poor impulse control, difficulty in retaining new information, emotional lability, lack of judgment, and impairment in social perceptions. Unfortunately, there are few outcome studies of long-term effects of such injury. In one report by Georgia Travis (1976), only 13 percent of severely injured children were normal neurologically. Personality change and mental retardation were serious residual effects, with only 16 percent able to return to normal school classes.

Special Considerations

In the hospital setting, there is a need for continuous diagnostic/prescriptive teaching as recovery progresses. Constant consultation with health professionals, physical therapists, and speech pathologists is necessary. Frustrated by the sense of loss, many children become angry or depressed. This is often complicated by the emotional lability that accompanies the injury, necessitating supportive counseling. Occasionally, the emotional sequelae, coupled by poor impulse control, necessitate close, 24-hour supervision of the child as a safety precaution. Structured environments are often necessary, and parental supervision needs to be constant. Such a situation causes severe strain on most families. In some cases, residential placement may be necessary if appropriate supervision is not available at home.

ORTHOPEDIC DISEASES

Special education needs for populations with the following diseases are not unlike those for other orthopedic handicaps in which temporary or permanent immobility results.

Legg-Calvé-Perthes Disease

This disease was first recognized in 1910 by three investigators whose names are associated with it: Legg, Calvé, and Perthes. It is likely to occur between four and eight years of age, with males diagnosed four times as frequently as females (Katz & Challenor, 1974). In a Blythdale Hospital study of 350 children with Legg-Calvé-Perthes disease reported by J.F. Katz and Y.B. Challenor (1974), a three percent incidence of familial association was found, although no genetic link has been identified. While the etiology is unknown, the condition occurs when there is tissue death at the end of a growing bone, caused by a decrease of blood supply. In Legg-Calvé-Perthes, the growth center (epiphysis) at the head of the thigh's long bone (femur) is affected, and the symptoms are related to the hip joint and the lower extremity (Bigge & O'Donnell, 1976). Symptoms include a pronounced limp, pain in the hip joint or knee, and a limitation of motion. In this disease, bone death in the growth center occurs first. This is followed by the growth of new bone, and eventually the epiphysis is reformed as the bone repairs itself. This process can take up to four years. The prognosis for full recovery is dependent upon the promptness of treatment, the age of onset, and the severity of the disease process. The younger the child, the better the prognosis. Older patients often suffer from a residual deformity (Silberstein, 1975).

Diagnosis is made by x-ray studies, usually by excluding the presence of other disease (Katz & Challenor, 1974). The disease usually occurs unilaterally, but can involve both hip joints.

Treatment

Treatment has been subject to a change of orientation in the last decade. Traditionally, the approach was prolonged relief of weight bearing, sometimes for up to two years. Patients were immobilized and often placed in traction for six to eight months. Casting or braces were sometimes used to stabilize the femoral head and decrease the chances of deformity as the healing progressed. Such casting or bracing also allowed earlier ambulation. A new approach that is gaining favor is surgery, which has been found to hasten the healing process by 6 to 12 months (Silberstein, 1975).

After surgery, the patient is encased in a body cast for six to eight weeks, followed by four to six weeks of intensive physical therapy.

Special Considerations

The casts or braces needed for treatment of this disease place the child in an uncomfortable position, with legs spread wide apart, held in place by a bar. This forced immobilization can be very frustrating to usually active children and necessitates inventive techniques for allowing them full partici- pation in school and recreational activities. Sometimes, the size of the cast hampers them from entering hospital schoolrooms. Special provisions need to be made to allow for such children's inclusion in programs. The section on educational strategies later in this chapter will deal with some of these issues in greater depth.

Osteogenesis Imperfecta

This disease is also known as *brittle bone disease*, in which bones formed improperly tend to break easily. The condition is hereditary and may be con- genital, present at birth, or latent, first appearing in childhood. The con- genital form is most severe, with many fractures present at birth. The condi- tion is generalized, involving tissues such as the teeth, skin, and whites of the eyes (Bigge & O'Donnell, 1976). Bones are fragile, and the limbs are thin and may be deformed. If the child lives to puberty, there may be a decrease in the fragility of the bones, and thus fractures are less likely.

Treatment and Special Considerations

Protection is the primary treatment. Braces, crutches, and wheelchairs may be required. Occasionally, surgery is conducted to correct deformities or provide support for bones. Frequent hospitalizations are common, due to the need for surgery or to treat repeated fractures. Fear of handling such children is real and makes their care by parents and health professionals dif- ficult. Parents frequently feel guilty when fractures result after routine han- dling, and they often fear the consequences of lifting and carrying their child. These children often attend special schools for the handicapped because of the school's barrier-free design, transportation, and support services. This segregation serves to isolate these children from normal classmates, which can further interfere with normal peer relationships. Frequent school ab- sences add to this isolation and increase the risks of academic delay and low- ered performance. Those children who survive to puberty face a serious de- velopmental crisis. As summarized by G. Fields (1974), "Bones are no longer fragile, and increased activity, perhaps an attempt at walking is indicated.

Abruptly, these previously highly protected teenagers are confronted with the world. At a time when they are hypersensitive about their body image, they must come to terms with deformities affecting both appearance and functioning" (p. 551).

JUVENILE RHEUMATOID ARTHRITIS

Juvenile rheumatoid arthritis (JRA) differs from adult-onset arthritis in a number of ways. Its onset usually occurs within the first five years of life, with the peak year of onset in the second year. Half of all cases occur by age five (Downey & Low, 1974). Up to two thirds of all children recover completely by the end of childhood.

The onset of JRA is insidious, usually beginning with swelling in one or more joints, accompanied by pain and sometimes by fever. The degree of severity varies widely, as does the involvement of one or more joints. The cause is unknown, the course unpredictable. One in 5,000 children is said to contract this disease by age 16 (Downey & Low, 1974).

Pain and stiffness result from the effects of the disease and are especially severe after periods of inactivity or at night (Travis, 1976). A frequent, severe complication is uveitis, an inflammation of the eye that can cause a serious loss of vision. Early and frequent ophthalmology exams are necessary to provide early detection and prevention of blindness.

In the early acute stage, pain, swelling, and fever are most common. Later, especially as a result of the child's tendency to favor the painful joint, flexion contractures may occur. These can be lessened by carefully monitored exercises and range of motion treatments by physical therapists and, under their supervision, by parents.

Children with JRA often are subject to growth disturbances caused by a number of factors: the disease itself, bone growth retardation, or prolonged course of steroid treatment (Travis, 1976). A less common but potentially severe complication is the development of heart problems. Again, careful medical supervision should be available to monitor heart function and to provide prompt treatment.

According to outcome studies reported by J.A. Downey and N.L. Low (1974), two thirds of all patients are expected to have a full recovery; 5 percent are reported to die due to complications of the disease or the therapy; 5 percent are left with severe, permanent handicaps, and 25 percent suffer from intermittent active flareups of the disease or minor residual disabilities.

Treatment

Aspirin is the most widely used medicine in the treatment of JRA. It provides both a pain-reducing component (analgesic) and an anti-inflammatory one. This second component is crucial, and parents must remember to continue to provide the recommended aspirin doses to their children, even if little pain is experienced. Aspirin in large doses can cause side effects that must be monitored. It can cause bleeding and irritation of the stomach, and high doses may result in a ringing sensation in the ears.

Steroids are often prescribed in severe cases. These must be monitored carefully because they have both physical and behavioral side effects.

Heat, in the form of warm baths or topical applications, is often used to relieve pain and swelling, especially in the mornings. Inactivity can also lead to a generalized muscle weakness; hence, carefully regulated exercises should be a part of the treatment regimen.

Surgery is now performed only cautiously to correct serious deformities and to help restore function. Surgery requires prolonged hospitalization, pain, and separation from family and school. As Downey and Low (1974) summarize, "Long periods in hospitals or convalescent institutions are countertherapeutic, leading to increased fear of returning to the normal life situation and increased anxiety and phobic avoidance when rehabilitation is attempted" (p. 21).

Special Considerations

Because JRA so often attacks young children who are just beginning to actively explore their environment, its effects on the child's development can be traumatic. Pain, which can be severe and unremitting, creates strong feelings of punishment, fear of activity, and prolonged dependency. Toddlers, confused by the association of pain with normal activity, may become excessively fearful and withdrawn. Parents and therapists are often seen as torturers as they attempt to move and exercise the painful joints. The unpredictability of the disease, especially in those children who experience frequent remissions and recurrences, can confuse a child. Parental expectations change as abilities change, and children who were allowed to sit-out chores one week may be held accountable the next, leading to inevitable conflicts. Some children begin to use their disability to avoid unpleasant or fearful tasks; others may rebel against the overprotection of parents.

As Travis notes (1976), continuous, recurrent pain is unique to JRA and can cause anxiety and depression in older children.

Pain in children is often ignored or downplayed by adults, an observation made by Dr. M. Robinson (personal communication), Director of Child Life at Children's Hospital, National Medical Center. She noted that physicians often prescribe less pain-relieving medicine to children, and parents and nurses often are heard to excuse a child's cries for relief as manipulative. Perhaps it is a sense of helplessness and inability to ease the pain that allows adults to rationalize in this way; nevertheless, the pain of children is real and should be respected and treated adequately.

When children attend school, they often face the frustration of being unable to keep up with peers, and the need to change classes frequently in the later grades, often involving stairs and long hallways, can be exhausting and painful. Morning routines take an unusually long time, and often children are needlessly kept home from school by parents unable to organize sufficiently to meet the time restraints of school schedules. Home teachers, thus assigned, may be able to assess the family's needs and suggest changes or seek the guidance of other support systems to expedite a return to school.

The choice of schools is a difficult one. Special schools for the handicapped are able to provide the needed transportation, barrier-free architecture, and therapy staff to help the severely afflicted child; they also, unfortunately, isolate the child from normal peers and from neighborhood social contacts. Often, assignment to special schools has the effect of labeling a child handicapped, a label that may be hard to erase for the majority of those children who recover completely. Even those who are left with mild disabilities may be more handicapped by social stigma than by the physical effects of the disease itself.

SPINA BIFIDA

Spina bifida is a term used to describe a group of congenital defects. It is considered to be the most prevalent birth defect causing paraplegia today, replacing poliomyelitis (Travis, 1976). Present at birth, it is a defect that occurs as a result of faulty embryologic development of the central nervous system. It results from a failure of the lower end of the spinal cord to close. The contents of the spinal column—nerve fibers, covering, and fluid—may protrude from the lower back in a sac, covered only by a thin membrane. The defect varies in severity. Occasionally, the skin may be intact, and the spinal cord undamaged. This relatively mild form, known as *spina bifida occulta*, usually results in little or no dysfunction. If only the covering bulges out in a sac, with no defect of the nerve fibers, surgery is usually performed to correct this defect, which is known as *meningocele*. Most serious is the form of spina bifida known as *meningomyelocele*, in which defective nerve fibers and the spinal cord lining protrude through an opening in the lower back (see Figure 6-3).

Hydrocephalus, a condition in which excess spinal fluid accumulates, is a frequent associated defect. This condition, untreated, creates severe enlargement of the head, increased pressure, and subsequent damage to the brain. Untreated, a meningomyelocele is an easy route of entry of bacteria into the spinal fluid, causing an infection, meningitis, that can result in death.

Figure 6-3 Spina Bifida

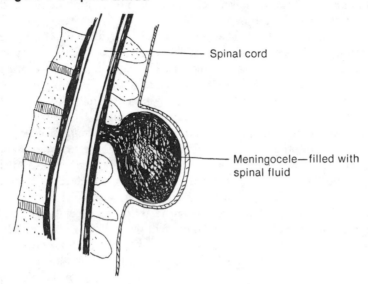

Spinal cord

Meningocele—filled with spinal fluid

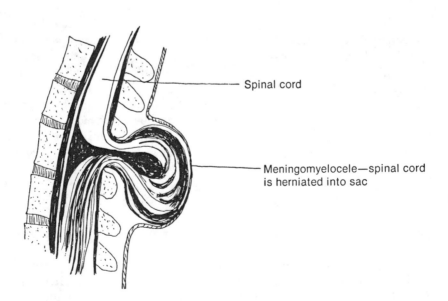

Spinal cord

Meningomyelocele—spinal cord is herniated into sac

Symptoms

The severity of the symptoms is variable, depending upon the extent of damage to the nerve fibers and the existence of other associated conditions, such as hydrocephalus. These symptoms include partial or full paralysis and deformities of the lower limbs; sensory loss below the level of the lesion; urinary and bowel incontinence; other orthopedic deformities, such as scoliosis (twisting) of the spine or kyphosis (humped deformity) of the spine; and lowered mental capacity, especially associated with hydrocephalus. The most common symptoms are described below.

Muscle Weakness

There is variability in the severity and extent of muscle weakness, depending upon the level of the spinal cord defect. Because the defect rarely occurs in the upper back, the areas of weakness or paralysis are nearly always confined to the trunk and lower limbs (Swinyard, 1964). The reader is directed to Figure 6-1 for the relationship between level of injury and mobility characteristics.

Sensory Loss

"There is a loss of awareness of touch, pain, pressure and heat or cold in those areas of the skin normally innervated by nerves which are involved in the spinal cord defect" (Swinyard, 1964, p. 12). Skin must be examined daily to make sure there are no pressure sores or red areas. The temperature of bath water needs to be checked carefully, and clothing should be checked for proper fit. Braces may also rub against legs, and the areas covered need to be examined often.

Bowel and Bladder

Due to a weakness of the muscles in the walls of the bowel and bladder, they are unable to contract to expel their contents. Sphincter muscles, which are usually tight around the openings of the bowel or bladder until relaxed during emptying, are unable to function properly. This creates problems of urinary reflux, or backup of the urine into the kidneys. This backup can cause serious kidney infections and potential kidney failure. The bowel incontinence can cause constipation, impacted stools, and constant leaking of excrement. Diet and a planned bowel evacuation program, consistently managed, can help to avoid these problems. Often these are the problems that interfere most with successful school placement.

Orthopedic Deformities

When bones are not used and do not carry any weight, they lose some of their mineral content. This loss can lead to a condition known as *osteoporosis*. Bones can become so fragile that even routine handling can cause fractures. This often necessitates school absence. Parents, teachers, therapists, and other caretakers become fearful of touching or moving such children, often increasing their sense of social isolation and differentness.

Other problems can occur from muscle or joint deformities that develop as a result of lack of movement. These can be minimized by treatment that employs standing tables, position changes, and frequent exercises to maintain range of motion.

Prevalence

Incidence figures vary, and there seems to be a variation in different populations, with higher rates reported for whites than for blacks in the United States (MacMahon, 1970). Irish populations have been reported to have significantly higher incidence rates than Japanese (4.2/1,000 in Dublin as opposed to 0.3/1,000 in Japan) (Coffey & Jessup, 1955). The cause for these differences is not known. The average incidence figures are reported to be approximately 1 infant in every 300 to 400 live births (Carmel, 1974).

Etiology

The cause of this severe birth defect is unknown. There is some indication of a familial tendency, with the risk of having a child born with spina bifida four to eight times greater in a family with one such child than in a normal family (Lorber, 1965). Research points to the interaction of intrauterine environmental factors with a genetic component (Swinyard, 1964).

Treatment Strategies

Within the last two decades, there has been a major change in the care and treatment of infants born with meningomyelocele. Prior to the 1950s, the vast majority of such children were untreated and often died of meningitis or hydrocephalus. With the advent of antibiotics to treat severe infections and aggressive use of surgical techniques in the early weeks of life, the survival rate has increased dramatically (Carmel, 1974). Dr. J.P. Reichmeister, an orthopedic surgeon working at the meningomyelocele clinic at Kernan's Hospital in Baltimore, Maryland, has suggested that 20 years ago, 90 percent of children born with meningomyelocele expired, while today, approximately 90 percent live (1980).

The decision as to whether to treat meningomyelocele has created considerable controversy. Some experts feel that all children should be treated surgically at birth, repairing the meningomyelocele and creating a shunt to treat hydrocephalus, if present, regardless of the prognosis. Others question such aggressive treatment when other serious defects exist and the prognosis is poor (Carmel, 1974). A group of physicians in England began to treat all cases with early surgical intervention in the late 1950s, a practice that has been widely adopted in the United States (Travis, 1976). Based on data collected from the English studies on over 1,200 cases, Lorber has questioned the practice of such unconditional treatment and has suggested that physicians examine each case to determine if the condition at birth is severe enough to adversely affect future survival and function. The four "adverse criteria" that he defined as being incompatible with a chance for survival with a "useful life" are: (1) severe paralysis, especially if the defect is above the small of the back; (2) severe enlargement of the head at birth; (3) kyphosis (spinal deformity); and (4) other severe abnormalities or birth defects (Lorber, 1972). The decision to treat each child thus becomes complex and raises serious ethical and legal questions (Holder, 1977). In addition to the medical criteria, the physician must consider the impact of this disease upon the whole family and must take into account social, psychological, and financial factors. In 1979, delegates to the Fifth Annual Conference of the Spina Bifida Association of America approved the following position statements:

POSITION ON MEDICAL/SURGICAL TREATMENT FOR INFANTS BORN WITH SPINA BIFIDA

— Whereas, it is the purpose of the Spina Bifida Association of America to set forth a positive image of the person born with the birth defect known as Spina Bifida,
— Whereas, the Spina Bifida Association of America has a deep concern for maximizing the potential of every person born with Spina Bifida,
— Whereas, the early medical/surgical treatment of infants born with Spina Bifida is essential to maximize those potentials,
— Be it resolved, that the position of the Spina Bifida Association of America shall be:
— That the Spina Bifida Association of America actively encourages the early evaluation and medical/surgical treatment of every infant born with Spina Bifida, and that the evaluation be performed by professionals experienced in the evaluation and treatment of myelomeningocele.

approved April 22, 1979
SBAA Annual Meeting
Washington, D.C.

POSITION ON TREATMENT OF ADULTS WITH
SPINA BIFIDA

— Whereas it is the purpose of the Spina Bifida Association of America to set forth a positive image of the person born with the birth defect known as Spina Bifida,
— Whereas the Spina Bifida Association of America has a deep concern for maximizing the potential of every person born with Spina Bifida,
— Whereas adequate and comprehensive treatment is often not available for persons over age 18,
— Be it resolved, that the position of the Spina Bifida Association of America shall be:
— That the Spina Bifida Association of America actively encourages continued, comprehensive and lifelong treatment/care for all persons with Spina Bifida.

approved April 12, 1979
SBAA Annual Meeting
Washington, D.C.

Once the decision to treat the child has been made, the family system is committed to years of surgical interventions, countless visits to hospitals and clinics, as well as the emotional, financial, and physical strains of caring for a handicapped child. The immediate treatment is neurosurgical, to close the spinal cord lesion and install a shunt if hydrocephalus is present. Frequently, orthopedic surgery is conducted at various intervals during the early years to correct orthopedic deformities or to enhance the possibility of ambulation.

The major cause of illness and death after the first three years is renal failure, and surgical interventions to prevent such complications are common. Ostomies are performed less often today, unless severe kidney damage is present, with modern management techniques of self-catheterization and consistent bowel programs preferred. (See section on spinal cord injury for details of these procedures.)

The long-term effects of meningomyelocele vary, depending upon the degree of the handicap, the presence of hydrocephalus, and the quality of care the child receives. Because of the relatively recent changes in treatment, little research has been done to study the long-term effects and life expectancy of these children. As summarized by P. Carmel (1974), "the quality of life for the child with spina bifida systica will depend on his locomotion, his intelligence and the condition of his renal tract" (p. 150). In a comprehensive study (Lorber, 1971), almost half the children 7 to 12 years after repair were largely or entirely wheelchair-bound, 18 percent walked with the assistance of braces and crutches, and 13 percent were independent of orthopedic aids but walked with a limp or a waddle. Many adolescents were reported to resort to wheelchair use after early years of ambulation, due to their increased weight and the slowness of mobility with crutches and braces. Frequently, the goal of orthopedic management to enhance more independent ambulation requires repeated surgical interventions, casting, and splinting in the child's early years. Such treatment again raises questions of the ultimate goals of management and the concomitant emotional and physical trauma that repeated surgical interventions inflict upon the child. Dr. Kopits, at the Johns Hopkins Birth Defects Center, espouses early and repeated orthopedic procedures, while the team at Philadelphia Children's Hospital postpones surgery until the child is walking (Travis, 1976).

Intellectual capacity has a crucial impact on the long-term outlook for children with meningomyelocele. In several studies reported by Carmel (1974), the major factor in determining the intelligence of survivors was the development of hydrocephalus. J. Lorber (1972), in his extensive studies, cites the following statistics: 49 percent were of normal intelligence (IQ 80 or above) but had a severe physical handicap; 18 percent had both normal intelligence and a mild to moderate physical handicap; 33 percent had a combination of severe physical handicap and mental deficits that would require total dependence on others for life. The isolation of so many children with meningomyelocele in homes or institutions and the educational discontinuity caused by frequent and prolonged hospitalizations often further affect the child's intellectual capabilities and future educational and vocational opportunities.

A criticism that is often raised by parents of children with spina bifida and by many of its victims concerns the common pitfall of fragmented care. An acquaintance of the author, a victim of spina bifida, now married, employed, and the president of the Maryland chapter of the Spina Bifida Association, talked of such fragmentation: having doctors who treated his legs, others who treated his various urinary problems, physical therapists who assisted him in ambulation training, teachers, nurses, and so forth. He described his mother as living in the car, traveling from one appointment to another.

Lifelong care is essential for those with spina bifida, and for such care to be beneficial, it needs to be well coordinated, centralized, and reflecting the philosophy that it is a person who is being treated, rather than a collection of disparate systems.

Special Considerations

The combined impacts of partial sensory deprivation, mobility limitations, frequent hospitalizations, separation from parents, pain from surgery and other therapeutic techniques, and social isolation cannot be minimized. Educational interventions and psychosocial supports should be available to children with spina bifida as early as the neonatal nursery unit stay. Infant stimulation programs and early preschool opportunities with mental-age peers can help to optimize the potential for these children. As they become mainstreamed into regular schools and programs, teachers need to be aware of the possibilities of social stigma for these children. Conferences and communication among teacher, nurse, and parent can help to develop contingency plans for urine and bowel elimination to avoid embarrassment and to allow the child to feel secure in class. Alternate physical education programs can also be arranged to encourage active participation. Periods of hospitalization should be scheduled, when possible, to coincide with school holidays or summer vacations, and home/hospital programs need to be set up to provide continuity if the school year is interrupted.

Frequently, parents and society respond to the sight of children crippled from birth with pity and overprotectiveness. They often fail to encourage such children to test their own limits, and they "do for" them. Discipline is hard to enforce on a child already handicapped, and parents, teachers, and peers may thus deprive children of reaping the rewards as well as the punishment of self-initiated actions. This can seriously affect their feelings of self-worth, and they may develop a sense of helplessness or loss of a sense of control over their own lives. Often, such children become dull and lazy, unmotivated to achieve, uncaring about their future. Hygiene is ignored, leading to medical complications and social isolation due to body odors, which further decreases self-esteem. As adolescents, these children often fail to take advantage of vocational opportunities and become dependent adults, a condition caused not by their handicap but by the lack of appropriate educational, social, and psychological intervention. As A.H. Lister (1970) asks, "What right have we to pay so little attention to the quality of life these people are being offered? Medical progress has made them survive. Social and educational progress must at least try to make them happy to survive" (p. 983).

BURNS

Severe burns constitute one of the most devastating disabilities in childhood. The burned child is thrust from normalcy to suddenly being faced with functional and cosmetic deformities, and the nature of the trauma often precipitates psychiatric disturbances as well. Rehabilitation begins at hospital admission and often continues for up to two years. Functional and cosmetic reconstruction can continue throughout the child's lifetime (Schmitt, 1980).

It has been estimated that 2 million people are treated for burns yearly, with one half of that group below age 20. Seven to eight thousand victims die yearly as a result of burn injuries (Cosman, 1974).

Burns in childhood result from the combination of poor supervision of the child and a poorly supervised environment (Cosman, 1974). The severe trauma that follows a major burn, the necessity for long-term rehabilitation, and the reality of permanent disfigurement and loss of function all combine to categorize major burns with other serious chronic disabling illnesses of childhood.

The severity of a burn is measured by the degree of depth of the burn, the amount of body surface that is affected, the parts of the body affected, and the existence of respiratory tract involvement or other disease or injuries. As a rule, first degree burns, which affect only the surface skin, are treated with simple first aid methods. Second degree burns are accompanied by blistering and can be classified as superficial or deep. The criterion is the amount of damage to the epithelial layer and the underlying skin structures (sweat glands, hair follicles, and sebaceous glands). In third degree burns, the tissues are so badly destroyed that no source for regeneration of the surface skin remains (Cosman, 1974). In children under age ten, burns that cover more than ten percent of body surface area are considered major and require emergency medical care. Burns of the hands, feet, joints, and face require special attention as well.

The speed of medical attention and the expertise of the staff can affect the eventual outcome of treatment and can prevent needless deaths. In large urban areas such as Baltimore, specialized regional referral centers have been instituted that can provide highly skilled medical teams trained in the latest techniques.

Treatment

Treatment and rehabilitation have basically three stages: initial treatment of shock and resuscitation, wound debridement and coverage, and restoration and reconstruction.

In the first critical stage, which lasts the first two to three days, the goal is to keep the patient alive and restore essential fluid balance. In severe burns, the skin damage causes damage to the capillary network, with resulting leakage of plasma. Fluid replacement is essential. Patients are kept immobile and receive constant intravenous therapy. In cases of facial or neck burns or respiratory involvement, an emergency tracheotomy may be needed to create an open airway.

In the second phase of treatment, dead skin needs to be removed surgically, and skin coverage must be begun to prevent infection and death. This is done by extensive skin grafting, since the patient's skin cannot regenerate naturally. Hydrotherapy for wound cleansing is also frequent. This phase can last for up to six to eight weeks, depending upon the extent of the burns and the speed of healing. During this period, the severe pain, the isolation of the patient, and the beginning realization of the extent of injuries can be severely traumatic to children. Treatments are given around the clock, in a hospital setting filled with strange lights, bizarre machines, and peculiar sounds and odors. Such a situation can cause profound confusion and panic in children. They may feel real or imagined guilt for causing the accident, and this may add to their anxiety. Often, burned children regress dramatically at this stage, unable to sort out feelings of pain, guilt, and anxiety. Many burn victims have been identified as risk-takers, with premorbid personality characteristics of poor impulse control and low tolerance for frustration. These traits can add to their difficulties in coping with the tragedy of their accident and make psychiatric intervention crucial. High technology burn centers, while helping to salvage the patient's life and function, can also lead to feelings of depersonalization. The child does, in fact, look bizarre, and staff may inadvertently being to treat burn victims as "things" to be cared for. Routines can help, as can sensitive psychiatric care and support to both staff and patient.

Exercise and movement therapy are begun early and are essential components of both short-term and long-term rehabilitative care.

The third phase of care, restoration and reconstruction, can take upwards of two years, both in inpatient treatment and outpatient care. It is a long and difficult process. As skin heals, it tightens and scars, causing contractures and limitation of movement as well as disfigurement. Body areas are often splinted to prevent contractures. Exercises are mandatory to increase range of motion and to maintain strength, normal movement patterns, posture, and gait. Open wound areas are frequent and need constant care to prevent skin breakdown and infection. Itching may be severe as healing occurs, which can reopen areas. Jobst elastic garments, worn over burn areas 23 hours daily, can help to reduce scarring by means of compressing the skin. Healing of scarred tissue can take up to 2 years to complete. Later, further hospitalization to increase function or improve appearance may be needed.

Special Considerations

The damage that a major burn inflicts on children's self-image may be as severe as the physical damage incurred. Their appearance is often monstrous. They look disfigured, often walk abnormally, and may have splints that create a crippling effect. The jobst garments, when worn on face and neck areas, give children a somewhat grotesque appearance at first sight. The early weeks and months of hospitalization provide a time for children to sort through their feelings of despair and self-denigration. Staff and family gradually accept their peculiar appearance and no longer respond with shocked stares. Patients begin to reexert some control over their lives in the hospital. Often, this takes the form of refusing to comply with exercise or hygiene regimens, which can frustrate staff. Hospital school programs can begin to help the child return to some aspects of normality.

For the child, returning to the outside world can present new problems. It is difficult to reenter the world drastically changed in appearance and abilities. This is especially hard for preadolescents and adolescents, for whom appearances are especially crucial. Hospital and homebound teachers can help such children by gradually allowing them to experience outsiders' reactions to their appearance. Visits to other hospital areas, to local stores, movies, and performances, and visits by former friends and classmates can help to ease them back into the world.

Compliance with exercise schedules is essential in order to reduce the risk of loss of functioning, especially in hand, fingers, or neck involvement. Teachers should become familiar with the child's exercise schedules and should know what functions are still available to the child. One burn patient, a master of manipulation, had led his teacher to believe he could not write with his right hand; thus he was excused from taking an important test. Lack of study, rather than lack of function, turned out to be the real limitation that day.

As burned children mature, vocational counseling can help to guide them into appropriate careers, and psychiatric counseling may be necessary to help them grow into adulthood with a minimum of psychological scars.

EDUCATIONAL STRATEGIES

General Issues

Prior to the recognition that all children were entitled to a free, appropriate education in the least restrictive environment, the vast majority of children enrolled in homebound programs were those with physical handicaps such as those described earlier in this chapter. Within the last decade, most children capable of benefitting from a school-based program have been offered this opportunity. Additionally, school districts are now required by law to provide specialized equipment, programs, and space to accommodate children, regardless of the degree of disability. Nonetheless, due to extended waiting periods while appropriate services are developed and frequent hospitalizations and periods of illness suffered by children with chronic illness, homebound/hospital teaching services are necessary to ensure educational continuity. Children with chronic illnesses that are accompanied by physical limitations present a complex challenge to the homebound/hospital teacher. Added to the need to provide continuity in academic programming and emotional support to the child, the teacher faces the task of having to adapt material and equipment or present it in alternative formats to fit the child's physical limitations. In some cases, the child's limitations are of a long-standing nature and the child has had training in specialized techniques, or the teacher has had prior training with children with physical handicaps. In others, the disability is new to both child and teacher, and neither has experience from which to draw. Specialized in-services can be of great benefit to teachers in such circumstances and can ease the feeling of frustration that such assignments often bring to the teacher unfamiliar with working with the physically handicapped. The following sections are an attempt to guide teachers in their efforts to help such children.

Task Analysis

As outlined by J.L. Bigge and P.A. O'Donnell (1976), task analysis is an essential tool for teachers. It allows them to start from the child's needs and abilities and determine (1) what to teach, (2) what steps are necessary for the child to learn the skill or task, (3) where the child is having difficulties in completing the assignment, and (4) what adaptations are necessary to aid task completion.

Abilities of the child can be assessed through a number of avenues: by informal observation, informal testing, or formal testing; error analysis; or diagnostic/prescriptive teaching. Steps that can be used as part of the process of task analysis are the following:

1. Define end criterion the teacher wants accomplished.
2. Analyze the component parts of the task.
3. Identify the skills each part requires.
4. Identify the prerequisites to each skill.
5. Identify those skills that the child
    a. already has
    b. can do with help
    c. can be taught to do
    d. cannot do (effects of the disability)
6. Change those aspects of the task to match the child's abilities.

Using this process, the teacher can often adapt curriculum and programs to suit the needs of each child. For example, a child who can read simple words and is currently working on a matching task may not have the motor ability to circle answers or to draw a line connecting the correct answers. The child may only be able to use the side of his or her hand to slide paper around. A board can be constructed containing cards of paper or cardboard marked with the matched items and their labels. Sectioned off at the bottom would be containers. The child then slides matching items into each container. By changing the information on the paper cards, many different learning skills can be taught in this way. For a more extensive discussion of these techniques, the reader is referred to J.L. Bigge and P.A. O'Donnell's text, *Teaching Individuals with Physical and Multiple Disabilities* (1976).

Adapting Equipment and Materials

Task analysis, described briefly above, can be used as a tool in adapting equipment and materials to match the physical limitations of children and help them function as independently as possible in academic tasks. Physical therapists and occupational therapists, skilled in methods of adaptation of equipment, can be invaluable to teachers in developing devices to assist in the learning process. Slant boards, velcro or gummed surfaces, pencil or pen holders, pointers, and magnetized wrist or arm holders can all help the child in fine motor tasks. (See Figure 6-4 for illustrated examples.) Consultation with physical therapists can help teachers become aware of positions that the child can assume for maximum functioning and comfort. Tape recorders, typewriters, and forced choice answers that can be pointed to or looked at all aid in teaching children with physical handicaps.

Hand-made or commercially purchased adaptive equipment, appropriate positioning of the child before beginning a task, and adaptation of the required mode of response to the child's abilities can establish an optimal learning environment for the child with a physically disabling illness. Examples of a variety of these adaptations can be found in Bigge and O'Donnell's text (1976). A list of some of the companies that make adaptive learning tools is provided in a latter section of this chapter.

Nonverbal Communication

Occasionally, children with physically disabling chronic illnesses are unable to use speech to communicate their wants or needs. This may be a temporary condition, such as that caused by head trauma. Being unable to communicate verbally adds to the frustration of the child, who is already sick or injured, and can seriously interfere with the provision of educational programming. Teachers working with such children can help them to express their feelings and continue their learning by providing or using alternative communication systems. Speech pathologists can assist teachers in developing communication boards or devising signals that can be used by the child to signify wants and needs or answers to questions. The following guidelines, adapted from Bigge and O'Donnell (1976) and prepared by Eileen Washington, Speech Pathologist, Mt. Washington Pediatric Hospital, may provide some helpful direction in educating nonverbal children:

1. Observe children in unstructured situations.
   a. Note the signs or signals they use to convey feelings or messages.

Figure 6-4   Adaptive Techniques for Writing

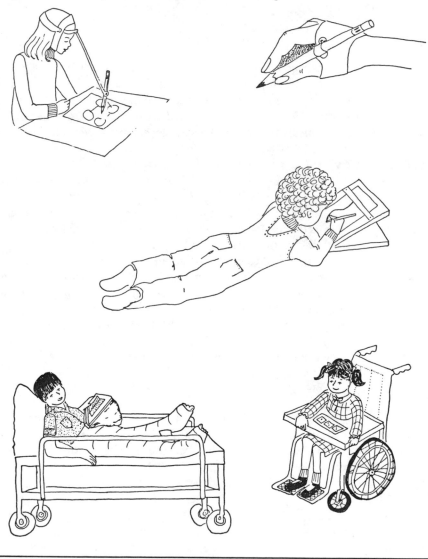

___

b. Listen to the "noises" or sounds that they make. They may be their
   way of attracting attention—"Hey I want to talk to you!"
c. "Bend" to the level of the children. Sit next to them (within their
   visual field) or in front of them so that you are at eye level.
2. Provide opportunity for interaction.
   a. Initiate conversation with a greeting; try to evoke a smile.

b. Maintain eye contact.

c. Observe the children and approach them about the activity in which they are engaged.

3. Ask questions one at a time.

a. Asking several questions in succession does not afford children the opportunity to respond immediately. They may not be able to process the information and formulate the expected response quickly.

b. Help structure decision-making situations by your question. Provide them with alternatives.

c. Ask simple, basic questions. Do not use complex vocabulary.

4. Allow time for expression of ideas and responses to your questions.

a. Be patient. Responses may be delayed.

b. Know their methods of expression (facial changes, gestures, pointing, and the context in which they are used).

5. Narrow options.

a. Begin with the immediate situation or environment. Ask questions requiring a yes/no response.

b. Find a classification or category (home, school, something about your appearance, something you want).

6. Avoid giving cues. Don't give away the correct answer (changes in vocal inflection, pauses, gestures, will give cues).

7. Accept only clear signals. That is important for confirmation of response. "I don't know" is acceptable.

8. Continue conversations until information is clarified.

a. Allow the "speaker" to choose whether to continue to pursue communication.

b. Encourage expression by asking: "Is there more? What do you think about that?"

c. Clarify notions: Ask "Am I close?"
"Is there more to it than that?"
"Is it too specific or too general?"
"Is that exactly right?"

9. Recognize deadlocks. There will be times when you will not be able to help children completely express their thoughts.

a. Say, "I'm really stuck. Do you want to go on?"

b. "Yes, it is frustrating for both of us, but let's keep trying."

c. "I have to leave, but I will think about it. You think too; I will be back."

10. Be aware of mistakes leading to deadlocks.

a. Do not reach premature conclusions.

b. Avoid erroneous assumptions by checking information phrase by phrase with the speaker.

c. Do not try to ask questions that the child does not wish to answer.

Remember, the nonoral child has no way to say "I don't want to talk about that right now."

d. Avoid discussing a topic that makes you uncomfortable.

Adaptive Games and Crafts

The hospital or homebound teacher should make an effort to provide physically disabled children with a full educational program, including motor activities and games. These will encourage the child to be actively involved and will afford the child an opportunity to engage in nonacademic activities with the teacher or peers. Many of these games can be played alone or with parents or siblings. See Exhibit 6-2 for examples of such adaptations.

Exhibit 6-2   Games Adaptable to the Physically Disabled

MOTOR GAMES
A. *Tossing and Catching—*
   Adaptations:
   1. Use bean bags rather than balls.
   2. Use velcro catcher's mitt and velcro balls. Child with limited use of arms can catch ball.
   3. "Pretend" to throw and catch. Verbalize what is being thrown.
   4. Use helpers to catch or throw.
B. *Soccer—*
   Use extra large ball that can be moved by wheelchair wheels or stretcher wheels. Confine area with benches or dividers on sides to define space.
C. *Bowling—*
   Adapted pins and balls can be invented, such as styrofoam frisbees and styrofoam cylinders. Position of pins can be adjusted to child's abilities.
D. *Ball games against a wall—*
   Tie ball to long rope on wheelchair or to arms of blind children so they can be independent and retrieve ball.
E. *Rope and ring—*
   Tie rope at one end to make circle; place ring inside. Everyone stands or sits in circle, holding rope with two hands. Leader slides ring between hands while music plays. Ring can be slid along rope under hands. Person who is "it" must guess who is holding the ring when music stops.

Exhibit 6-2 continued

MUSICAL GAMES
A. *Moving to music—*
Move various body parts with or without rhythm instruments.
B. *Musical chairs—*
Adaptation: Have children move to various corners of the room in their wheelchairs, traveling in a circle to designated areas. They lose if music stops when they are in open area.
C. *Passing sounds—*
This is especially good for children with very limited movement. Place children in a circle. One person passes a sound to player on his or her right, and sound goes around. Second player (at random) passes another sound the opposite way. Sounds can catch each other, change direction, be sent clear across the circle. Sounds can even chase each other!
BODY IMAGE ACTIVITIES
A. *Move body parts—*
Have children try to isolate movement and move as many different body parts as possible. Have them open and close their eyes and mouth, smile and frown, shake or wiggle limbs, swing limbs, bend and straighten different body parts. Try it in different body positions: in the chair, on the stomach, on the back, and on the side.
Helper: Before asking a child to bend his arm, stretch it gently as straight as possible. Before asking a child to straighten a limb, bend it gently as far as possible.
B. *Hand touching other body parts—*
Help children to touch their dominant hand to other body parts and parts of the head and face, using direction words such as front, back, up, down, right, and left.
Helper: If children cannot touch these parts, take a piece of ice and touch body parts for them. Ask them if they can feel the ice.
C. *Trace the child—*
Have children lie on a piece of butcher paper. Trace their whole bodies talking to them: "Now, I'm going around your foot." Hold the tracings up for them to see. If possible, have them help draw in features and details of clothing. If they are not able, have them watch while it is being done

Exhibit 6-2 continued

and describe to them what is being drawn.

Helper: Repeat this activity with children lying on their sides. Place arms and legs in different positions while tracing. Use the drawings to indicate progress in gaining range of motion.

D. *Shadow play—*
Place children between a light source and a wall or suspended sheet. Encourage them to move and watch themselves move. If a sheet is hung (across a doorway, between two poles, and so forth), the rest of the class can be an audience on the other side of the sheet. The shadow only will be visible. They can try to guess who it is.

Helper: Play music and let the children dance or do exercises as they watch the shadows. Ask them to make animal shapes that the audience can guess.

E. *Reinforcement—*
When exercises or moving to music gets old, try attaching bells or balloons to the limbs with tape or elastic. This will give children more feedback about where their body parts are in space.

F. *Mirror—*
Ask the children to explore their range of motion in front of a mirror so they can watch themselves. Have them assume different shapes (stretched, curled, wide, narrow, crooked, twisted); ask them to balance in different poses (sitting, prone and facing mirror, prone looking back over shoulder, on either side, on knees, standing, walking or crawling toward); and have them move their faces to show different emotions.

G. *Body parts' prints—*
Using water paint or washable ink, have children make prints of their hands, fingers, thumbs, feet, elbows, knees, nose, chin, and bottom. Temporary prints can be made with plain water on an absorbent surface.

H. *Photographs and videotape—*
Depending on resources, take prints, slides, movies, or make a videotape of children as they participate in some of their favorite activities, indoors and outdoors. Show them to the children as soon as possible. Have them participate in a skit if possible and show it back to them. Videotape or film participation in aquatic activities.

Exhibit 6-2 continued

AQUATIC ACTIVITIES
A. Paint with water on a wall or sidewalk outdoors.
B. Pour water from and into different types of containers.
C. Blow through a straw into water, trying different kinds of straws.
D. Splash with different body parts (hand in basin, foot in bucket).
E. Blow at Ping-Pong balls, walnut shell boats, or corks.
F. Make bubbles with commercial or soap solutions and wave rings or blow through pipes, straws, or commercial bubble toys.
G. Squirt water with squirt toys, detergent bottles, rubber syringes, water-filled balloons, trick rings, or roses from a magic shop.
H. Sponges, cotton balls, and washcloths are fun to squeeze, wring, feel, throw, and catch.
I. Colored water doubles the fun of all the above activities, especially if using transparent containers. Use food coloring.
SENSORY PLAY
A. Use a variety of fabric on cardboards—
   Touch and name games (soft, hard, fuzzy)
B. Use feely boxes to encourage recognition of various shapes, textures, and sizes.
C. Remember *all* the senses when playing any game—touch, sound, smell, taste, and kinesthetic sense.
D. Use sand and water play with a variety of mixing and pouring vessels.
BOARD GAMES
Cards, simple board games, and the like can help pass the time when hospitalized. The key is to adapt the rules to suit the disability.
Cards. For example, if the child has visual problems, get cards that have enlarged numbers. (Blank cards are available commercially for maximum adaptability.)
If the child's arms are not available for use, due to casting or poor motor control, set up cards in holders, on tray, or with a partner who acts as the child's hands.
If the child cannot read, change the rules to make games simpler. If cards slip off the table, use magnetic or velcro backing.

Exhibit 6-2 continued

ART ACTIVITIES

Any art activity can be analyzed and its steps broken down as described above. Simple activities could include:

A. Cutting and pasting. Use adapted scissors and tape paper to table or trays so that it doesn't slide when in use.

B. Crepe paper can be cut up and even very young or physically handicapped children can crumple it and paste it on precut form for an attractive display.

C. Paint with any available body part!

D. Paint can be put in roll-on deodorant bottle for easy application.

E. Finger paint with pudding (edible!) or ivory soap flakes.

Source: The sections on body image games and aquatic activities were adapted from a recreational therapy workshop given by Sharene Smoot, Fulton County Schools, Florida at the 1979 annual council for Exceptional Children's Convention, Dallas, Texas.

Preschool

The preschool years represent a child's first exposure to a school setting. A child's attitudes toward school, teachers, and learning develop in these early years. The nature of these first experiences influence and help to shape the child's future responses.

In order to encourage the development of a positive attitude toward school and learning, these early experiences need to be supportive, providing a nurturing environment in which young children learn to accommodate to their disabilities, gain cognitive mastery of skills, and develop a sense of self-worth.

Preschoolers with a physically disabling chronic illness face a lifetime of limited mobility. At a time when the need for active exploration of their environment is greatest, these preschoolers find themselves immobilized by splints, casts, wheelchairs, or braces. They need to be encouraged to participate in normal activities and to be provided with alternative motor experiences. Games of ball or bean bag throwing should be encouraged, using any available extremity. A preschooler in one center was encouraged to use her head to "throw" a soft sponge ball to a partner when all her other limbs were casted or in traction. Assigning partners can help the preschooler join in physical play, as one runs or swings a bat in place of another. Velcro-covered balls, darts, or gloves can allow a weakened child or one with poor coordination to practice throwing and catching skills. Preschoolers should be placed in the thick of the action, whenever safe, to play alongside peers. Puzzles can be done by all the children on the floor or on a mat, or tables can be bought or adapted to allow a child in a wheelchair to be placed at the table alongside the other children.

Children with chronic disabling illness are frequently hospitalized for surgery or other intrusive treatment regimens. Hospital school programs can offer preschoolers the opportunity to express their fears and anxieties through the medium of play, while continuing to provide developmentally appropriate experiences.

The issues of dependence and independence are central to preschoolers. Hospital school programs and preschool community programs can afford children with chronic illnesses the chance to develop independent skills to the fullest extent possible. Self-help skills such as feeding and dressing do not come naturally to many preschoolers with physical disabilities. Early education in these skills as part of a preschool curriculum is important so that these children can gain a measure of independence and mastery. The wheelchair-bound preschooler who learns to retrieve a fallen toy or button a shirt has gained a sense of efficacy that can carry over into later academic learning. The feeling that "I can do it," that frustrations and defeats can be overcome, is essential in later educational settings. Feeling pity for the "poor helpless" children and doing tasks for them that they can accomplish with help and training leads to a defeatism and overdependency that can be very hard to reverse as the child matures. The sensitive teacher always must walk a thin line between helping the child, so that tasks are not overwhelming and impossible to achieve, and allowing the child to do things independently.

In many hospitals or special schools, preschoolers must undergo many hours of therapy. Consultation with therapists can often allow the teacher to integrate treatments with educational activities. Thus, if a child needs to be kept on a prone board for a few hours, cognitive tasks such as puzzles, sorting games, or matching games can be offered to use the time effectively. Children can often be encouraged to do range of motion exercises if they are encorporated into group activities. Many such activities can be integrated into the preschool program in hospitals or special schools.

The issue of mainstreaming needs to be raised at this point. Hospital school or playroom programs or special schools that are staffed with teachers experienced in working with the physically handicapped often provide excellent programs and are able to integrate education with the other therapeutic services that are provided in those settings. The question to be raised is whether such settings meet the full range of needs of the child with severe burns, arthritis, or orthopedic disease. Many of these children will partially or fully recover and will be expected to return to the mainstream for their future educational and social experiences.

Because other preschoolers are often expected to react negatively toward wheelchairs, prosthetic devices, jobst stockings, and the like, adults may see their open comments about these as indications that they would be cruel to handicapped children. In fact, the reactions of preschoolers to handicapped children are usually aimed at the devices, not the child. A sensitive teacher can recognize this as natural curiosity and use it as part of the curriculum. Children can borrow a wheelchair and see how it feels to push one, or they can write a language experience story about going to the hospital. The teacher needs to follow the lead of the child in such cases, sensing the child's willingness to demonstrate special abilities (wheelies) or special devices (hooks to pick up crayons, lap boards to write on). The aim is to encourage others to feel comfortable around the child's adaptive devices, but not to embarrass the child. Such openness can go a long way toward encouraging children to accept one another with or without special equipment.

There are a number of considerations that have to be taken into account in the decision to include a physically handicapped child in a regular preschool program. Preschoolers are naturally curious and may attempt to play with a physically handicapped child's medical appliances. Thus, a child just learning to manipulate fine motor objects may try to pull out the tracheotomy or ostomy bag of a peer. Children immobilized by casts or splints may be walked over or ridden over by impulsive classmates, and prone-standing tables may be toppled by children running through the room. Staff-child ratios need to be adjusted downward in such cases, in order to provide the appropriate supervision necessary to ensure the child's safety.

Specialized preschool programs that provide intensive therapeutic services in conjunction with a curriculum that includes a good balance of normal developmental activities may allow a child to receive maximum therapeutic intervention in the early years. Such centralization of services also benefits the family, since they can avoid costly and time-consuming outpatient trips for therapy after the child's school day is over.

The issues that should be taken into account in determining the best school placement should focus on the most appropriate educational program and the availability of needed therapeutic services. These should be provided in the least restrictive environment. The free, individualized, open atmosphere of most preschool programs that follow a developmental model are often most appropriate for successful mainstreaming of physically disabled children, even if they will later attend a special school program.

School Aged

Hospital School*

One of the first major concerns when working with physically handicapped children is dealing with the space available. The physical plant or schoolroom

---

*This section of the text was contributed by Celeste Klima.

area is an important part of the successful, motivating experiences with children in an academic setting. The room needs to be large enough to hold wheelchairs, stretchers, and other adaptive equipment. At times, when a schoolroom is filled with 14 children and 7 of them are in wheelchairs or stretchers, the room becomes a maze. One of the best techniques is a simple one: proper planning. This helps by ensuring that each chair or stretcher will be placed in the most efficient and advantageous position. It eliminates problems such as having to empty out the whole room when a child leaves for a scheduled appointment. Another problem arises when a child's cast is too big to fit through a normal sized door. Then the teacher has to use turning techniques under proper supervision or place the child just outside the open door. To ensure inclusion in the group, the teacher needs to arrange the room carefully.

A similar problem is arranging for appropriate adaptive desk tops for wheelchairs that do not fit under the desk or table or for stretcher patients on their stomachs. Padded desk pillows are available, made on a slant with a hard surface on top to use for writing (see Figure 6-4). They are equipped with a lip along the bottom to hold the paper in place. Also, maintenance departments can be asked to cut and finish pieces of plywood to fit over wheelchairs as removable desk tops. A heavy rope can be attached to hold them in place. These are cheap and effective pieces of equipment that can serve numerous purposes.

Children with physical handicaps present various types of problems for the teacher planning individualized programs. Some are normal mentally but have had to deal with a physical handicap since birth. Others have been handicapped recently and are still dealing with the anger and frustration of the new restrictions they are now facing. This will usually occur whether the handicap is permanent or temporary; however, the degree may be different depending on the child's ability to realize and rationalize the condition realistically. Some are mentally limited and have been handicapped since birth. These children have serious problems in self-help skills, learning to control their bodily functions, and relating to other children. They have different needs than the healthy child, and their programs should be individually designed accordingly. Most programs will require materials that are functional and that meet each child's physical and mental needs and limitations. It should be noted that many regular school materials can be adapted, such as putting pencil grips on pencils, placing desks on sides of patients, folding ditto sheets so that only a section can be seen at a given time. Manipulative materials are available in abundance through commercial supply houses and publishers. The teacher's task is then to design the appropriate programs and select the necessary materials for each child. At times, needed materials will have to be hand-made or designed to meet the student's physical limitations.

Peer relationship is another area that needs to be addressed in the hospital school. Many times children feel well accepted in this group because they are not the only ones that look "different." But at times, one or more normally functioning children may not appreciate other children's inability to control their bowel or bladder. Accidents that result in foul odors frequently occur to such children. This can lead to name-calling and/or a child's refusal to come to school out of embarrassment. A teacher needs to limit this type of behavior in an understanding but firm way and be supportive to all patients.

Another major problem is in the area of restrictions placed on a physically handicapped child. Many children are able to become excellent drivers of stretchers and wheelchairs. They actually end up with few limitations because they can easily maneuver their equipment anywhere, even when this may not be safe or medically advisable. Since these children need to feel they have control and do not want to be left out, this can cause problems. It is very hard for seven year olds in casts to understand why they can't swim when everyone else is swimming or take a walk down a steep hill when they think they can safely do it.

In such instances, supervision is needed to protect the child, and attempts need to be made to adapt activities to include the child whenever possible. Thus, at swimming time, the casted child may be given a basin of water and water toys to manipulate. Other adaptations can be found in manuals, in books, and in the teacher's own personal store of games. Many games can be adapted with a little imagination. Wheelchair children can play volleyball, baseball, catch, circle games, organized line games, or run relays if some forethought precedes the activity. Some safety training, good sense, a book of games, and a little practice are all that is needed. The reader is directed to the earlier section on task analysis for further explanation. This opens the door for more appropriate peer relationships, group interaction, and good socialization skills, and it increases the child's ability to both compensate for and deal with his physical handicap whether it is temporary or permanent.

The teacher must make a few personal adjustments in dealing with the physically handicapped child. First, the teacher must explore personal fears and anxieties in handling this type of child. It is also necessary for the teacher to learn to tend to these children in ways that may not be previously thought of as a teacher's responsibilities. This may include transferring patients to chairs, beds, stretchers, prone stands, and so forth. It could also include wiping around tracheotomies or mouths or readjusting bags that children have hooked to them after they are accidently detached or broken. Everyone finds some of these tasks unpleasant, but they usually can find some way to successfully deal with these unavoidable situations. In the end, such help allows the child to feel less different and often saves valuable time. If the teacher needs to interrupt the education process to obtain the services of a nurse each time such a situation arises, school becomes little more than a string of disruptions, separated by occasional teaching.

Children with physical handicaps are often in need of the services of other medical departments. This requires flexibility on everyone's part and identification of each child's limits of tolerance for activity or pain. Rest periods need to be fit into all schedules. Even the best arranged schedule can be thrown off because of the extensive time required for maneuvering the child in and out of positions and performing basic care routines.

Any staff member working directly with physically handicapped patients should be familiar with accepted practices and protocols. One way to gather this information is by attending all in-services offered and making use of the consulting services of various disciplines.

In summary, the hospital teacher of children with physical handicaps must provide a setting and experiences that are positive and that stimulate growth. The teacher must be able to coordinate peer interactions, design or adapt equipment and programs, and meet the children's social and emotional needs. Experience, understanding, and training are the best tools available to the teacher.

Homebound

Education for the school age child with physically disabling chronic illness should be conducted in school settings whenever possible. Homebound programs for this population should be short-term, and the teacher should make every effort to help the child become reintegrated into a less restrictive program. Often, home teaching is arranged for this population when the child is recovering from surgery or awaiting repair or the reordering of essential adaptive devices. Occasionally the child is at home while awaiting placement in a more appropriate school setting. At such times, home teachers may find that they are serving the needs of the child best by acting as the child's advocate, pushing for speedy delivery of a wheelchair or expediting a screening meeting. For school age children, physical limitations often interfere with normal opportunities for socialization. Forced isolation at home further limits their social experiences and thus further handicaps them.

Constant efforts to help children view themselves as a part of the class can help to ease some of this isolation. Telephone contacts should be arranged with classmates, and the children can keep up with projects and can be asked to submit work done for display on bulletin boards. Academic preparations should be closely tied to children's class assignments, and they should be encouraged to keep up with the group without undo pressure or a sense of unhealthy competition. In cases in which children have had an accident, leaving burn scars or requiring adaptive equipment, photographs of their changed condition or tape recordings of their voice, shared with classmates through the teacher, may make the return to class less frightening for both these children and their classmates. This should be done only with the consent and support of the injured child. Photos of the class and hand-drawn get well cards can also help children feel less isolated.

Transition back to a home school should be made with careful preparation. The school may, for example, be essentially barrier-free, but the bathroom doors may be too narrow for wheelchairs. The child may need to visit the health suite and meet the staff, so that if the need to use the suite arises, the child feels comfortable in using this resource. This can be helpful in cases in which the child may need to perform self-catheterization or in other circumstances that are likely to prove embarrassing to the child.

If the child has had a severe head trauma, with resulting loss of memory or impulse control, careful assessments should be made to ensure that the child is placed in a program that provides supervision and remediation.

Recovery from head trauma is a slow process. Children may continue to gain new skills for up to two to three years following the accident. Continued reassessments of their academic skills, physical abilities, and social judgment need to be made, and school placements may need to be changed frequently during this period. A number of criteria need to be taken into account when reintegrating children with head trauma into a school setting. These include their physical limitations and need for continued physical therapy, their distractibility and tolerance for working in a group setting, their overall level of academic functioning, their current communication skills, and their need for supervision.

Adolescents

Hospitalized

There are a number of issues that need to be examined that affect hospital educational programs for adolescents. They include the nature of the disability and whether it is temporary or permanent, new or long-standing; the prior educational programs and goals of the adolescent; the nature of the hospital program available, and whether it involves individual or group instruction; and available resources for inclusive programming of secondary education curriculum.

Adolescents who have been disabled by disease for much of their lifetime have, by puberty, usually accommodated themselves to their disability. The impact of puberty, however, brings with it new concerns and fears, which often affect educational programming. If hospitalizations have been recurrent, the adolescent often views the hospital as a second home, and staff are seen as peers. Motivation to make plans for future jobs may be lacking, and the hospital teacher may be able to use the educational program to explore career choices and examine realistic options. In addition to providing regular curriculum offerings, hospital schools should attempt to include career information and leisure activity training in their program, especially in rehabilitation or long-term care hospitals.

Such offerings are crucial for those adolescents newly disabled by disease or injury, such as those with spinal cord damage or burns. For these patients, exploration of changing future goals within the hospital setting can provide a chance for them to verbalize frustrations, anger over the destruction of their plans, and fears of failure. Visits to rehabilitation units or visits by disabled young adults to the hospital can help to introduce the adolescent to a new set of future options. Patience and understanding are needed, however. Adolescents, newly disabled, may not be able to accept their fate or make plans for their future for a considerable period after the accident. Educational staff should make vocational information available to them but should not force them to face the reality of their changed circumstances. Adolescents who were performing marginally in schools and were planning a career that required an able body may be especially devastated by sudden disability. Careers in sports or in the armed forces, plans to be firemen or policemen or construction workers are all crushed by the cruel twist of fate that befell these adolescents. Time and support are needed to help them regain a sense of hope and a new identity.

The struggle to see oneself as normal yet different, as different yet worthy, is a lifelong psychosocial task for the physically impaired. Its initial emergence as a core issue occurs during adolescence (Kaplan, 1981).

Hospital school programs for adolescents vary from state to state and from setting to setting. In some large medical centers, there is a large enough adolescent patient population to support a grouped secondary school program. Adolescents thus have the opportunity to engage in essential peer interactions, to learn in a group context. This affords them the chance to do group projects and to thus learn essential skills of cooperation and teamwork. In smaller settings, tutors are assigned to each adolescent on an individualized basis, for different subject areas. This kind of programming is most common, and unfortunately, it provides only fragmented and partial secondary education. Academic subjects such as biology and chemistry can be very difficult to teach in such a setting, although the very environment of the hospital may afford a unique opportunity for the imaginative teacher to assemble and demonstrate applied science techniques. The teacher may be able to use old x-rays to teach basic anatomy; the laboratory may be borrowed for simple chemistry experiments with the help of a sympathetic and interested technician; lectures by experts may be arranged by tactfully asking a doctor, nurse, or therapist to share their expertise with the adolescent.

With flexibility in programming, reading assignments can include material, fictional and biographic, about physically handicapped people. A variety of books for or about people with handicaps can be used by the teacher to help adolescents identify with problems and fears familiar to them (Mullins, 1979). Again, caution should be exercised to avoid pressuring adolescents to accept and adjust to their disability before they are emotionally ready to cope with it.

For the adolescent receiving individual tutoring, a schedule should be developed that fits into the student's hospital therapy programs and that is agreed upon by the student. Adolescents in hospitals are afforded very little opportunity to control their lives and the decisions that affect them. Their willingness to cooperate in their hospital education program can be increased if their right to consultation and choice in scheduling times for tutoring can be recognized and taken into account. Goals for the achievement of specific education skills, such as completing a book report or a math assignment, can also be made via a contract between the teacher and the adolescent. The teacher can share with the adolescent the overall curriculum goals, and together they can plan for the timing and content of the material. Adolescents usually are more likely to finish academic tasks if they feel that they had a choice in the development of the material, and they may be able to give the teacher a realistic sense of the amount of time each assignment might take for them and the amount of time they have free in the hospital.

Vocational planning can be started in the hospital school setting, especially if the adolescent has suffered a recent accident that has caused permanent physical disability. The local school district should be contacted to provide a full battery of vocational assessment tests, so that educational planning can be started. A meeting with the adolescent, the parents, a social worker, and the teacher should be planned to review the results and evaluate the best strategies for helping the adolescent. Recommendations may be made for continued services at a residential or outpatient rehabilitation center. The availability of services, the child's age and degree of impairment, and the family's capacity to provide supervision, transportation, and support all play a role in determining the best options for the adolescent.

Vocational planning is a team function, but the hospital teacher can play an invaluable role in coordinating the various efforts and in helping the adolescent identify strengths, weaknesses, interests, and abilities that can ensure a successful adaptation to the larger world. For some, the severity of the accident or illness precludes independent living and career planning. For these students, a realistic approach is necessary to prevent them and their parents from developing misconceptions as to their true potential. Children who are quadriplegic and who cannot feed or dress themselves without assistance should not be encouraged to plan for an independent job, but should be helped to investigate alternate supportive living arrangements, such as group homes, supervised apartment living, or foster care. In such cases, educational goals can be established to develop a variety of skills in leisure activities and limited sheltered workshop jobs. Since the majority of these adolescents will be essentially homebound as adults, home catalogs should be a part of the curriculum materials. Lessons should emphasize shopping for value, budgets, sizing by a catalog, and how to return unwanted items.

Home-based jobs can be investigated as well. Some quadriplegics can be trained, for example, to read books into machines for tapes for the blind, via use of electronic push buttons, page turners, and other adaptive equipment.

These skills can help to make the physically handicapped adult a contributing member of society, with a consequent increase in self-esteem.

For all categories of hospitalized adolescents, a primary goal for the teacher is to bring the curriculum into perspective with the illness and with the adolescent's abilities, interests, and future needs, while complying with state and local regulations. Although this may seem to be an impossible mission, it is a goal worth aiming for, one that can help a disabled adolescent to reenter the community with new skills and a sense of hope and self-worth.

Homebound

As with the school age child, homebound programs for adolescents with physically disabling chronic illness should be used sparingly. Adolescents isolated at home often become severely depressed and lack motivation to engage in any pursuits. They often sleep long hours, neglect their hygiene, and lose interest in the world outside. The home teacher often arrives to find the adolescent asleep, unwilling to spend the time with the teacher. Assignments are often left undone, and the adolescent's parents usually respond with a sense of frustration and despair. As one mother expressed sadly, "I give up. He stays up till 4 A.M. watching T.V. movies, sleeps all day, never showers or bathes, and his room stinks." In this family, the boy, newly paralyzed after an accident, was awaiting school placement and the repair of a wheelchair. The teacher used her contact to arrange for a speedy school assignment and began using a "loving tough guy" approach on the adolescent. The family was encouraged to arrange for friends to visit, and the boy was taken to a swimming program for disabled adolescents by the staff of the rehabilitation hospital that had treated him. Psychiatric counseling was recommended. Many of the tasks performed by this home teacher went well beyond her assigned duties. Without them, however, she had been unable to provide any educational programming and was, in fact, on the verge of asking to have him removed from her rolls.

Placement decisions are crucial in planning an educational program for the physically handicapped adolescent. The decision as to the choice of schools should be made by consultation, including the parents, school personnel, and, if old enough, the child. All factors should be considered: the child's age, physical limitations, academic needs, social-emotional needs, availability of services in the schools and community, and the family's needs. Finally, whatever the placement, it should be reevaluated periodically or whenever any of the conditions, such as prognosis, change.

The psychological impact of physical disability on adolescents is a major factor in educational planning. An adequate adjustment to the handicap and its consequent effects allows the adolescent to take full advantage of educational and vocational planning, and thus move on toward adulthood.

Table 6-1 Elements of Adequate Adjustment for Handicapped
Adolescents

While the relatively well-adjusted will not manifest all of the behaviors, there will be
a preponderance of these features.

Behavioral:

1. Self-care at an adequate level.
2. Regular school attendance and at least moderate achievement commensurate with
   ability.
3. Compliance with medical treatment.
4. Participation in a social/recreational activity.
5. Maintenance of a close relationship.
6. Willingness to enter new social situations.

Psychological:

1. Acknowledgment of disability, its limitations, and responsibilities.
2. Motivation toward self-care and social experiences.
3. Sense of differences and commonalities with others.

Source: Reprinted from The Psychosocial Adjustment of Visibly Physically Handicapped Adolescents by Chaya Kaplan. Unpublished paper, 1981.

Table 6-1 presents suggested components of an adequate adjustment for handicapped adolescents and can serve as a guideline in establishing educational,
vocational, and social goals for physically handicapped adolescents.

SUMMARY

This chapter examined a variety of visible illnesses and presented curriculum materials aimed at enhancing the educational experience of children
with physically handicapping conditions. Because these conditions typically
result in some degree of physical limitation, methods of task analysis were
briefly presented, as well as guidelines for working with nonvocal children.

Suggestions for adaptations of games, equipment, and the environment
were also presented, with the aim of increasing the reader's repertoire of educational strategies.

RESOURCES

Alpha Chi Omega Fraternity, 3445 Washington Boulevard, Indianapolis, Indiana 46205. *Alpha
Chi Omega Toy Book: Self-Help Toys to Make for Handicapped Children.* 38 pp. Single Copy
free.

American Automobile Association. *Vehicle Controls for Disabled Persons.* Published by the
American Automobile Association; available from Traffic Engineering and Safety Department, AAA, 1712 G. Street, NW, Washington, DC 20006.

American Printing House for the Blind, P.O. Box 6085, Louisville, Kentucky, 40206. Supplies books and educational materials to schools and classes. Manufactures talking books.

B.O.K. Sales Company, Box 32, Brookfield, Illinois 60513. Catalog of items to adapt devices for eating and drinking.

Bare, C., Boettke, E., and Waggoner, N. *Self-Help Clothing for Handicapped Children*. Chicago: National Society for Crippled Children and Adults, 1962.

Bell Telephone Company. (Supplies: school to home telephone service, electric larynx, volume control for amplification on the telephone, bone conduction telephone receivers, watchcase receivers for the deaf, light and amplified telephone rings.)

Braille books (American Foundation for the Blind).

Braille Magazine. Contains articles on education, science, culture, and communications. The Braille Review, published in English, French, and Spanish contracted Braille. Visitors Information Center, Information Division, UNESCO, 7 Place de Fontenoy, 75700 Paris, France.

Closer Look. The National Information Center for the Handicapped, Box 1492, Washington, DC 20013.

Haycraft, Howard. *Books for the Blind and Physically Handicapped*. Division for the Blind and Physically Handicapped, Library of Congress, Washington, DC 20542.

Hoffman, Ruth B. *How To Build Special Furniture and Equipment for Handicapped Children*. Charles C Thomas, 1974. 100 pp. $6.50.

Iowa State University Cooperative Extension Service, Ames, Iowa 50010. *Clothes to Fit Your Needs*. Jacqueline Yep et al. 13 pp. No charge.

J.A. Preston Corporation. *Self-Help Devices for Rehabilitation*. 71 Fifth Avenue, New York, New York 10003. Catalog of adaptive devices for eating, games, etc.

Kamenetz, H.L. *The Wheelchair Book*. Springfield, IL: Charles C Thomas, 1969. This book gives complete descriptions of all wheelchairs made, plus many other kinds of equipment.

Library of Congress, Division for the Blind and Physically Handicapped, Taylor Street, NW, Washington, DC 20542. Includes talking books, Braille books, playback machines, tapes. Publishes selected reading lists (also on large type).

Mealtime Manual for the Aged and Handicapped. Institute of Rehabilitation Medicine, New York University Medical Center.

Medic Alert Foundation International, Turlock, California 95380. At cost—bracelet with identifying medication information, emergency answering service—call collect from anywhere in the world, 24 hours a day, (209) 634-4917.

New York Times, P.O. Box 2570, Boulder, Colorado 80302. Weekly large type editions.

Elwes, Nicholas D.B. *Aids for the Handicapped*. Spastics Society, 1973. 64 pp. $1.50 (paper).

Oster Vibrator, Jr. Model. Oster Company, a hand-held vibrator helpful in lung clearance.

George Peabody College for Teachers, Nashville, Tennessee 37203.

Prosthetic and Sensory Aids Service, Department of Medicine and Surgery, 810 Vermont Avenue, NW, Washington, DC 20420.

Robinault, Isabel P. (Ed.). *Functional Aids for the Multiply Handicapped*. Harper & Row, 1973. 233 pp. $12.50.

Rosenberg, C. *Assistive Devices for the Handicapped*. Minneapolis: American Rehabilitation Foundation, 1968.

Talon Velcro Consumer Education and Velcro Corporation. *Convenience Clothing and Closures*. 41 East 51 Street, New York, New York 10022. A free book of clothing adaptations for the handicapped (illustrated).

United Cerebral Palsy Association, Inc., 66 E. 34th St., New York, New York 10016. Cerebral palsy equipment and accessories patterns are available for making large size diapers, support vests, safety helmets, and improvised thigh or waist cuffs.

United Cerebral Palsy Research and Educational Foundation. *Nonvocal Communication Resource Book.* Baltimore: University Park, 1978, 228 pp.

United Cerebral Palsy Association, 66 E. 34th St., New York, New York 10016. *Recreation for the Homebound Person with Cerebral Palsy.* Morton Thompson, 30 pp. $.25.

U.S. Government Printing Office, Washington, DC 20402. *Feeding the Child with a Handicap.* 19 pp. $.40.

Zimmerman, Muriel E. *Self-Help Devices for Rehabilitation. Parts I & II.* Published by William C. Brown Company; available from publisher at 135 Locust Street, Dubuque, Iowa.

REFERENCES

American Public Health Association. *Accident Prevention.* New York: McGraw-Hill, 1961.

Azarnoff, P., & Flegal, S. *A pediatric play program: Developing a therapeutic play program for children in medical settings.* Springfield, IL: Charles C Thomas, 1975.

American Alliance for Health, Physical Education, and Recreation, 1971, *1.*

Bigge, J.L., & O'Donnell, P.A. *Teaching individuals with physical and multiple disabilities.* Columbus, OH: Charles Merrill Publishing Company, 1976.

Carmel, P. Spina bifida. In J.A. Downey & N.L. Low (Eds.), *The child with disabling illness.* Philadelphia: W.B. Saunders Co., 1974.

Coffey, V.P., & Jessup, W.S. The incidence of spina bifida. *Irish Journal of Medical Science,* January 1955, pp. 30–48.

Cosman, B. The burned child. In J.A. Downey & N.L. Low (Eds.), *The child with disabling illness.* Philadelphia: W.B. Saunders Co., 1974.

Diem, L. *Who Can?* (4th ed.) Frankfort, Germany: M.W. Limpert, 1964.

Downey, J.A., & Low, N.L. *The child with disabling illness: Principles of rehabilitation.* Philadelphia: W.B. Saunders Co., 1974.

Epstein, M. Head trauma. Symposium, Mt. Washington Pediatric Hospital, November 25, 1980.

Fields, G. Social implications of long-term illness in children. In J.A. Downey & N.L. Low (Eds.), *The child with disabling illness.* Philadelphia: W.B. Saunders Co., 1974.

Hanrigan, K. Protocol for bowel and bladder management. Unpublished, 1980.

Haslam, R. Teacher awareness of some common pediatric neurologic disorders. In R. Haslam & P. Valetutti (Eds.), *Medical problems in the classroom.* Baltimore: University Park Press, 1975.

Holder, A.R. *Legal issues in pediatrics and adolescent medicine.* New York: John Wiley & Sons, 1977.

Kaplan, C. *Psychosocial adjustment of visibly physically handicapped adolescents.* Unpublished paper, 1981.

Katz, J.F., & Challenor, Y.B. Childhood orthopedic syndromes. In J.A. Downey & N.L. Low (Eds.), *The child with disabling illness.* Philadelphia: W.B. Saunders Co., 1974.

Lister, A.H. Future for children with spina bifida. *Lancet,* 1970, *2,* 982–983.

Lorber, J. Results of treatment of myelomeningocele. *Developmental Medicine and Child Neurology,* 1971, *13,* 279–303.

Lorber, J. Spina bifida cystica. *Archives of Disease in Childhood,* 1972, *47,* 854-872.

Lorber, J. The family history of spina bifida cystica. *Pediatrics,* 1965, *35,* 589-595.

MacMahon, B. Environmental influences on congenital defects. *Medical Opinion and Review,* 1970, 58.

Mealey, J. *Pediatrics head injuries.* Springfield, IL: Charles C Thomas, 1968.

Mullins, J.B. *A teacher's guide to management of physically handicapped students.* Springfield, IL: Charles C Thomas, 1979.

Myers, S.J. The spinal injury patient. In J.A. Downey & N.L. Low (Eds.), *The child with disabling illness.* Philadelphia: W.B. Saunders Co., 1974.

Reichmeister, J.P. Seminar on chronic illness, presented by Mt. Washington Pediatric Hospital, Baltimore, MD, 1980.

Rigoni, H.C. Psychological coping in the patient with spinal cord injury. In D. Pierce & V. Mickel (Eds.), *The total care of spinal cord injuries.* Boston: Little, Brown & Company, 1977.

Robinson, M. Personal communication.

Rose, S. *The conscious brain.* New York: Vintage Books, 1976.

Schmitt, M.A. Pediatric burn rehabilitation. Unpublished summary, undated.

Silberstein, C.E. Orthopedic problems in the classroom. In R. Haslam and P. Valetutti (Eds.), *Medical problems in the classroom.* Baltimore: University Park Press, 1975.

Spina Bifida Association. Position statements, 1979.

Swinyard, C.A. *The child with spina bifida.* Chicago: Spina Bifida Association of America, 1964.

Travis, G. *Chronic illness in children.* Stanford, CA: Stanford University Press, 1976.

BIBLIOGRAPHY

Association for the Care of Children in Hospitals. *Guidelines for the development of hospital programs and for the personnel conducting programs for therapeutic play for pediatric patients,* 1971. (Available from ACCH, 3615 Wisconsin Avenue, NW, Washington, DC 20016)

Cratty, B.J., & Breen, J.E. *Educational games for physically handicapped children.* Denver: Love Publishing Co., 1972.

Diem, L. *Who Can?* 1967.

Fluegelman, A. (Ed.). *The new games book.* Garden City, NY: Doubleday, 1976.

Kennedy Foundation. *Let's play to grow.*

Wessel, J. *I can.* East Lansing, MI: Michigan State University.

Chapter 7

Degenerative Diseases

OVERVIEW

This chapter will review two degenerative diseases and discuss the implications of such conditions for educational and vocational planning. The diagnosis of a degenerative disease is devastating for the child and family, and the family's focus is most often toward the medical considerations. Educational and vocational planning is usually seen as secondary and often nonessential. Earlier diagnosis and increasingly sophisticated medical technology have created a core of children whose life span, while significantly shortened by the disease, is considerable. It is therefore not appropriate to forego education and vocational planning for a child who may well be alive for 10 to 20 years after the initial diagnosis is made.

For the child, each day presents time that he or she exists, and each day should be filled with learning and pleasure and growth.

FRIEDREICH'S ATAXIA

In discussing Friedreich's ataxia, the most common of the inherited degenerative conditions, the emphasis will be on the characteristics common to central nervous system degenerative diseases and the special educational and vocational issues that such diseases create.

Friedreich's ataxia can be transmitted as either an autosomal recessive trait or an autosomal dominant trait, and it affects both sexes equally. It is equally distributed racially and nationally. The recessive trait has its onset around age 10 or 11, while the dominant trait usually presents later, between ages 18 and 22 (Menkes, 1980). The recessive form is ten times more common than the dominant. The presence of the disease in more than one sibling occurs in about 18 percent of affected families (Menkes, 1980).

189

Symptoms

The distinguishing symptoms are gradual ataxia (muscular discoordination); disturbed speech patterns, sometimes exhibited in explosive speech or hesitant speech; nystagmus (involuntary movement of the eyeballs); and gradual spinal deformities.

Etiology

The exact etiology is unknown, although current research seems to point to a complex metabolic disorder. In the disease, neurons gradually lose their myelin covering and die, beginning at the nerve cell's periphery and progressing toward the center, with gradual disappearance of the cell (Greenfield, 1954). In early life, these children may be slow in learning to walk and may begin to stumble frequently. As noted by John H. Menkes (1980), "Neurological symptoms advance relentlessly. Although the disease evolves rapidly in a few children, progression is slow in the vast majority, and occasionally long stationary periods occur" (p. 120).

Gradually, the child's muscle weakness of the lower limbs and unsteady gait increase, necessitating more dependence upon crutches, walkers, and eventually a wheelchair. As the condition progresses, sensory modalities become affected, with gradual loss of feeling in the extremities. The upper extremities eventually become involved, and involuntary movements of the head and extremities become common. Pains, cramps, and areas of sensation loss are also frequent. Degeneration of the nerves associated with the eye and ear may occur, leading to loss of vision or hearing acuity. Speech difficulties are also common, with a gradual slurring of speech. Bladder and bowel control is frequently impaired, and over half the patients are reported to suffer gradual mental deterioration (Menkes, 1980). In advanced cases, patients may be totally bedridden. Death usually occurs as a result of congestive heart failure, although secondary infections or severe malnutrition can precipitate death.

Treatment

Death usually occurs by the time the child reaches young adulthood. Children are encouraged to remain active as long as possible to postpone the inevitable deterioration of muscle control. Physical therapy is recommended to maintain mobility and avoid contractures. In addition, as the child becomes dependent upon a walker or wheelchair, physical therapy is necessary to train the patient in independent transfers and self-help skills. Emotionally, this training is crucial to allow the child to retain as much independence and control as possible, as long as possible.

Special Considerations

Degenerative diseases present a complex picture. For the child, the prospect of increasing dependence and a drastically shortened life span is traumatic and grim. The normal developmental progression from dependency to independence is reversed, creating increasing psychological conflicts. That the illness becomes debilitating in adolescence is even further devastating, since it breaks the pattern of autonomy and throws the child back upon the family's resources at a time when separation is natural. The loss of smooth function in the upper extremities and the gradual slurring of speech combine to frustrate the youngster, adding to feelings of depression and helplessness. If an older sibling has had the disease, the child may begin to measure his or her symptoms against those that occurred in the sibling. Often, this can precipitate premature acceptance of immobility without regard to individual variability of onset or type of symptomotology. A lack of motivation to continue school, job training, or therapy often occurs as the disease progresses. It becomes very difficult for the child or adolescent to relate to future plans, in light of the debilitating and terminal nature of the condition. Teachers and counselors are often beset by similar feelings of futility. These issues and their effect on educational programs will be discussed in greater detail in Chapter 9, which deals with the dying child.

For families, the presence of a degenerative inherited disease creates intense feelings of guilt, blame, and anxiety. Looking for answers, parents often look to each other's families to explain the disease. Clear, repeated genetic counseling can help to alleviate early confusions over etiology and can clarify the issue of blame. It is difficult for parents, faced with the diagnosis of an inherited disorder, to separate the feelings of blame and guilt from the realization that their genetic makeup played a role in their child's disease.

The parental anxiety that accompanies degenerative diseases such as Friedreich's ataxia involves the possibility of other siblings developing the disease, as well as fears surrounding the diagnosed child's prognosis. Increasingly, parents' physical, emotional, and financial resources are drained as the child becomes less independent and in need of a host of support services, medical care, and adaptive equipment.

School programming needs to take into account the constantly changing nature of the condition. The need for periodic reevaluation is essential to monitor motor skills, mental ability, and hearing or vision loss and to revise educational programming in accordance with the findings.

MUSCULAR DYSTROPHIES

There are a group of muscular diseases that are inherited and that show a gradual onset in early life. The most common and severe is Duchenne's muscular dystrophy, which is transmitted via sex-linked recessive genes; hence, females are carriers, but usually asymptomatic. In the disease, there is a gradual degeneration and wasting away of muscle tissue. The disease usually has its onset between two and five years of age and becomes progressively worse. It is relatively common, with prevalence of 1 case per 25,000 live births (Menkes, 1980).

The onset is gradual, and often initial signs are overlooked. These include difficulties in climbing stairs, rising from the floor, and other signs of pelvic weakness. The disease progresses in stages, marked by the child's decreasing abilities and independence in the usual activities of daily living, such as walking, dressing, and toileting (Peterson & Cleveland, 1975). The rate of progression is rapid and symmetric. In the later stages, heart enlargement and heart failure are common, occurring in 50 to 80 percent of patients, as are contractures (Menkes, 1980).

Defective intelligence, which is nonprogressive, has been noted in some cases. The course of the disease is invariable and progressive, with death usually occurring during adolescence. Death is often due to heart failure or secondary infections.

There are other forms of muscular dystrophy that are only slowly progressive and that may be compatible with a near normal life span.

Diagnosis of Duchenne dystrophy is made by a study of the symptom patterns, a positive family history, and blood analyses. These identify abnormal elevations of enzymes associated with muscle deterioration (Peterson & Cleveland, 1975).

Treatment

While there are no specific treatments to slow or stop the deterioration, a treatment goal is to help the child maintain as much independence for as long as possible. Treatment usually consists of frequent reassessments of the child's abilities and the prescription of and training to use adaptive devices such as standing boards, braces, crutches, and wheelchairs. Exercises to keep muscles from becoming stiff and positioning to prevent contractures are also helpful.

Special Considerations

Children with muscular dystrophy should be encouraged to be as independent as possible, for as long as possible. Early clumsiness in school or at home should be a sign to seek medical advice. After diagnosis, children should be allowed to continue in regular class programs for as long as they can and to continue to receive educational programming for as long as they are able. It would be a disservice to the child to lower teacher expectations or to abandon all future expectations, since individual symptoms are variable, and the disease progression may be slower than expected. On the other hand, teachers need to establish realistic goals and must recognize the likelihood of a severely shortened life span, with drastic limitations in the child's mobility in the later stages.

With degenerative conditions such as muscular dystrophy, educational orientation needs to be redirected, away from planning for future career goals and more toward the enhancement of the quality of life each day. The child's interests and genuine abilities should form the core of the curriculum, with emphasis on short-term goals, leisure pursuits such as literature, art, music, hand work (when possible), and practical, functional skills in areas like cooking, sewing, and budgeting. In some cases, training for a high school equivalency diploma may allow children to pursue a simple career with a high school diploma while they are still physically able to perform a job, rather than spend four full years in high school. In other cases, continued attendance in regular schools allows the child to remain in social contact with peers through adolescence and avoids the isolation so common in children with a degenerative disease.

For the child, the family, and the teacher, coming to terms with the inevitability of the condition and facing the reality with a degree of acceptance and fortitude become paramount tasks.

EDUCATIONAL STRATEGIES

The diagnosis of a degenerative disease may be the cruelest and most devastating experience a child and family must face. Usually, the child is young and the symptoms subtle, so that the full impact of the inevitability of the condition can only be imagined. Parents look at their preschooler, who may be clumsily running in the living room or backyard, and find it hard to envision that child wheelchair-bound, unable to feed or dress himself or herself, unable to grow toward independence and autonomy. The tendency for parents is to shelter and protect their children, occasionally to the extent of failing to enroll their children in school or even removing them from school when symptoms become obvious and mobility is impaired. The feelings of futility in future planning and the tendency toward overprotectiveness typical of parents of children with degenerative disease often hasten the child's descent into dependency.

Educationally, the child's program needs to be planned with a number of objectives in mind:

- All planning should be based upon short-term goals.
- There should be an established mechanism for periodic reevaluation of the child's skills and medical condition.

- Independence in all skills should be encouraged for as long as possible.

- The areas of socialization and training in leisure activities should be considered high priorities in educational curriculum planning.

- Placement decisions should be made on the basis of the least restrictive environment philosophy.

For the teacher, the quality of each day's activities should be taken into account. As Mullins (1979) sensitively suggests:

> When a student has probably a shorter life expectation, the teacher may pay a little more attention to the quality of his life each day. If he hates mathematics and loves reading, it might be better to encourage a literature course instead of calculus. Enrichment courses can be used to stimulate new interests such as music appreciation, creative writing, arts and crafts, and skills such as playing a musical instrument, balancing a budget, repairing household gadgets, typewriting, sewing, and weaving. The development of these skills and interests helps the child to utilize constructively the large amount of leisure time at his disposal rather than spend an excessive amount of time watching television, which many homebound children do. (p. 299)

Preschool Child

Although the prognosis in degenerative diseases is usually poor, medical technology continues to make strides, and major medical breakthroughs are not inconceivable. Even with a shortened life span, preschoolers can look forward to 10 to 20 more years of life. The preschool period is a crucial time for the child to develop a sense of self-worth through mastery of skills and a repertoire of coping strategies that can profoundly affect the child's future.

Children in the early stages of degenerative diseases can benefit from early educational intervention programs designed to enhance socialization skills and to recognize and support the expression of individual differences. Preschoolers should become familiar with neighborhood stores, community programs, and the like, so that when they become increasingly visible by their gait or by the use of adaptive devices, they will be less afraid to appear in public. Positive early school experiences increase the likelihood that when children are older, they will be willing to continue to attend school, even as their physical condition deteriorates.

School Age Child

The school age child may begin to exhibit increasing weakness or other physical signs of degenerative disease. Often, this is accompanied by feelings of despair, anxiety, and anger as the prognosis slowly begins to dawn on the child. Parents may be hesitant to share with the child the full medical realities of the condition, and the child may begin to question the teacher, searching for facts. This creates a dilemma for teachers, who may be uncertain what course to follow. Should they obtain fact brochures about the illness and share them with the child? Should they avoid the issue and stick to teaching, in spite of the child's obvious preoccupation? A conference with parents, teacher, and health professionals is necessary to sort out these questions and to provide the child with both knowledge and support. Hospital school teachers face this situation most often, but teachers in regular schools and home-based programs may have to confront the issue as well.

A complicating factor in this situation relates to the mechanism of denial, so common in such cases and often necessary for the emotional stability of the child and parents. Thus, children may ask their teachers for answers, hoping to hear different ones than those presented to them by their parents or physicians. Parents may be unwilling to discuss the condition with their child and may be resentful of the teacher attempting to break through their denial. The child may have overheard a conversation and be confused by the terminology used or by the meaning of certain words. Finally, teachers often feel uncomfortable discussing medical questions that are unfamiliar to them, and they are often naturally reluctant themselves to face the painful issues brought up by such questions. The following guidelines may be helpful to the teacher when such discussions are inevitable:

- Recognize that a part of the teacher's job is to provide emotional support to the children. Such discussions should, therefore, be considered a part of the teacher's role.

- Arrange for a conference with the parents and health professionals involved. It is important that the teacher be aware of how much children know, what the parents and doctors have told them, and what emotional reactions they have exhibited. For example, some children may show no emotion when discussing their condition, while others may cry or withdraw.

- Honesty is essential. While teachers may not be willing or able to tell children all the facts, they should never lie or distort the truth to protect them. At worst, saying nothing is better than not telling the truth.

- Don't tell children more than they can handle. Watch for signals such as tears or a sudden change of subject.

- Listen. That is often all the child wants or needs. The teacher can reflect back what the child is saying, rather than replying. For example, if the child says "My legs are going; I'll never be able to walk again, right?", the teacher may just respond by reflecting, "You're afraid you'll never walk?" Such active listening is a useful tactic and often helps the child sort out feelings.

- Be natural. Often, children will attempt to shock the teacher with a question or a gory description of a surgical procedure that is contemplated. Teachers should examine their own biases and fears and try to react to the child with sympathy and sensitivity. "That's disgusting!" is not an appropriate response to a child's fear-filled but brazen comment, "I'll be out of school next week—they are going to cut me open and chop off a tendon in my knee," even though the teacher may be revulsed.

- Find time to talk to the child alone, away from interruptions and other children.

- Be patient, supportive, and understanding. The child is attempting to deal with a traumatic experience. The fact that the child chose to confide in the teacher puts a heavy responsibility on the teacher to provide support and a sympathetic ear.

Adolescent

The child with a degenerative disease is usually suffering from some degree of physical limitation by puberty. While most adolescents are concerned with decisions involving future goals in relationship to careers, education, and marriage, these adolescents must face a future filled with dependence upon others and eventual death. If they remain in school or in hospital schools, they often exhibit depression, poor motivation, and a general sense of helplessness and hopelessness. Occasionally, their condition may appear to be degenerating rapidly, with a drastic loss of abilities that may be attributed to a general sense of defeat, rather than to any physical progress of their condition. Inconsistent responses are also common, and careful reevaluations should be made to accurately assess the adolescent's current functioning.

At times, an observed loss of functioning may be due to a period of depression, rather than to true physical deterioration. In one instance, a 17-year-old boy hospitalized with Friedreich's ataxia began to lose considerable function in his arms and required help in feeding for the first time. His obvious deterioration alarmed the staff, who requested a neurologic reevaluation. A team meeting with the adolescent's child life specialist, social worker, and other health professionals revealed that the anniversary of the death of his older brother (a victim of Friedreich's ataxia) was approaching, and the patient had begun to talk about his own "timetable" in counseling sessions and in the playroom. With supports and a concerted effort on the part of the staff, the patient was encouraged to take more trips out of the hospital, especially for meals. His ability to feed himself independently returned, without the need for intrusive testing.

Early realistic vocational planning should be developed, and the adolescent should be encouraged to share in goal setting and the investigation of educational and vocational opportunities. Vocational training programs, funded through state and federal subsidies, can provide short-term job training and job placement opportunities. The longer adolescents remain in school, the more likely that they will be eligible for job training programs because of their increased academic abilities and their expanded social experiences.

While marriage may not be a realistic future goal, friendships with a wide range of people should be encouraged, and opportunities for continual social experiences should be provided, along with supportive counseling. Recreation programs for the disabled are available in most areas, and many rehabilitation centers offer a wide variety of social opportunities. In the final stages of degenerative illness, the adolescent may be unable to remain at home. Residential settings ought to provide continued occupational and physical therapy services, social and recreational opportunities, and educational and vocational programs. Unfortunately, funding for such an array of services is often lacking in residential placements, and the adolescent spends countless hours alone without resources or activities, awaiting death.

SUMMARY

In this chapter, the special problems associated with degenerative diseases have been examined. Friedreich's ataxia and muscular dystrophy are the most common of the degenerative conditions, and educational strategies for such conditions were reviewed, emphasizing the importance of maintaining learned skills and setting short-term, achievable goals.

As noted in the beginning of the chapter, prognosis for these diseases has improved, and programs are needed to expand and enhance the quality of life for affected children within the still-limited bounds of their existence.

REFERENCES

Greenfield, J.G. *The spino-cerebellar degenerations.* Oxford: Blackwell, 1954.

Menkes, J.H. *Textbook of child neurology.* Philadelphia: Lea & Febiger, 1980.

Mullins, J.B. *A teacher's guide to management of physically handicapped students.* Springfield, IL: Charles C Thomas, 1979.

Peterson, R.M., & Cleveland, J.O. (Eds.), *Medical problems in the classroom.* Springfield, IL: Charles C Thomas, 1975.

Chapter 8

Childhood Cancers

OVERVIEW

Today, cancer ranks second only to accidents as the major cause of death in children. Few families have been spared personal experiences with cancer, and it is estimated that one in four persons will contract cancer in his or her lifetime (Shimkin, 1980). Medical advances have changed the course of cancer in recent years, but complete cures or permanent control have yet to be achieved. "What were once acutely fatal illnesses have become chronic life-threatening ones" (Koocher & Sallan, 1978, p. 283). While death is no longer an inevitable outcome in all cases, it still looms as a potential threat for all children afflicted with cancer, and it is a reality for many. The premature death of any human is dismaying and sad; the death of a child is "one of the outrages of nature" (Schowalter, 1970, p. 51).

This section will examine the most common childhood cancers and suggest educational approaches for children thus afflicted. Chapter 9 will explore the effects of death and dying in childhood on the child, the family, and the caregivers.

Cancer is a term that describes a group of diseases. It can arise in any organ or tissue of the body. As described by Shimkin in the National Cancer Institute's Publication, *Science and Cancer* (1980),

> Its main characteristics include an abnormal, seemingly unrestricted growth of body cells, with the resultant mass compressing, invading and destroying contiguous normal tissues. Cancer cells then break off or leave the original mass and are carried by the blood or lymph to distant sites of the body. Cancers are classified by their appearance under the microscope, and by the site of the body from which they arise. (p. 3)

At least 100 different cancers have been identified. Each of the childhood cancers has its own cause, treatment modality, and prognosis. The two general categories are hematologic malignancies, or cancers of the blood, and solid tumors. The following pages will discuss the most common disease entities in each category.

LEUKEMIA

Leukemias account for approximately 35 percent of all deaths due to malignancies (Miller, 1980). It is estimated that 7,000 new cases of cancer will be diagnosed yearly in the United States; of those, 2,500 children will have leukemia.

Leukemia seems to afflict whites more frequently than nonwhites, and it is more prevalent in boys than in girls (Travis, 1976; Miller, 1980). It is most common in children under ten, with a peak between ages three and ten (Miller, 1980).

There are different forms of leukemia, and usually the forms found in adults are different than those in children. Of these, the most common and most serious form in children (80 to 85 percent) is acute lymphoblastic or lymphocytic leukemia. The classification of the kind of leukemia is made on the basis of the type of white blood cell that is affected.

Leukemia is a disease of the blood-forming organs. The name itself is derived from the Greek words, *leukos* and *haima*, meaning *white blood*. Blood cells form in the bone marrow, and their components perform various essential functions: lymphocytes are formed in the lymph nodes; red blood cells carry oxygen throughout the body; platelets prevent abnormal bleeding; and white blood cells, leukocytes, defend the body against infection. A severe decrease in red blood cells will cause anemia, while a severe decrease in platelets results in excessive bleeding. In leukemia, abnormal white blood cells replace normal bone marrow, and their rapid growth inhibits the production of normal white cells, red cells, and platelets (Travis, 1976). This results in anemia, excessive bleeding, and a severely lowered resistance to infections. The early symptoms of leukemia thus include the pallor and fatigue that accompany anemia; joint pain; excessive bleeding or bruising or distinctive pinpoint red spots on the skin (petechiae) caused by a lowered platelet count; and an increased susceptibility to infection.

Early diagnosis and prompt treatment often make a crucial difference in the final outcome. Unfortunately, the early symptoms are often easily confused with other, nonthreatening childhood illnesses. Once more severe symptoms are present, the disease may be moderately advanced. Diagnosis is not difficult and usually consists of a series of blood tests and a crucial bone marrow examination. Blood tests can determine the level and type of existing blood cells, while the bone marrow tests often pinpoint the existence of abnormal leukemia cells in the marrow. The marrow is extracted from a large bone, usually the hip bone, by means of a needle inserted while the child is awake, but under local anesthetic. The examination and the implications of a positive diagnosis make such a test unusually traumatic for the child and family.

Etiology

While the cause of leukemia is not known, a number of agents have been implicated as causative factors. Radiation is one such factor, and the significant increases in cases of leukemia that resulted from the 1945 atomic blast in Hiroshima give weight to this theory. Viruses have been explored as a cause of leukemia as well, although no evidence of transmission or contagion has been found. The presence of a genetic component is suggested by the unusually high incidence of leukemia in children with Down's syndrome, a condition that results from chromosomal abnormality. Further research is needed to shed light on the cause of leukemia. It is possible that a combination of causes exists, which will make research even more complex.

Prognosis

The outlook for leukemia-stricken children has changed drastically in the past decade, a circumstance that has had profound effects on all those who are touched by the diagnosis. Until recently, the diagnosis of leukemia was associated almost invariably with the prediction of death in a relatively short span of time. Even today, untreated leukemia almost invariably results in death within six months. The dramatically improved outlook has been attributed to a number of factors, including more accurate diagnosis, better supportive care, new advances in drug therapy and the use of drug combinations to reach and maintain remission, and the use of prophylactic therapy to prevent central nervous system involvement (Miller, 1980). Estimates of survival vary from a conservative 40 to 50 percent of long-term remissions of at least five years (Sherman, 1978) to 65 to 70 percent in complete remission after five years. Further, estimates of survival seem to imply that the risk of a recurrence decreases from the fifth to the ninth year, with the prediction that approximately one-half the children alive after five years will pass the ten-year barrier (Sherman, 1978). Prognosis differs according to a number of predisposing factors. D.R. Miller (1980), in a multifactor analysis, suggests that the following factors contribute to the prediction of a good or poor prognosis: initial white cell count, platelet count, hemoglobin, age, sex, and the enlargement of glands. Most favorable prognosis occurs in females, over the age of three but under the age of ten, with no gland enlargements, no central nervous system involvement, and moderate decreases in blood count. The prognosis for a first extended remission also increases when initial treatment is done in large, centrally located cancer research and treatment facilities.

These facilities have available to them the latest therapeutic protocols, and often the funding for treatment in such centers is provided in whole or part by federal grants. The implications of having a child treated at such a place, which is usually large, impersonal, and often far from home, will be examined later in this chapter.

The changing prognostic picture in leukemia has created a dilemma for the professional staff as well as for the child and family. As Georgia Travis notes (1976), the old problem, that of living with and accepting death, has been replaced by a new problem, that of living under a shadow. For Dr. Allen Schwartz, pediatric hematologist at the University of Maryland Oncology Center, it was relatively easy to help a parent accept the inevitability of death, compared to the confused message that must now be given—"your child may be spared, or may not; or remission may last longer, with death still to come" (personal communication).

Treatment

Diagnosis of leukemia is usually made in a hospital setting. This is followed by a short-term hospitalization, designed to evaluate the child's overall medical status and to initiate drug therapy. The goal of treatment is to obtain a total remission of symptoms for as long as possible. The function of chemical therapy is to interfere with the reproductive processes of leukemia cells. Drug therapy, which was begun in 1947 by Dr. S. Faber of the Children's Cancer Research Foundation in Boston (Sherman, 1978) has become a highly complex process today. Effective treatment strategy today consists of a number of key components. Initially, drug combinations are administered in large doses to produce prompt remission. Ninety percent of all children go into their first remission within a few weeks of initial treatment (Sherman, 1978). These drugs are often toxic and produce considerable adverse side effects. These include pain, swelling, nausea, hair loss, loss of appetite, and occasionally kidney damage. Supportive measures are often needed to allow the child to survive the treatment. The child may receive blood transfusions or increased transfusions of platelets. Certain drugs severely reduce the body's resistance to infections, and patients need to be placed in reverse isolation, so that they are protected from all germs. Radiation therapy to the head and spinal cord usually is provided to prevent nervous system involvement. After remission, the child often appears well and can return to home and school. Frequently, the child continues to receive maintenance doses of medication and must have periodic checkups at outpatient clinics, where blood tests and bone marrow examinations are conducted. As Sherman (1978) notes:

> The child is a child who was, is, or has the potential for being sick; frequent medical check-ups and blood tests, and possible daily ingestion of medication, remind the child that he is not as he once was. Older siblings, even if not acquainted with the diagnosis, will inevitably realize that their brother or sister requires special medical attention. The parent is now the parent of a leukemic child. (pp. 51-52)

While children show variable reactions to the various treatments, remission is often a time of relative normality, a time of hope and patient waiting. Even with the sense of normality, parents often continue to perceive their child as vulnerable (Sherman, 1978). With extended remissions now more common, questions are being raised by research institutes as to the length of time that maintenance drugs should be used and the necessity of radiation therapy for all patients. The longer the remission, the more the child and family begin to hope for a cure.

Relapse

The first relapse, if it occurs, is necessarily devastating for child and family. Hopes dashed, they begin to face the prospect of pain and death once again. When relapse occurs, new drug combinations are tried, but later remissions usually take longer to achieve and usually last a shorter time. Relapse means hospitalization, new drugs, transfusions, further tests, and greater anxiety. Sometimes the first relapse ends in death; sometimes a second remission occurs, followed by further relapses, hemorrhages, infections, or central nervous system involvement. Each child's experience is unique, and each family must face a "sequence of several different experiences" (Travis, 1976, p. 373). For one family, death may come quickly at the first relapse; for another, death comes only after years of agony and repeated cycles of hope and despair; for some, a relatively normal life span is likely. Sensitive professionals need to recognize the varieties of experience and provide support for the child and family through all the stages of their experience.

The major causes of death in leukemia are infection and hemorrhage. Blood transfusions are often provided to prevent hemorrhage, and they often allow for the prolongation of life by allowing the child to become strong enough to withstand more vigorous chemotherapy (Van Eys, 1976). Good general health is therefore an important component in treatment, and well-balanced meals are essential. The interaction between nutrition and cancer is very complex. The disease and the side effects of treatment often affect the child's appetite. Cancer may also interfere with the body's absorption and use of food. Malnutrition thus creates additional problems and may be a detrimental factor in the body's ability to withstand the treatments necessary to cause remission (Van Eys, 1976). The National Institute of Health's publication, *Diet and Nutrition: A Resource for Parents of Children with Cancer* (NCI, 1979) is an excellent source book and contains many useful suggestions for parents.

The changing picture in the treatment of leukemia is dramatic and hopeful. New experiments in bone marrow transplantations and continued basic research aimed at uncovering the etiology of leukemia continually hold out hope for higher remission and cure rates. However, a significant proportion of children still die as a result of leukemia. Some questions need to be raised concerning the attitudes and philosophy of care espoused by the professionals. Is the ultimate goal to prolong life, even if that in fact means no more than the prolongation of suffering and the process of dying? Should drug protocols be rigidly adhered to, regardless of the child's reactions? Is treatment at a central pediatric cancer center still best if it involves a major family disruption due to excessive distance from home? Has the disease been treated at the expense of the child? As J. Van Eys (1976) notes, "If we do not support the whole person we may find a biologically cured child who has not developed mentally, and who has not learned the experiences a normal child needs to learn to be competitive with his peers" (p. 221).

Special Considerations

In spite of the encouraging outlook for leukemia today, the diagnosis of the disease has a devastating impact upon the family. Their lives will never again be the same. Frequently, the diagnosis is made by a family physician or local pediatrician; often the child is initially hospitalized in a local hospital. The parents, still in shock over the implications of the diagnosis, must quickly make a vital decision: to continue to have the child treated locally, or to seek out a larger comprehensive pediatric cancer center. Clearly, factors such as finances, geography, and family resources affect this decision. The supportive care of a well-known family doctor may be crucial in the early weeks; equally crucial is the availability of the latest treatment methods. Sometimes a compromise can be achieved, with intensive care provided by the large clinical center and maintenance care offered closer to home. Hospitalization, usually traumatic, becomes even more devastating when leukemia and its treatment are the cause. The impersonal nature of a large medical center may be especially hard for the child and family. The helplessness parents feel when they watch their child's responses to massive drug therapy often leads to despair and hopelessness. In cases of severe drug reactions, parents may question their decision to approve the treatment, seeing death as the lesser of two evils. The mourning process may thus begin too soon and may interfere with future decisions regarding treatment.

With leukemia, the family faces not one but a series of critical decisions. At which medical center should the child be treated? Should the child be told of the diagnosis? Who else should be told? Should the child return to school? In cases of repeated relapses, how many times should new drugs be tried? If the child is to die, should it be in the hospital or at home? In children who have frequent remissions and relapses, the effects can be psychologically devastating, with the family always preparing anew for death.

If parents choose to take their child some distance from home, there is a need to find lodging for the family if they are to be near the child. Increasingly, rooming-in is becoming a standard option in large hospitals, allowing one parent to spend the night at or near the child's bedside. This is crucial for young children, for new admissions, and for children near death. The hospital atmosphere can, however, become stifling to a parent.

Local hotels, on the other hand, are often costly and impersonal. In some cities, a humanistic alternative is being offered. Usually with the support of local organizations, homes for parents of children with serious illnesses are being opened in the vicinity of large medical centers. Many, under the partial support of the McDonald's Company, are termed *Ronald McDonald Houses.* They are a new concept and one that is universally needed and appreciated by parents. They provide a respite for parents: a place to stay, to be among peers, and to escape the hospital. Often, leukemic children in town for outpatient services can stay in these houses with their parents, rather than being admitted into the hospital. Ronald McDonald houses are in existence in over two dozen cities in the United States, as well as in Canada and Australia.

Repeated hospitalizations in the later stages often occur with a mixture of renewed anxiety and a sense of returning to a familiar place. Frequently, parent groups, either informal or coordinated by the clinic staff, provide parents with an opportunity to share feelings.

Should the Child Know?

There is much disagreement over how much to tell children. Some feel that telling children that they have leukemia and may die will lead to despair and hopelessness. Often, parents avoid telling their children as part of their own denial of the reality. With the current ambiguity of long-term prognosis, it is probably unwise to suggest the possibility of death to the child at the time of diagnosis. On the other hand, the reactions of parents, the discomfort of the disease symptoms, and the severity of the reactions to treatment make total denial and silence unreasonable. Children almost always know something serious is wrong. In her study of the private worlds of dying children, M.B. Langner (1978) quotes a five year old:"Everybody cries when they see me. I'm pretty sick" (p. 8) as proof of even a young child's awareness of crisis. A fairly common approach espoused by Miki Sherman (1978), herself the mother of a leukemic daughter, is to explain, at the children's developmental level, that they have a serious blood disease. Afterwards, questions should be answered as simply and as honestly as possible, but no child should be told more than he or she asks. The sophistication of many children after a few months in the hospital or at outpatient clinics is often astounding. "That's John. He's on vincristine; his hair is falling out. See"; "She's going in for another bone marrow; she must be in relapse" are comments often heard in playrooms and waiting areas. Sick children often share a bond with one another, and new friendships are often formed.

Families often hesitate to tell relatives and friends of their plight, although some need to tell everyone they know. Again, this decision is personal and individual. It is important to remember, however, that if all the neighborhood knows that a child has leukemia, the child is likely to learn about it informally and may be unnecessarily avoided or teased by peers.

Siblings need to be taken into parents' confidence as well, especially if they are old enough to be aware of the family crisis. Again, their age, personality, and relationship to the sick sibling needs to be taken into account. Treatment of the sick child as special creates feelings of jealousy in siblings, and they often feel abandoned by parents, especially if the leukemic child and one parent spend time far from home.

When children are in remission, the question of how to treat them arises. While they are essentially well, they are still vulnerable. Parents often tend to avoid disciplining such children and may overprotect them and shower them with excessive gifts. A sense of "time running out" may be prevalent, and parents may try to pack all the loving and giving they can into a few years. This often creates additional problems. The other siblings may feel left out; the child may begin to fear that such treatment can only mean impending death; the child may become a tyrant, manipulating the household, running parents ragged with excessive demands. Finally, the prospect of long-term remissions and possibly a cure makes a return to normal behaviors more appropriate, albeit with a heightened sense of the fragility and temporary nature of human existence.

Dealing with Dying

Even with the present state of medical technology, at least half of the children with leukemia face a premature death. The reactions to death are highly personal and are unique for the child, the family, and the caregivers. The physical strain on the child and family in the terminal stage is great: the need for hospitalization; the use of experimental medications to try one last time to ward off death; the all-night vigils at the child's bedside; and the child's growing weakness. The experience of dying for the child, the family, and caregivers will be dealt with at length in the next chapter.

Dealing with Living

Since death has been a typical outcome in leukemia until recently, there is little literature on living with leukemia or other cancers. In a study conducted in 1976 on the psychological response of adult patients cured of cancer, B.J. Kennedy, A. Tellagen, S. Kennedy, and N. Havernick report that such patients' overall attitude toward life and the future was positive. They had a greater appreciation of life, people, and interpersonal relationships and were less concerned about nonessentials. The age of the child, the awareness of the potential for death, the child's personality structure, the family system, and other factors all play a role in the child's reactions. From examples of children who, even at the brink of death, were not without humor and acceptance, one would expect recovered children to display resiliency. This may not always occur, and children recovered from a life-threatening disease often need professional counseling.

The child's return to school may be difficult. In the early stages of the disease, the child may be fatigued easily and may be wearing a wig or hat to hide baldness. Children may feel differently about themselves and their peers; an argument over who is wearing the most "in" clothes may have little meaning to an adolescent who is grappling with issues of mortality. Many clinical workers have described leukemic children as "older than their years": somber, serious, and lonely (Mullins, 1979). Many children exhibit a new awareness of life's fragility and are excessively concerned with the health and safety of peers, family, and pets. The death of a pet often triggers the need for ornate rituals of burial, with much pomp and circumstance. This may reflect children's own wishes to be properly mourned and may also afford them an opportunity to act out their own process of grieving.

School should remain a critical part of the child's life, regardless of prognosis. The child needs to feel a part of the world and needs continuity in both academic and social experiences. A letter written by an 11-year-old leukemic girl a month before her death reaffirms this crucial need. She writes:

> I have acute lymphoblastic leukemia. But please don't feel sorry for me. I live a perfectly wonderful life.
> I go to parties, play games, swing on swings, and, for the most part I am able to do whatever I want. I think that this is an important part of life which some parents of children who have leukemia overlook, and I think they should not! I think that children who

have leukemia should be able to play when they feel up to it, unless they have a cold or have just had a shot that makes them sick.

(American Journal of Nursing, 1975, p. 988, reprinted in Journal of Pediatrics, 1976)

In a footnote to the letter, the physician who forwarded it for publication noted:

Amy Timmons wrote this in May 1974, and died one month later, on June 14. In spite of her illness, she was an honor student, president of her class, and active in the Girl Scouts. She left the hospital to attend her sixth-grade graduation, and to go on a four-day vacation with her family. The day before she died she had enjoyed swimming and playing on the beach, and that night, she had stayed up until 11 p.m., playing games with her family. Amy died in a coma the day she was to return to the hospital.

(Journal of Pediatrics, 1976, p. 147)

A final issue relating to the education of the child with leukemia needs to be raised. A growing clinical picture is emerging among children treated with a combination of radiation and chemotherapy that raises the specter of learning disabilities occurring as a result of such treatment. In research on the effects of chemotherapy on cancer patients, P.M. Silberfarb, D. Philibert, and P.M. Levine (1980) identified chemotherapy as a major variable associated with cognitive impairment in patients who were normal prior to treatment. While these findings are still only suspected and preliminary and there is little documented research, physicians and parents familiar with the issue attest to its growing prevalence (Grace Monaco, president of Candlelighters, personal communication; Dr. Allen Schwartz, pediatric hematologist, University of Maryland Hospital, personal communication). In light of this, careful periodic psychoeducational reassessments of children with leukemia who have received such treatment should be made, and educational remediation should be provided, if necessary.

SOLID TUMORS

Solid tumors arise as a result of excessive, abnormal cell growth. Solid tumors differ from hematologic malignancies in a number of ways. They usually occur in one or more distinct organs of the body, and symptoms thus may be more visible and localized. Tumors may be benign and may not endanger life unless they are located in such a way as to interfere with the body's functioning. Such tumors can usually be surgically removed and do not recur. Malignant tumors, on the other hand, are invariably life-threatening if not removed or treated. They may spread to other parts of the body through the bloodstream or lymphatic system and form secondary tumors, or metastases. Approximately 40 percent of all cancers in children are due to tumors (Mullins, 1979), with the most common tumors occurring in the brain, the kidneys (Wilms' tumor), or the bone. In solid tumors, the most common therapy is surgical, with the goal of removing the entire tumor. This often creates body changes and the consequent need to provide rehabilitation or "adaptation" to the surgically acquired handicap (Koocher & Sallan, 1978, p. 288). Often, such surgical intervention is followed by radiation therapy, and occasionally chemotherapy, to prevent the spread or metastasis of the cancer to other sites in the body. The prognosis for different types of solid tumors varies widely, depending upon the site of the tumor, the stage of development upon diagnosis, and whether the tumor has metastasized to other organs.

Brain Tumors

Brain tumors represent 17 to 20 percent of pediatric cancers, second only to leukemia in frequency (Koocher & Sallan, 1978). They usually are contained within the central nervous system. The prognosis for successful surgical removal is highly dependent upon the location of the tumor: some are relatively small, localized, and easily reached; most are difficult to remove without destroying vital brain tissue. For this reason, radiation therapy is a common adjunct to surgery and is occasionally the primary therapeutic mode if the tumor is inoperable.

Symptoms and Prognosis

Symptoms vary, depending on the location of the tumor, and usually are similar to those associated with head trauma. They may include headaches, vomiting or nausea, unsteady gait, weakness, or sensory changes. In certain cases, shunts may be placed to drain off excessive buildups of spinal fluid in the brain, preventing added pressure on the brain. (See the section on spina bifida for a detailed description of shunting procedures.)

In children with brain tumors, residual effects may be as disabling as the cancer itself. Depending upon the area of the brain affected and the degree and success of surgery, children may suffer from communicative disorders, sensory impairments, and/or motor limitations. Problem-solving abilities and short- or long-term memory may also be affected. Children may become impulsive, distractible, or emotionally labile. The resulting disabilities may themselves create additional emotional disturbances in the child, who is suddenly faced with the prospect of serious intellectual and/or motor disabilities, in addition to the original diagnosis of cancer.

Rehabilitation and educational planning are often similar to that for children who have suffered from head trauma. There is, however, the additional prospect of the possibility of the tumor's recurrence, resulting in a significantly shortened life span.

Neuroblastoma

Neuroblastomas are solid tumors of the neural tissue, most commonly found in the adrenal gland (abdomen) and the sympathetic nervous system (chest or abdomen). They account for an additional seven to ten percent of childhood malignancies and usually occur in infancy or early childhood (Koocher & Sallan, 1978). They are unusual in that they may spontaneously regress or disappear, especially in infants.

Symptoms, Treatment, and Prognosis

Symptoms usually occur in relation to the site of the tumor, with abdominal masses or chest pains and breathing difficulties most common. Biopsy of the tumor or of bone marrow is necessary to make a diagnosis. The outcome depends upon the degree of spread of the tumor. Neuroblastomas are divided into stages, reflecting the degree of spread or dissemination of the tumor, which determines the prognosis. Stage I thus refers to a completely enclosed, operable tumor, with the likelihood of survival after five years better than 90 percent in infants (Koocher & Sallan, 1978), while stage IV indicates that a tumor has widely spread, and the survival rate for children over two years is estimated at less than 7 percent (Koocher & Sallan, 1978).

Special Considerations

In cases of early diagnosis and prompt treatment, with continuing remission, the most serious effects are similar to those of an infant or young child suffering from a serious, acute illness. The effects of early separation, surgical intrusion at a vulnerable age, and unexplained pain need to be mediated by continuous nurturing parental support. In cases that have a less promising outlook, the pain and resulting irritability and confusion make the child especially helpless and often leave parents feeling impotent, unable to alleviate the suffering of their child.

Kidney Tumors (Wilms' Tumors)

Cases of kidney cancer in children are almost always Wilms' tumors. They are thought to start in immature cells that would normally become mature kidney cells and may arise while the child is still in the uterus. The usual age of onset is from infancy to age five; it is rare in older children or adults.

Symptoms are usually not remarkable and most commonly are first noticed as an abdominal mass. Occasionally, bloody urine is present as well. Children may have low-grade fever, fatigue, anemia, weight loss, or loss of appetite. In some cases, Wilms' tumors are associated with a few developmental anomalies. The most common is the absence of the iris of the eye (the colored portion). Abnormal enlargement of a body part is another abnormality sometimes encountered in Wilms' tumor patients.

Treatment and Prognosis

Treatment combines the use of surgery for removal of the tumor and often the involved kidney and surrounding tissue (radical nephrectomy), radiation for either the presurgical shrinking of the tumor or preventively after surgery to control new growth, and chemotherapy in virtually all cases. The side effects of both chemotherapy and radiation are similar to those encountered in leukemic children and are usually reversible when treatment is discontinued. Because of the extreme youth of most Wilms' tumor patients and the immaturity of bone growth, radiation may affect the growth and development of the spinal column, and the newest therapeutic approaches are aimed at substituting chemotherapy for radiation in children under two years (National Cancer Institute Publication, *Wilms' Tumor*, 1980). Prognosis for a positive outcome in Wilms' tumor is quite good, with suggested figures of eight of ten children attaining the long-term disease-free status that is considered a cure in cancer treatment (NCI, 1980). Long-term care must include prevention of urinary tract infections, which could endanger the remaining kidney if not treated. Limited contact sports are suggested for any patient with only one kidney.

Bone Tumors

Bone tumors are most prevalent in late childhood and adolescence and represent fewer than one percent of all malignancies. The most common of these, osteogenic sarcoma, is often first suspected when the child suffers pain at the site of the tumor. Early diagnosis is often delayed when the child or adolescent attributes the pain to a bruise or accident incurred as a result of normal activities. Untreated, the tumor typically metastasizes to the lungs and results in death. Treatment usually consists of limb amputation, followed by chemotherapy and sometimes radiation to prevent spread of the disease. Occasionally, limb preservation is attempted by replacing a section of bone with an internal prosthesis (Koocher & Sallan, 1978). Whatever the treatment, the child often faces the prospect of partial physical handicap and may need extensive rehabilitation. The sudden removal of a limb, especially during late childhood or adolescence, brings with it a whole array of emotional reactions as well as physical ones. Often, the remarkable coping skills of a child such as Ted Kennedy, Jr. are looked to as a model for all children. His resiliency and fortitude, while exemplary, may not always be present in every child. Depression, hopelessness, and despair are often seen after amputation in young adolescents. Sensitive counseling is needed to help them reach a point at which they are willing to participate in the difficult task of rehabilitation.

Modern prosthetic devices are often remarkable, and after a period of rehabilitation, the child or adolescent is usually able to resume all normal activities. Recurrence of the cancer, in the form of lung metastasis, is especially cruel for these who have arduously learned to use a prosthetic arm or leg and returned to home and school. Preventive chemotherapy is an attempt to avoid such a relapse and is presently showing some degree of success, although with not nearly the promise for extended cures that had earlier been thought possible (Koocher & Sallen, 1978).

EDUCATIONAL ISSUES

Children continue to grow and develop in spite of their disease. Apart from the need for continued medical supervision, the need for educational continuity remains a central issue in their lives, one that should not be ignored. Children with cancer may have many symptom-free years, and many may conquer the disease and live out relatively normal lives. Even for those whose lives are drastically shortened by cancer, each day's activities are important in their own right and should be enjoyable and meaningful to the child. Schoolwork represents normality for children, and its continued role in their lives is a signal that hope is not lost, that they may, in fact, continue to live for many months or years to come. Children or their parents or well-meaning friends may suggest that the child should not be forced to continue in schoolwork drudgery and recommend that they stay at home, do what they want to, have fun. But is staying at home, isolated from all social contacts, engaged in no meaningful pursuits, really fun for the child? Often, after an initial feeling of freedom, boredom and anxiety occur. The child has endless hours alone to worry and feel frightened. If the goal for education is to help children develop a sense of efficacy, mastery of their environment, and self-worth, continued educational experiences are essential. One needn't question the temporal nature of such pursuits if the process is seen as equally important as the goal; each day is taken and used to the fullest, regardless of outcome.

For all these reasons, children with cancer should be encouraged to attend school in the least restrictive environment whenever possible. There are a number of obstacles to school attendance and performance that need to be addressed and resolved, but they are not insurmountable. Children with cancer may have frequent absences due to medical relapses, clinic appointments, or periods of unusual fatigue. The regular classroom teacher needs to be aware of these problems so that work can be sent home or, in cases of planned absences, schoolwork can be assigned in advance. Home teachers or hospital teachers can be helpful resources to the regular classroom teacher at such times, providing continuity of programs and assisting the child in mastering appropriate academic skills and concepts.

When the child has been newly diagnosed after an initial absence from the class, the teacher should be invited to a conference with parents and health professionals to help prepare for the child's return. L. Kagan-Goodheart (1977), in a discussion of a cancer victim's reluctance to return to school, recommends that reentry issues, such as class preparation, schedules, embarrassment, and fatigue, be an integral part of the team treatment plan. In the National Cancer Institute's resource handbook for educators (1980), it is suggested that the teacher gather the following information, if available:

- Specific type of cancer and how it is being treated;
- Treatment the student is taking when it is administered, what potential side effects are, and effects on appearance and behavior;
- Approximate schedule of upcoming treatment, procedures, or tests that may result in the student's absence from the classroom;
- Limitations, if any, on the student's activities (Periodic up-dates from parents are also helpful);
- What the student knows about the illness (although current policy is to be honest with young people who have cancer, there are exceptions);
- For younger students, what the family would like classmates and school staff members to know;
- For adolescents, whether the student wishes to talk directly with teachers about any of the above points. (p. 6)

Children with cancer inevitably face a serious emotional crisis; much of their attention and energy may be focused upon their disease and their attempts to develop ways to successfully cope with the tragedy they face. This shifting of energy away from their normal developmental tasks may hamper their ability to concentrate in school and to keep focused on their academic tasks. This is often the case with children old enough to fully realize the implications of the disease. They may need to take a short leave of absence from school or receive professional counseling at this point.

Classroom teachers face a real challenge when a child in class is diagnosed as having cancer. They need to come to grips with their own feelings of disease and death; they may feel overwhelmed at the prospect of having to explain the child's disease to the class or prepare extra material for the sick child or monitor the class's reactions to the child. Should classwork be judged equally? Should discipline be uniform? It is generally felt that children with cancer should be treated as normally as possible. They should be judged on their work with the same standards used before the onset of the disease, although time limits for completed work may need to be adjusted to the child's energy level and schedule. The cancer should not be ignored, since it is an essential part of the child's life, nor should it be an overwhelming concern to the neglect of other aspects of the child's life (NCI, *Students with Cancer*, 1980).

Children with cancer can engage in activities suitable to their age and abilities. A conference with parents and the health care team can clarify this area, and special limitations or restrictions can be explained and programs accordingly adjusted. Children on chemotherapy for cancer are unusually susceptible to infection, and the presence of shingles (herpes zoster), chicken pox, or regular measles in the child's class or the class of a sibling should be immediately reported to the parents. Children may be kept at home during periods of exposure to monitor their health and prevent their contracting these diseases. Schoolwork should be sent home at these times to avoid having the child fall behind.

Children with cancer rarely have a medical crisis in the classroom (NCI, *Students with Cancer*, 1980), and the minor effects of fatigue, headache, or nausea can be treated in the school's usual manner.

Unexplained absences by the child can provoke anxiety in the teacher and the class. Families should be encouraged to keep in touch with the teacher. The class should be helped to maintain the relationship by frequent phone calls, cards, or special class projects.

In addition to the classroom teachers' need to recognize and manage their own feelings of anxiety and depression, they must also act as a model and counselor to the child's classmates. If a class is prepared for the return of their peer, teasing or isolation due to embarrassment or fear may be lessened. The teacher needs to consult with the child and parents prior to any class discussion to obtain permission to share information. In some school districts, each class member's parents must also consent to the discussion. The discussions should be geared to the class's developmental level and should allow for individual responses and expressions of feelings. The following suggestions from the NCI resource handbook (1980) may be useful:

- Begin by asking students in the class how they want to be treated when they are ill or how they feel when they are around someone (of any age) who is sick. Use answers to these questions as bases for discussing how classmates might treat their friend with cancer.

- Explain to classmates the type of cancer their friend has, the kind of treatment he receives, and the ways the disease and treatment may affect his appearance and/or behavior. This is particularly useful in dealing with embarrassing side effects such as temporary weight gain or hair loss. Classmates who know that these changes come about because of the lifesaving therapy their friend is receiving are less likely to tease and may even defend him against the ill-considered remarks of outsiders. Also, reassure classmates that they can't "catch" cancer and emphasize that no one knows what causes it.
- Prepare a health or science unit for the study of cancer. Assign groups of class members to develop research reports on a specific type of cancer treatment, and side effects, making sure that source material is up-to-date. When completed reports are shared with the class, students will have basic knowledge about cancer as well as their classmate's disease.
- Invite personnel from the treatment center or another organization (one teacher involved the social worker from the local American Cancer Society office) to make a presentation to the class. This approach should be a supplement, rather than substitute, for class discussion led by the teacher (pp. 9–10).

M.B. Sachs (1980), in a description of a rehabilitation demonstration project designed to aid the child with cancer return to school, reaffirms the importance of classroom preparation programs. Team visits of hospital personnel to the child's school to meet with school staff and classmates have, in her words, "replaced rumor and fear with fact, have provided positive learning experiences about cancer and have promoted peer and school personnel support for the child with cancer" (p. 331).

Children with bone cancers who have suffered from amputations may need extra assistance in reentering school. Classmates may assist in acting as temporary aides for the child, helping with lunch trays or carrying school equipment. This should be done with the agreement of the students and should come out of a natural friendship rather than a forced assignment. The decision as to whether a child with an amputation is best served in the regular school or a school especially designed for children with physical handicaps is a complex one. Factors such as the child's physical limitations, the regular school's accessibility, the child's needs for regular physical or occupational therapy, and the child's own wishes should all be taken into account. Again, the objective is the greatest degree of normality in the least restrictive setting.

Special problems occur in secondary schools. The schools are larger and often less personal. Classes change each hour, and the child is not as well known to the school personnel or to the other students. Students with prosthetic devices or hats or wigs may be subject to unnecessary teasing by peers or unwarranted discipline by staff. In one large school, a student was berated for wearing a hat in the halls, and its removal by a strict teacher precipitated a round of jeers as the adolescent's baldness became apparent to all. Such incidents can damage the already fragile self-esteem of an adolescent and lead to a reluctance to return to school. Adolescents with amputations may be unwilling to risk the reaction of peers and may choose to remain on home teaching to avoid painful social contacts. For such adolescents, counseling and short visits to the school or the homes of peers may help them to take the first step back into the community.

Children in Isolation

For many children with cancer, short periods of hospitalization are common. Occasionally, these are required while the child undergoes chemotherapy or radiation therapy, and often the child is placed in isolation to prevent infections.

Children in isolation are usually able to be ambulatory, although their energy levels may be low. They can benefit from active games that allow them to move about freely. Such activities can also serve to release pent-up tensions and frustrations in positive ways. Isolation requires that all equipment brought in be sanitized and either resanitized or discarded after use. Handmade games that the child can keep are a good alternative to commercial materials, since they are less expensive and can be owned by the child. Punching bags, ring toss games, and bowling pin sets can all be used for the preschooler or young child. The adolescent might enjoy a regular program of calisthenics or aerobic dance exercises to music. All exercise should be coordinated with the medical and nursing staff to make certain that restrictions are observed.

Art projects that can be used to help children decorate their rooms, making them more personal, are an important component of the hospital school program for the isolated child (Dooley & Coppock, 1979).

School materials should be duplicated on paper or xeroxed so that books need not be discarded after use. The assignment of a hospital teacher during these periods allows the child to feel more secure that the prospects of getting well again are good. It also affords the child a regular routine and interesting varied activities, which are essential in isolation to avoid boredom and severe depression.

The Death of a Classmate

Inevitably, a large number of children with cancer die. Their death affects all those who had contact with them and has special meaning for their classmates and peers. In the final weeks, the classmate may have been absent from school or may have attended only sporadically. When a classmate dies, students respond individually, as does the teacher. The responses also vary with age and with each person's understanding of the meaning of death and its irreversibility. Feelings of loss, helplessness, and frustration are common in teachers. While it is difficult to discuss such issues with the class, especially in light of the teacher's own grief, it is necessary. Classmates will react to the death in a wide variety of ways; some may openly cry, others may withdraw or avoid any discussion, and a few may appear indifferent or act out their anger and sense of confusion. The full effect of the information may take a while to be felt, and reactions may be delayed for days or weeks. While the teacher needs to acknowledge the child's death openly, classmates should not be pressured into responding in certain ways, and no child should be forced into a discussion. In a sensitive discussion of the reactions of preschoolers to the death of a classmate, M. Rudolph (1978) relates the variety of reactions that the news evoked in her class, from frank questions concerning the nature of the child's demise and comparisons to animals who had died, to questions that expressed concerns about their own safety. These children reacted openly to the information, and their responses reflected their understanding of death and its meanings. "They showed feelings about their own protection from death, they showed empathy with grief and some realism about adjustment for the living" (Rudolph, 1978, p. 16).

Older children may find that attending a funeral or special memorial service allows them to express their sorrow and bid their friend farewell. A special school project, such as the planting of a tree, the establishment of a scholarship fund, or donations made to a charity may provide an outlet for the class to express their grief and may provide closure for the class. The family is usually touched by such a gesture, as it provides them with evidence that their child is remembered and loved by peers.

Class discussions, even months later, may reflect a classmate's lingering sense of loss or fear of death, and the subject should be handled much the same way as is any significant event in the context of the class. The following chapter will examine, in greater depth, the effects that a child's death has on parents and caregivers. Teachers who have had the experience of working with children with cancer often find that they are involved in a rich, meaningful relationship in which learning is reciprocal. The teacher can provide the child with an enhanced quality of life and days filled with learning and ideas; the child can provide a heightened sense of the value of life and a model of courage and fortitude in coping with tragedy.

SUMMARY

This chapter has examined the major childhood cancers—leukemia, brain tumors, neuroblastoma, kidney tumors, and bone tumors. The widespread prevalence of cancer, and the extentions of life made possible by new technological achievements have created a large core of children who are chronically ill with cancer. This puts special pressures upon the child, family, teachers, and friends. This chapter has reviewed these pressures and suggested a variety of approaches to educational planning, as well as examining the issues of working with the child who is in remission or cured of cancer.

BOOKS FOR CHILDREN ABOUT DEATH AND ILLNESS

Abbott, Sarah. *Old Dog*. New York: Coward, McCann & Geoghegen, 1972. $4.29.

Alcott, Louisa. *Little Women*. New York: Macmillan & Co., 1962. $1.50 (originally published, 1869).

Anglund, J.W. *Love Is a Special Way of Feeling*. New York: Harcourt Brace Jovanovich, 1960. $2.95.

_____. *Morning Is a Little Child*. New York: Harcourt Brace Jovanovich, 1969. $5.95.

_____. *Spring Is a New Beginning*. New York: Harcourt Brace Jovanovich, 1963. $2.95.

_____. *What Color Is Love?* New York: Harcourt Brace Jovanovich, 1966. $2.95.

Armstrong, W.H. *Sounder*. New York: Harper & Row, 1969. $5.95. (paperback, $1.25).

Bartoli, Jennifer. *Nonna*. Irvington-on-Hudson, N.Y.: Harvey House, 1975. $4.99.

Bawden, Nina. *Squib*. Philadelphia: J.B. Lippincott, 1971. $1.95.

Berger, Terry. *I Have Feelings*. New York: Human Science Press, 1971. $6.95.

Birnbaum, Abe. *Green Eyes*. Racine, WI: Western Publishing Co., 1973. $4.95. (originally published, 1953).

Blue, Rose. *Nikki 108*. New York: Franklin Watts, 1973. $4.90.

Borack, Barbara. *Someone Small*. New York: Harper & Row, 1969. $4.43.

Brenner, Barbara. *Baltimore Orioles*. New York: Harper & Row, 1974. $4.95.

_____. *Bodies*. New York: E.P. Dutton & Co., 1973. $6.95.

_____. *Year in the Life of Rosie Bernard*. New York: Harper & Row, 1971. $4.79.

Brooks, J. *Uncle Mike's Boy*. New York: Harper & Row, 1973. $5.79.

Brown, N.E. *The Dead Bird*. Reading, MA: Addison-Wesley Publishing Co., 1958. $4.50.

Buck, P.S. *The Big Wave*. New York: John Day, 1973. $6.50. (originally published, 1948).

Carrick, Carol. *Accident*. New York: Seabury Press, 1976. $6.59.

_____ and Carrick, Donald. *Swamp Spring*. New York: Macmillan, 1969. $4.95.

Cleaver, Vera, and Cleaver, Bill. *Grover*. New York: New American Library, 1975. $1.25.

Coburn, J.B. *Anne and the Sand Dobbies*. New York: Seabury Press, 1964. $7.95.

Cohen, Barbara. *Thank You Jack Robinson*. New York: Lothrop, Lee & Shepard Co., 1974. $5.49.

Coutant, Helen. *First Snow*. New York: Alfred A. Knopf, 1974. $5.69.

Craig, Jean. *Spring Is Like the Morning*. New York: G.P. Putnam's Sons, 1965. $4.97.

DePaola, Tomie. *Nana Upstairs and Nana Downstairs* (New ed.). New York: G.P. Putnam's Sons, 1973. $4.99.

Dobrin, Arnold. *Scat!* New York: Scholastic Book Services, 1971. $4.95.

Dunn, Phoebe. *Feelings.* Mankato, MN: Creative Education Society, 1971.

Eunson, Dale. *The Day They Gave Babies Away.* New York: Farrar, Straus & Giroux, 1946. $3.95.

Fassler, Joan. *My Grandpa Died Today.* New York: Human Science Press, 1971. $6.95.

Fitzerald, J.D. *Me and My Little Brain.* New York: Dial Press, 1971. $5.95.

Greene, C.C. *Beat the Turtle Drum.* New York: Viking, 1976. $5.95.

Greenfield. E. *Sister.* New York: Thomas Y. Crowell, 1974. $5.50.

Grollman, E.A. *Talking About Death: A Dialogue Between Parent and Child.* Boston: Beacon Press, 1976. $3.95.

Harnden, Ruth. *High Pasture.* Boston: Houghton Mifflin Co., 1964. (out of print)

Harris, Audrey. *Why Did He Die?* Minneapolis: Lerner Publications Co., 1965. $3.95.

Holl, Adelaide. *The Wonderful Tree.* Racine. WI: Western Publishing Co., 1974. $5.95.

Kantrowitz, Mildred. *When Violet Died.* New York: Parents' Magazine Press, 1973. $5.95.

Klein, Norma. *Confessions of an Only Child.* New York: Pantheon Books, 1974. $5.95.

Krauss, Ruth. *Growing Story.* New York: Harper & Row, 1947. $4.95.

Lee, Virginia. *The Magic Moth.* New York: Seabury Press, 1972. $6.95.

LeShan, Eda. *Learning to Say Good-by: When a Parent Dies.* New York: Macmillan, 1976. $6.95.

McNulty, Faith. *Woodchuck.* New York: Harper & Row, 1974. $4.95.

Miles, Miska. *Annie and the Old One.* Boston: Little, Brown & Company, 1971. $5.95.

Molloy, A.S. *The Girl from Two Miles High.* New York: Hastings House Publishers, 1967. $4.68.

Orgell, Doris. *Mulberry Music.* New York: Harper & Row, 1971. $5.79.

Parker, B.M. *The Wonders of the Seasons.* Racine, WI: Western Publishing Co., 1974. $3.95.

Pringle, Laurence. *Death Is Natural.* New York: Scholastic Book Service, 1977. $5.95.

Rock, Gail. *The House Without a Christmas Tree.* New York: Alfred A. Knopf, 1974. $4.95.

_____. *The Thanksgiving Treasure.* New York: Alfred A. Knopf, 1974. $4.95.

Shecter, Ben. *Someplace Else.* New York: Harper & Row, 1971. $4.79.

Shotwell, L.R. *Adam Bookout.* New York: Viking Press, 1967. $3.95.

Simon, Norma. *How Do I Feel?* Chicago: Albert Whitman & Co., 1970. $4.75.

Smith, D.B. *A Taste of Blackberries.* New York: Thomas Y. Crowell, 1973. $5.50. (paperback, 1976. $0.95).

Stein, S.B. *About Dying: An Open Book for Parents and Children Together.* New York: Walker & Co., 1974. $5.95.

Tresselt, Alvin. *The Dead Tree.* New York: Parents' Magazine Press, 1972. $5.95.

Viorst, Judith. *The Tenth Good Thing About Barney.* New York: Atheneum Publishers, 1971. $1.95.

Warburg, S.S. *Growing Time.* Boston: Houghton Mifflin Co., 1969. $7.95.

White, E.B. *Charlotte's Web.* New York: Harper & Row, 1952. $4.95.

Wiggin, K.D. *The Birds' Christmas Carol.* Boston: Houghton Mifflin Co., 1941. $5.95.

Zim, H.S., and Bleeker, Sonia. *Life and Death.* New York: William Morrow & Co., 1970. $5.09.

Zolotow, Charlotte. *My Grandson Lew.* New York: Harper & Row, 1974. $4.95.

REFERENCES

Dooley, A., & Coppock, L. *Child life programming for immobilized and isolated patients.* Johns Hopkins Hospital, 1979.

Kagan-Goodheart, L. Re-entry: Living with childhood cancer. *American Journal of Orthopsychiatry.* 1977, *47,* 651-658.

Kennedy, B.J., Tellagen, A., Kennedy, S., & Havernick, N. Psychological response of patients cured of advanced cancer. *Cancer.* 1976, *38,* 2184-2191.

Koocher, G.P., & Sallan, S.E. Pediatric oncology. In P. Magrab (Ed.), *Psychological management of pediatric problems* (Vol. 1). Baltimore: University Park Press, 1978.

Langner, M.B. *The private worlds of dying children.* Princeton, NJ: Princeton University Press, 1978.

Miller, D.R. Acute lymphoblastic leukemia. *Pediatric Clinics of North America.* 1980, *27*(2), 269-292.

Monaco, G. Personal communication.

Mullins, J.B. *A teacher's guide to management of physically handicapped students.* Springfield, IL: Charles C Thomas, 1979.

National Cancer Institute. *Diet and nutrition: A resource for parents of children with cancer.* NIH Publication No. 80-2038, 1979.

National Cancer Institute. *Students with cancer: A resource for the teacher.* NIH Publication No. 80-2086, 1980.

National Cancer Institute. *What you need to know about Wilms' tumor.* NIH Publication No. 80-1570, 1980.

Rudolph, M. *Should the children know? Encounters with death in the lives of children.* New York: Schocken Books, 1978.

Sachs, M.B. Helping the child with cancer go back to school. *Journal of School Health.* 1980, *50,* 328-331.

Schowalter, J.E. The child's reaction to his own terminal illness. In. B. Schoenberg et al. (Eds.), *Loss and grief: Psychological management.* New York: Columbia University Press, 1970.

Schwartz, A. Personal communication.

Sherman, M. *The leukemic child.* U.S. Department of HEW, Public Health Service, NIH Publication No. 78-863, 1978.

Shimkin, M.B. *Science and cancer.* National Cancer Institute, NIH Publication No. 80-568, 1980.

Silberfarb, P.M., Philibert, D., & Levine, P.M. Psychosocial aspects of neoplastic disease II: Affective and cognitive effects of chemotherapy in cancer patients. *American Journal of Psychiatry.* 1980, *137,* 597-601.

Timmons, A.L. Is it so awful? *American Journal of Nursing.* 1975, *75,* 988. (Reprinted in *Journal of Pediatrics,* 1976, *88*(1), 147-148.

Travis, G. *Chronic illness in children.* Stanford, CA: Stanford University Press, 1976.

Van Eys, J. Supportive care for the child with cancer. *Pediatric Clinics of North America.* 1976, *23*(1), 215-224.

Chapter 9

The Dying Child

OVERVIEW

Today, dying is no longer the inevitable outcome after a brief terminal illness. New technologic advances that can prolong life, offer long-term symptom-free remissions, or merely hold off death have made dying a complex process. "Dying in childhood now tends to be more prolonged and much more obvious" (Easson, 1970, p. 4). Medical procedures frequently affect the timing and nature of the child's death, to the extent that it can almost be programmed and orchestrated by the treatments received (Easson, 1970, p. 5). The growing concern with the quality of life and the legal, ethical, and psychological implications inherent in the new technologies have been expressed in research, as well as in the media and the arts. A number of relevant critical issues have been raised: How much care is enough? Should treatment be discontinued? When? Should the child be allowed to die at home or in a hospital? Should life be prolonged? Who makes these decisions, and who should make them—the child, the parents, or the caregivers? This section will explore these issues and examine the effects of death and dying on the child, the parents, and the caregivers.

THE CHILD'S PERSPECTIVE

The dying child is giving up an uncompleted life. Thus, death for a child is very different than for an adult. Children's perceptions of their own death and its meanings depend upon a number of factors: the child's age, the nature of the illness, the reactions of parents and other relatives, and previous experience with death. Children's understanding of death cognitively is similar to their understanding of other abstract concepts. Preschoolers, who have only a vague sense of time and causality, may view death as temporary. Older children may see death as more final, but distant from themselves (Nagy, 1948). For children who have reached a stage of formal abstract operational thought, death is understood as a universal inevitable process, and adolescents must come to terms with their own acceptance of mortality. These stages of understanding death do not, however, imply that young children cannot understand death or do not fear their own loss of life. The meanings become personal, and although loss is often concretized for the young child, it is no less real. Young children often act out their responses symbolically in play, while older children may verbalize their feelings.

In an attempt to understand death and its meaning for children, researchers have identified stages of awareness or reactions to death. These models are meant to help explain the process of dying and can serve as guidelines in relating to children. Two models will be presented briefly in the following pages, since they seem to clarify major reactions and are well documented. One represents a summarization of the classic stages of dying as delineated by Elisabeth Kübler-Ross (1969); the other was developed by Myra Langner (1978) to identify stages of awareness of children's concepts of death and their concomitant changes in self-concept. A few words of caution are necessary. Stages in a process as complex as dying are necessarily simplified and symbolic. People are complex, everchanging individuals. Children may linger in one stage or move back and forth between stages hundreds of times. They may skip a stage or respond to situations as if they are in two or more stages simultaneously. Stages, then, are simply guideposts to help one understand the child's reactions. When perceived in this way, they can be helpful to the caregiver and can make some reactions more understandable.

In her classic work, *On Death and Dying* (1969), Elisabeth Kübler-Ross identifies five stages of dying that she argues are universal:

1. Shock and denial. There is a strong urge to continue life. Visiting many doctors or clinics, "shopping" for a better diagnosis, is frequent. Patients may react with disbelief and try to shield family. Sometimes, family shield patients, reinforcing denial.
2. Anger. "Why me?" is often the cry out of anguish as the impact becomes more evident.
3. Bargaining. Often, this involves making promises to God in return for health, such as "If I get better, I'll give up cigarettes," or "I will be a better person." Patients often work to finish unfinished business, "put their house in order."
4. Depression. Losses are mourned. The patient often loses interest in the outside world and people. Saying goodbye and dissociating from others is common, as is preparatory grief.
5. Acceptance. This represents peace and closure.

M.B. Langner (1978), in her exploration of dying children's concepts of themselves and their world, sees the children's acquisition of information about their disease and their own mortality as part of a larger socialization process. The stages of acquiring information about the disease process after diagnosis are identified as:

1) "it" is serious;
2) drugs have names and are associated with side-effects;
3) purposes of treatments and procedures are understood;
4) disease is seen as a series of relapses and remissions, without death;
5) disease is seen as a series of relapses and remissions, including death. (p. 166)

Associated with these stages is a gradually changing self-concept:

1) well before diagnosis;
2) seriously ill;
3) seriously ill and will get better;
4) always ill and will never get better;
5) dying (terminally ill). (Langner, 1978, p. 169)

In discussions with children and in observations of their play, a sensitive caregiver can begin to recognize children's expressions of fears or concerns about illness and death and help them to cope with their feelings. Central in their growing awareness of the implications of death is a persistent feeling of anxiety that is manifested in a variety of ways. Younger children may express their growing sense of anxiety in more subtle and symbolic ways (Morrissey, 1964), and their anxiety may be compounded by fears of abandonment or separation. As children become more conscious of a personal identity and thus more devastated by its potential destruction, anxiety may be overwhelming at times.

As the children attempt to come to terms with this anxiety, they face their last, and perhaps their most profound, learning experience. Too often, instead of helping children to successfully master this task, parents and caregivers add to the children's burden because of their own grief and anxiety. What follows is often a complex drama of interaction between the child and close relatives or caregivers, a game of "mutual pretense" (Glaser & Strauss, 1965) in which children protect others from having to talk about the illness and death by not admitting to any awareness of it themselves. Such pretense, when supported by the anxiety of parents or caregivers, often leaves the child feeling a loss of relationship, a loss of intimacy, which can translate into feelings of abandonment. In the end stages of dying, this abandonment may extend beyond the verbal realm, as parents and caregivers begin a process of anticipatory mourning (Lindemann, 1944) and begin to avoid the child as much as possible. Care is given quietly and impersonally, family visits become shorter and less frequent, and the child is left alone in the final days and moments of life. While such reaction may serve the family as a coping process, it can be very destructive to the child, creating an "increasing emotional distance and accompanying sense of loneliness as the illness progresses" (Koocher & Sallan, 1978, p. 299). The need for emotional supports and the continued physical presence of those close to the dying child is crucial. It is illustrated by a poignant story, told by Dr. Mary E. Robinson, Director of Child Life, Children's Hospital, National Medical Center. She tells of a dying child who needed the comfort and attention of a close friend, the child life specialist, but was too tired to talk. The child life teacher held her hand and the child responded by squeezing in answer to questions. Quiet conversation occurred for a few minutes this way. Then the child life specialist's attention was drawn away by a visitor. She resumed her hand holding when the visitor left and felt no response when asking the child a question. Fearful that death had occurred, she jumped up and looked closely at the child's face. "Dummy," the child responded, "you're holding the wrong hand." The child died moments later, holding onto her friend, with a childlike sense of humor and wit to the end.

Finally, as death approaches, the child begins to feel more helpless and dependent upon others. This may cause resentment and anger on the child's part, especially in adolescence. Often, such temporary reactions become excuses for family or caregivers to avoid the child, thus increasing the loneliness.

When the death of a child is inevitable, one of the most important goals is to allow it to occur naturally, in the presence of close family, with no last minute heroic lifesaving efforts. It should occur in a setting familiar to the child and family—the home or the much frequented hospital—among known professional staff. Both the parents and the child need continuity, and neither is prepared for new relationships.

Death at Home Versus Death in the Hospital

The decision to allow a child to die at home or in the hospital is difficult. The family's "psychological strengths and physical resources" (Travis, 1976, p. 401) must be evaluated, as well as the availability of visiting health professionals. The child's wishes should also be taken into account, as well as the effect such an experience will have on siblings.

In a study of the option of home care for children dying of cancer, I.M. Martinson, G.D. Armstrong, D.P. Geis, M.A. Anglim, E.A. Granseth, H. MacInnis, J.H. Kersey, and M.E. Nesbit (1978) identify a number of factors that need to be taken into consideration. The costs of dying at home are considerably lower than in the hospital, although most health insurance plans to date do not cover the bulk of out-of-pocket expenses in home care, while hospital care is often totally reimbursed. Secondly, the parents, rather than the health professionals, become the primary caregivers. This may put an excessive burden on the family's emotional resources, but it can often help the family to overcome the feelings of helplessness and loss of control that accompany a death in the hospital setting. The stress of being torn between the care of the dying child in the hospital and the needs of the rest of the family at home is greatly relieved. The administration of pain medication and other treatment procedures must be taken over by parents, thus entailing a training period as well as frequent home visits by health professionals to provide necessary supervision and support. As summarized by Martinson et al. (1978):

> The real key to making the program work, however, rests with the individuals involved. Each of the four principals—the child, the parents, the physician, and the nurse—needs to perceive that home care is a viable alternative. Fear of the children about adequacy of pain control, ambivalence about providing care on the part of the parents, only partial cooperation by physicians, or lack of flexibility on the part of the nurses makes home care much more difficult. (p. 111)

Given the right set of circumstances and supportive help for the family, a death at home can be more comfortable and more personal for both the child and the family. It can represent closure and a personal leave-taking among familiar surroundings that can help to sustain family members after the child's death.

Hospitals, by their very nature, are more impersonal, organized settings, guided by many rules and regulations. Such an institutional framework often leads to the increased dependence upon technologic procedures, and decision making is often predicated upon technical know-how in such settings. Staff consistency is usually lacking, and the child may be cared for by as many as 20 to 30 nurses, physicians, and technicians in a single day. In spite of this, many children do die in hospitals. Parents and support staff need to counteract this inconsistency and depersonalization of hospitals by pressing for primary nursing care arrangements and rooming-in whenever possible. Psychosocial support services, such as those provided by social workers, psychiatrists, psychologists, chaplains, and child life specialists, can be invaluable to the child and family in helping to create a humane environment within the hospital.

The child and family need to be assured the services of a coordinated, supportive health care team, the right to privacy, and the right to play a part in all decisions regarding the dying child, regardless of where the child spends his or her last days.

FAMILY REACTIONS

When parents learn that their child has a terminal illness, they are suddenly thrust into a maelstrom of emotions—shock, disbelief, and numbness. In the event of the sudden death of a child, these reactions are the first steps in the process of managing grief and bereavement; with the diagnosis of terminal illness, they become the early reactions in a frequently protracted, roller-coaster process of grief that may last for years before the actual death of the child. Unlike sudden death, the child's needs must be met during this extended period as the illness gradually takes its toll upon the child. During this process, the family begins to face the reality of eventual death and the loss of an extremely meaningful relationship (Easson, 1970). The child is a part of each family member, and the anticipated death thus represents the death of a part of them all. As Harriet Schiff (1977) notes, "To bury a child is to see a part of yourself, your eye color, your dimple, your sense of humor, being placed in the ground. It is life's harshest empathetic experience and must therefore be the hardest one with which to deal. In reality, when children die, not only are we mourning them, we are also mourning that bit of our own immortality that they carried" (p. 23).

This identification with the child can make it very difficult for parents to accept the slow deterioration, the disfigurement by scars or amputation or tumor, of their loved child.

Parents may begin to feel profoundly sad and pained by their children's illness and their inability to help them, to make them better. They often begin to blame themselves for actions taken or not taken: letting the child go out to play in the cold or failing to take a headache or nausea seriously; marrying a spouse who carries an inherited disease; failing to check the child's temperature. As the illness continues, with pain for the child and emotional and financial strains on the family, parents may find themselves wishing for a quick death, then feeling overwhelming guilt for such thoughts (Fischoff & O'Brien, 1976). In the face of such conflicting emotions, parents may begin to feel helpless and angry: at the child, for forcing them to undergo such trauma; at God, for failing to protect them; at friends, for having a healthy child; at the child's doctors or nurses, for failing to heal their child. Anger at the child produces even more guilt, and often the anger and helplessness is directed outward—toward a spouse or toward the child's caretakers. Doctors, who are seen primarily as experimenting with their child, trying one new treatment after another, are often viewed with distrust (Kirkpatrick, Hoffman, & Futterman, 1974). Parents see caretakers as unfeeling, and they may find fault with the condition of the child's room or the sloppiness of the bed or the unkemptness of the child's appearance. During this time, parents may question the hospital's practices or focus on what they may feel are unreasonable hospital costs or routines. While much of this anger is a result of the natural mourning process, parents' complaints should not be automatically dismissed as unreasonable. In some cases, anger and resentment at the impersonality of hospitals are justified, and parents' concerns need to be addressed and, if necessary, responded to by changes in the hospital's management of the child's care (Beuf, 1979).

In many terminal illnesses, the period between the initial diagnosis and the final death is extended, with long stretches of remission or plateaus in the child's condition. During these times, the families may begin to pick up the pieces of their lives as the child returns to school, the parents to work schedules. Undercurrents of anxiety, sadness, or disbelief continue to exist. For some families, prolonged symptom-free periods lead to feelings of hope or denial of the ultimate death of the child. For others, the early grief work may be resolved by prematurely accepting the child's death and becoming gradually divorced from the child emotionally, in anticipation of the eventual final separation. If this occurs too early, the child may feel isolated and rejected and may begin to withdraw from family involvements. In some tragic cases, the child may literally be abandoned, left in the care of the hospital personnel to wait out the remaining days or months of life.

This premature adjustment to the death of a child can be especially damaging to the child who has an extended remission or an unexpected cure. In such a situation, the child must often be reintegrated into the household as a new person, with a new role. The child and family must then face the difficult task of adjusting to this new circumstance (Easson, 1970).

Family members who must undergo the long, slow process of watching a child die face other strains as well. Financial burdens become enormous, and parents often need to take on extra jobs to pay for expenses. Family routines are interrupted as the child spends increasingly more time in hospitals, and parents must take turns playing multiple roles in both the home and the hospital—father preparing meals, mother driving home alone in the late evening or sleeping in the hospital and returning home to relieve father of the babysitting chores in the early morning. Parents who take an occasional day off to enjoy a movie or a picnic often feel guilty at having a good time. Friends and relatives can add to this feeling by criticizing the parents for not meeting their own expectations of appropriate mourning behaviors. Others may feel helpless or afraid to interact with parents, thus isolating them at a time when they most need support.

Parents may also become excessively overprotective of their other children and generally fearful of new family crises. Family discord may result, leading to marriage breakups or isolation and noncommunication within the marriage. S.B. Lansky, N.U. Coins, R. Hassanein, B.A. Wehr, and J.T. Low-man (1978) found no increase in divorce rates among families of children with cancer but did find heightened marital stress, with feelings of low self-esteem, helplessness, and unmet dependency needs prevalent. At the time of death, parents need to cope with a myriad of practical problems: Should an autopsy be performed? Who will be involved in funeral preparations? What kind of funeral should be held? As Harriet Schiff (1977) notes, "When their child is lying there dead, there can be no really "nice" funeral. In most cases, all but the most religious have not yet been reconciled to their grief. The funeral then becomes a matter of getting over the most treacherous ground" (p. 10).

Religion is a source of strength for many parents at this time, as is the support of friends and family. Parents who have remained with the child to the end usually feel less guilt afterwards and often hold onto the last memories of the child as a source of strength (Travis, 1976).

Parents almost uniformly describe feeling empty and numb for the first days and weeks after the death of their child. They may have difficulty eating or sleeping and often have physical symptoms of fatigue, shortness of breath, or an empty feeling in the pit of the stomach (Easson, 1972). They may have periods of forgetfulness and listlessness or periods of restlessness and irritability. Parents may find it difficult to return to daily routines and may find themselves preoccupied with thoughts of their child (Miles, 1978). The mourning process, which may have begun after the initial diagnosis was made, continues for an extended period of time. Parents may have difficulty making decisions and may find that they have lost interest in life. Some parents even express the fear that they are going crazy (Miles, 1978). For most parents, such a process is normal and self-limiting. While the time frame for the mourning process varies among individuals, and the pain eases only gradually, recovery and reorganization occur in most situations. Families do become re-involved with life and with future plans and gradually adapt to the loss.

> The pain of the loss becomes less intense, the good days outbalance the bad ones, and the child can be discussed and remembered with more happiness. Recovery isn't "being one's old self again," for parents are never their old selves after the loss of a child. They are always different from what they were before. Tragic loss can, in time, give rise to renewed meaning and personal growth. (Miles, 1978, p. 5)

In the early weeks, parents may need to relive the last days or hours of their child's life and may need to review the process of the child's entire illness or life over and over again. Feelings of anger and guilt may resurface and need to be vented.

Occasionally, parents may be at different stages in the mourning process and may feel resentful at a spouse's seeming insensitivity or frequent outbreaks of crying. Each family member mourns alone, even when supported. Parent self-help support groups, such as the Candlelighters and the Compassionate Friends, are invaluable in helping parents work through the process of bereavement. Through a national network of support, such local groups offer parents the comfort and sharing that is essential at such a time. Exhibit 9-1, prepared by Lee Schmidt and circulated widely by various chapters of the Compassionate Friends, represents guidelines for friends, relatives, and caregivers in their relationships with bereaved parents. The following letter to the staff of Mt. Washington Pediatric Hospital, written by the mother of a child who died of Huntington's chorea, exemplifies the reactions of parents in a way that no textbook description can match (Exhibit 9-2).

Siblings

When a child dies, he or she often leaves behind siblings. When an illness has been of an extended nature, siblings often feel abandoned and confused by the loss of parental attention. In some instances, parents have attempted to protect the siblings from pain by hiding their own fears of impending death or in the mistaken belief that the siblings are too young to understand (Miles, 1978). Heffron et al. (1973) describe a cycle of behavior and reactions typically seen in siblings when a terminal illness had been of long duration. Feelings of jealousy due to the special needs of the ill sibling lead to teasing, which inevitably leads to guilt as the sibling's condition worsens. Very young siblings may not fully understand the death of their brother or sister, but the expressions of grief and mourning that are present in the family are nonetheless frightening. If the child dies in the hospital, the siblings may be confused about the finality of the death. The comings and goings to and from the hospital may seem to have occurred with no rhyme or reason before the death, and the young sibling may expect an eventual return and even question the whereabouts of the child months after the death, causing fresh pain for the parents. In some cases, children may believe that the hospital, rather than the disease, was at fault in killing their sibling. "In this regard," as I.M. Martinson et al. (1978) note, "having the sick child at home during illness and death may help to establish the causal link between illness and death for the younger siblings" (p. 112).

Children often experience grief reactions similar to those of their parents, although they are more likely to express these feelings in their behaviors or in play (Miles, 1978). Seeing a young child act out a funeral procession or draw picture after picture of dead flowers and dead animals may cause additional pain for the family, although such activities are vital for the child in order to work through feelings of mourning.

Exhibit 9-1 Do's and Don't's for Helping Bereaved Parents

DO	DON'T
• Do let your genuine concern and caring show.	• Don't let your own sense of helplessness keep you from reaching out to a bereaved parent.
• Do be available . . . to listen, to run errands, to help with the other children, or whatever else seems needed.	• Don't avoid them because you are uncomfortable (being avoided by friends adds pain to an already intolerably painful experience).
• Do say you are sorry about what has happened to their child and about their pain.	• Don't say you know how they feel (unless you have lost a child yourself, you probably do not know how they feel).
• Do allow them to express as much grief as they are feeling at the moment and are willing to share.	• Don't say "you ought to be feeling better by now" or anything else which implies a judgment about their feelings.
• Do encourage them to be patient with themselves, not to expect too much of of themselves, and not to impose any "shoulds" on themselves.	• Don't tell them what they *should* feel or do.
• Do allow them to talk about the child they have lost as much and as often as they want to.	• Don't change the subject when they mention their dead child.
	• Don't avoid mentioning the child's name out of fear of reminding them of their pain (they haven't forgotten it!)
• Do talk about the special, endearing qualities of the child they have lost.	• Don't try to find something positive about the child's death (moral lesson, closer family ties, etc.).

Exhibit 9-1 continued

- Do give special attention to the child's brothers and sisters at the funeral home, during the funeral, and in the months to come (they too are hurt and confused and in need of attention which their parents may not be able to give at this time).

- Don't point out that at least they have their other children (children are not interchangeable; they cannot replace the child who is gone).

- Don't say, "You can always have another child." Even if they wanted to and could, another child would not replace the child they have lost.
- Don't suggest that they should be grateful for their other children (grief over the loss of one child does not discount parents' love and appreciation of their living children).

- Do reassure them that they did everything that they, could, that the medical care received was the best, or whatever else you know to be *true* and *positive* about the care given their child.

- Don't make any comments which in any way suggest that the care given their child at home, in the emergency room, hospital, or wherever was inadequate (parents are plagued by feelings of doubt and guilt without any help from their family and friends).

Source: Reprinted from "Do's and Don't's for Helping Bereaved Parents" by Lee Schmidt, Parent Bereavement Outreach, Santa Monica, CA, 1979.

Added to their grief, siblings may become fearful of being abandoned by their parents or of becoming separated from them as in the case of the dead child. They may be more demanding of attention and may be clinging or dependent. This fear of abandonment may be exacerbated if parents, in their own grief, are temporarily unable to give the remaining children the love and attention they need.

Exhibit 9-2 Letter from a Parent to the Staff at Mt. Washington Pediatric Hospital

To the Staff,

Thanks is such a small word to write at the end of a two year period that my son spent at Mt. Washington. His involvement was with many staff members, most of whom I knew but some I only knew by name and never met. I feel I don't have to mention names, anyone that worked with M. contributed to his total care and happiness and now at the end of the road I am saying thanks from the bottom of my heart for his care, your support and also for getting me through a difficult time in my life.

If I backed up to two years ago, I truthfully would have to say when I brought M. to the hospital it was the saddest day of my life. I never did let go of him, I was frustrated, remained so and made a point to oversee everything that was done with him. Sometimes, I think I was unreasonable but I hope in time you will realize M. was my heart and soul and just to sit quietly with him brought me happiness.

I probably broke most of the rules at your hospital such as my walks off the grounds with M. in a wheelchair, riding through the side streets of the community. I needed this—I had to be alone with him—we shared some of our greatest moments together on a little side street with a stretch of trees, no houses, just him and I—these are memories I will always cherish.

In time I hope to make a new life for myself and as the pain eases only the good memories will remain. God did bless me with a child—a child that was born out of a beautiful love—I loved M. every day of his short life here on earth but now he has returned to an even greater love. To be a Mother and to have enjoyed it was one of the most rewarding experiences of my life.

GOD BLESS EVERYONE FOR
ALL THEIR HELP

Source: Reprinted with permission from Mrs. Curtin, 1981.

At times, children may appear to be unaffected by the death or may exhibit what has been termed a "short sadness span" (Wolfenstein & Kliman, 1965). Well before the parents have ceased to mourn their loss, the siblings may be asking for the dead child's room or belongings or reengaging in social contacts. This may anger or distress parents, who do not fully understand their children's need to postpone grief until they have adequate concepts to help them explain their feelings (Koch, Kermann, & Donaldson, 1974).

Siblings can be helped to deal with their feelings, and parents can make the process less painful. The following guidelines, adapted from *The Grief of Parents* (Miles, 1978), can serve as tools:

- Children need to have an understanding of physical death, geared to their developmental level, and repeated often.
- Explanation of death in terms of religious meanings can be supportive to the child, especially if the parents rely upon such supports.
- Children should be involved in the rituals of death and allowed to participate in decision making, when possible.
- Children's fears about death should be allowed to be discussed openly, and children should be made to feel that parents will listen to them, will tell them the truth, will love and reassure them, and will allow them to resume normal activities as soon as possible.

STAFF REACTIONS

People trained to serve others—doctors, nurses, teachers, physical therapists, social workers—typically are expected to help their clients, to make them well or brighter or happier. Caring for the dying child often seems to negate all of their training and expertise. Often they are left with feelings of helplessness and guilt at being unable to do what they were trained for: helplessness in the face of death, guilt for having failed to avert it.

The staff members' own concepts of death, their personal acceptance or rejection of its finality, also play a role in their reactions to a dying child. The physician may feel a strong sense of failure and may be reluctant to spend time with the family and child, providing emotional support and comfort. Physicians may avoid coming to terms with these feelings by acting coldly or always rushed or by recommending more and more instrusive life-threatening treatments in an effort to stave off death. Occasionally, these last-ditch efforts are ordered more for the benefit of the medical team's sense of helplessness than for the child's welfare, and some may even shorten the child's life or cause the child undue pain or discomfort (Easson, 1970).

The nursing staff face the difficult tasks of simultaneously caring for the dying child's physical and emotional needs, reacting to the child's family and being reacted to by them, all the while mourning for their patient and re-sponding to their own sense of failure and helplessness. Often, the conse-quences of such turmoil lead to a covert agreement on the part of the treat-ment team to isolate dying children (Glaser & Strauss, 1965): to place them in private rooms, or in the back of a ward; to visit only when necessary, and only for short periods; to avoid confrontations with the reality of the child's pain and suffering. Parents may turn on nursing staff, expressing the anger they cannot contain, further alienating the staff from the patients and their families. Often, as the child approaches death, familiar staff have difficulty in continuing to provide primary care, since they feel the pain of death and are not able to separate those feelings from their professional responsibilities. At times, staff may develop close emotional ties to the family after long months of visits, of sharing coffee and a cry together. As W.M. Easson (1970) points out, such close relationships may not be helpful to the family after the child's death, since the family needs to complete the process of mourning by sepa-rating from the hospital and its staff.

To help staff deal with this complexity of reactions and continue to treat the child with the sensitivity and nurturing that is essential, staff supports must be strong and continuous. Staff must be given time to share their feel-ings with one another and should be allowed opportunities for expressing their emotions in private and for working through their reactions to the death of a patient they cared for. Until the child's actual death, children need to feel supported. Staff need to be helped to see that children remain children even while dying. Both children and parents need to rely on familiar faces and established relationships at this time, making the need for staff support even more crucial.

Teachers face an additional dilemma. What a nurse does for a child may not keep that child alive, but it does provide the child with essential physical care. The teacher's role is less clear and may seem superfluous to many. Why bother to teach a child who will be dead in a week or a month? Why invest precious time in this child, when dozens are waiting to be taught? These doubts are valid, but they fail to take into account the broad purpose of education. Is it merely a set of skills to be mastered for future productive labor, or a re-ciprocal process, a total therapeutic social milieu, in which both teacher and pupil learn from each other in countless ways?

Other reasons exist for abandoning the role of educator for the dying child. Again, the need to protect oneself from pain by isolating the patient is ap-parent, as the teacher no longer feels comfortable approaching the child's bedside with schoolwork. While the maintenance of a formal curriculum is clearly impossible, a few moments spent reading with or to a child or sharing a project can be therapeutic for both child and teacher. Until the child's ill-ness is severe enough to preclude all formal schoolwork, the provision of such tasks gives the child hope and a chance to escape from the anxiety of waiting. Teachers can play a crucial role in providing support to the dying child's classmates as well. Provisions can be made for continuing contact and, after the child's death, the teacher can help the other students to work through their own feelings of grief, as detailed in the previous chapter.

The teacher, less involved than the hospital staff, nevertheless needs a support system and an opportunity to vent feelings. The needs of the caregivers are great and often are unrecognized by the systems that care for the patient or pupil. The letter in Exhibit 9-3, written for an in-house nursing newsletter by a staff nurse at Mt. Washington Pediatric Hospital, exemplifies the dilemmas caregivers face.

Exhibit 9-3 My First Day

It was my first day on my first job in a hospital. The charge nurse pointed to a private room across the hall from the nurses' station where, wearing my new white uniform and starched cap, I had just reported. "Mr. J. in that room is dying. You take care of him tonight."

"What am I supposed to do?" I asked in a voice as shocked and shaky as I felt.

"There isn't much to do. Just check his vitals once in awhile," she said as she turned away to other duties.

I'm a nurse. I'm supposed to *do* something. How could I sit in that private room and do nothing but take a blood pressure every fifteen minutes? I was afraid to touch the man, but I felt guilty about just letting him lie there. So I kept myself very busy learning where supplies were and how equipment worked and every fifteen minutes I hurried in and out of Mr. J.'s room, closing the door behind me after I had recorded another blood pressure.

That was a long time ago. There has been a lot written about the dying patient since then. There has been a lot of controversy about treatment. But I wonder if care for the dying in most hospitals is really very much different now from what it was when I was assigned that patient so many years ago.

Very recently I was told by the mother of one of our patients, "You know that I work in another hospital." According to her, when someone is dying there, he is put in a private room and someone peeks in every now and then to see if he's still breathing. "I was so afraid that would happen to my son," she told me in anguished tones. She went on to say that our contin-

Exhibit 9-3 continued

uing to bathe and to change and to do all of the other ordinary things we had done day after day for her son had comforted her during her child's last hours. That we had not left him alone, isolated and out of sight, had eased a little of her pain.

I was glad that she could share her feelings with me for it comforted me to know we had helped. And I needed to be comforted. We're different here at Mt. Washington Pediatric Hospital from that other hospital she described. But that difference takes its toll. We spend long months, even years, caring for these children, and we come to love them. When they die, it hurts.

Yet when we see them dying, and that helpless feeling of "I'm in nursing. I'm supposed to do something" begins to overwhelm us, we can look back and realize that we've been "doing something" all along. We have been caring for the child, his parents, and each other in very ordinary and human ways, and it's in these ordinary and human ways that we give and receive the comforting that we call "nursing."

Source: Reprinted from *Professionally Speaking* by Mary Platt, February 1, 1981, with permission.

In her conclusion, Mary Platt seems to resolve the dilemma that often faces caretakers as she recognizes the fact that ordinary care and sensitive support are indeed vital services.

PROLONGATION OF LIFE

The preceding pages have touched on the issues of when to stop treatments and the right to refuse treatments. These issues have become more pertinent today as new hopes for prolongation of life are found in the new technologies. Quality of life has become a recent concern as a result of this new technology, and the question is raised over and over again: What kind of life is prolonged? At what costs?

In the past, when the body was ill beyond a certain extent, the person lapsed into unconsciousness and soon died. Today, such states of coma or semicoma can be extended by machines indefinitely. Treatments can be provided for secondary infections, such as pneumonia. Resuscitation can even be attempted after the heart stops beating. How far should we go, assuming we can technologically go that far, to prolong a life?

One reason that has been postulated for the expanded use of technology to prolong life is the medical community's conception of death as the enemy, a belief system often fostered in medical education programs (Charmaz, 1980). Operating under such a conception, the inability to avert death, to "win the battle," becomes for the physician a failure, a defeat. In this context, "attempting to keep the patient alive then becomes the physician's personal responsibility...." (Charmaz, 1980, p. 103).

K. Charmaz suggests that, in the state of high technology that exists today, moral decisions are being replaced by technical ones. Thus, instead of asking the question, "Is this patient ready to die, by nature of the illness?", the question becomes "How long can we prolong life by using machine 'A' versus machine 'B'?"

In the wake of such technologic expertise, a countermovement has developed that calls for "death with dignity" and that asserts the person's right to die without extraordinary measures being taken to prolong life.

Against this background, a number of issues need to be examined. They include the legal criteria, the child's and/or parents' rights, and the issue of research and experimentation.

No clear legal statutes have been developed to guide physicians in helping parents and children make decisions regarding prolongation of life. Legal precedents are being established slowly, case by case, and give some direction to physicians and families.

The provision of ordinary treatment that will not cause undue discomfort or permanent handicap is clearly the right of all patients, including the child with a diagnosis of terminal illness. If the child will suffer from the effects of extraordinary treatment, such as full paralysis or blindness after excision of a brain tumor, and would live more normally, although for a shorter time, without such surgery, the refusal of such surgery is considered legal (Holder, 1977). The issue in question becomes the relative benefits of extraordinary treatment versus its costs in terms of handicap or severe discomfort. The permanence of the handicap or discomfort also plays a role in decision making. Chemotherapy for leukemia, while it causes fairly severe side effects, is now considered ordinary treatment, and its success in prolonging normal life has been well documented. Such is also the case in bone cancer. The loss of a limb is ordinarily a reasonable, although traumatic, price to pay for the continuation of a normal life. Senator Edward Kennedy's son is a testament to such a choice, and when observing him on the ski slopes or among his college friends, one would be hard pressed to suggest that surgery was cruel.

Many treatments, however, represent last-ditch efforts, experimental approaches to save lives at considerable cost to the child in terms of pain or handicap.

A patient, aged 13, who had successfully undergone leg amputation and had spent two symptom-free years, developed lung involvement. She was hospitalized in a chronic care setting after she and her parents decided that she not undergo chemotherapy, which had a ten percent chance of success. She was not able to face the prospect of severe discomfort for such a risk, and her parents concurred. In this instance, she and her family chose a higher quality of life, essentially pain-free until the last days, rather than the prolongation of life in extreme discomfort.

Informed decisions such as this one, carefully made, are becoming more frequent as medical procedures become more extreme and more varied. What are the legal implications of such a decision? For adults, legal precedents exist that affirm the right of mentally competent adults to refuse treatment that prolongs a life of misery and pain (Holder, 1977). A.R. Holder argues that this concept should be extended downward. He states that "a parent should be able to make the same decision for death with dignity for his child. As long as ordinary care is provided, it would appear that the parents have a legal right to refuse extraordinary care" (p. 128).

The decision to choose an earlier but more comfortable death necessarily involves a great many complex factors: the family's religious and ethical philosophy; their belief in life after death; the conditions of life at the present time; and their definition of the quality of life.

The age of the child is also a consideration. A ten year old who would "rather die than lose a leg" may have only a vague notion of the finality of death but may be devastated by the prospect of being unable to keep up with peers. A 16-year-old girl, on the other hand, who has had two unsuccessful kidney transplants and who is increasingly unresponsive to dialysis, may fully understand the choices and may be unwilling to extend her pain beyond a few more days.

Holder suggests that the key issue in cases such as those cited above lies in the child's ability to fully understand the finality of death and thus revolves around the concept of informed consent. Hence, ability to understand the abstract concept constitutes ability to make decisions that are based on informed consent (1977).

In cases in which the child and parent disagree, the issues become cloudier. Here, Holder states that:

> It is perfectly sound logic and law to conclude that if a terminally ill child wants treatment and his parents do not, a physician is entitled to abide by a wish to preserve life and, if necessary, do so by court petition. The same principle should apply if one or both parents want to have the treatment given and the child does not. (p. 130)

Thus, the conflict should be resolved in favor of the preservation of life.

It is very difficult for parents to refuse treatment for their child, especially when a concerned physician recommends it strongly. Parents' guilt and helplessness feed into such situations, making them uncertain and fearful of angering the physician or harming their child. In some cases, they may even recognize that the treatment has little hope for success for their child but may aid in experimental research. Such decisions become doubly hard for parents. Legal responses to counter this pressure toward extraordinary treatment and to attempt to resolve the dilemma that high technology has created have been developing slowly throughout the country. A series of "right to die" laws have been enacted in a number of states in an attempt to return to patients some rights in respect to their impending death. To date, these laws are still ambiguous and represent a variety of problems (Veatch, 1976). Definitions of key terms, such as *death* and *dignity* and *competence,* are not yet adequately clarified. Many of the laws passed are cumbersome to administer, and some even contradict existing patients' rights (Charmaz, 1980).

The questions that are thus raised as a result of increasingly complex medical options are themselves complex, and simple answers are not readily available. Unfortunately, parents and children are often not in an emotionally strong state when faced with choices such as those raised above. Decisions become clouded by factors such as fatigue, guilt, financial pressures, family crises, and the like.

Parents and children faced with such critical issues should be afforded the opportunity to work through the issues, reviewing the risks involved, the consequences for the child, and the costs, both financial and emotional, for the child and family. Time is needed for such deliberations, and professional support by social workers, psychologists, chaplains, or other health professionals may help families work through this difficult process.

Families that have been supported and encouraged to weigh all the issues find it easier to cope with the child's eventual death or handicap and are often able to return to a reasonably normal pattern of functioning more quickly. They have been allowed to take some control over their lives and the lives of their children and are thus left with less of a sense of futility and guilt or anger at staff for a decision made by others that affected their child's life.

SUMMARY

Central to the issue of prolongation of life discussed in this chapter are the concepts of informed consent and patient autonomy. In an increasingly technological context, the patient and family need to be intimately involved in all of the decisions made in the process of dying. The finality of death and the unique tragedy of the death of a child make such decisions difficult and painful to consider. For the caretakers, helping a family or a child through such a process involves working through one's own feelings of mortality and death. For parents, the seemingly senseless destruction of a life that they created takes its toll in grief and a permanent sense of loss.

Hopefully, out of such tragedy can come a heightened sense of life's fragility and a respect for human life and its value. Being touched by death may help many to know how to live.

REFERENCES

Beuf, A. *Biting off the bracelet*. Philadelphia: University of Pennsylvania Press, 1979.

Charmaz, K. *The social reality of death*. Reading, MA: Addison-Wesley, 1980.

Easson, W.M. *The dying child*. Springfield, IL: Charles C Thomas, 1970.

Easson, W.M. The family of the dying child. *Pediatric Clinics of North America*, 1972, *19*, 1157-1165.

Fischoff, J., & O'Brien, N. After the child dies. *Journal of Pediatrics*, 1976, *88*(1), 140-146.

Glaser, B., & Strauss, A. *Awareness of dying: A study of social interaction*. Chicago: Aldine, 1965.

Heffron, W.A., Bommelae, K., & Masters, R. Group discussions with parents of leukemic children. *Pediatrics*, 1973, *52*(6), 831.

Holder, A.R. *Legal issues in pediatrics and adolescent medicine*. New York: John Wiley & Sons, 1977.

Kirkpatrick, J., Hoffman, I., & Futterman, E.H. Dilemma of trust: Relationship between medical caregivers and parents of fatally ill children. *Pediatrics*, 1974, *52*(2), 169-175.

Koch, C.R., Kermann, J., & Donaldson, M.H. Supportive care of the child with cancer and his family. *Seminars in Oncology*, 1974, *1*(1), 81-86.

Koocher, G.P., & Sallan, S.E. Pediatric oncology. In P. Magrab (Ed.), *Psychological management of pediatric problems* (Vol. 1). Baltimore: University Park Press, 1978.

Kübler-Ross, E. *On death and dying*. New York: Macmillan, 1969.

Langner, M.B. *The private worlds of dying children*. Princeton, NJ: Princeton University Press, 1978.

Lansky, S.B., Cains, N.U., Hassanein, R., Wehr, B.A., & Lowman, J.T. Childhood cancer: Parental discord and divorce. *Pediatrics*, 1978, *62*(2), 184-188.

Lindemann, E. Symptomatology and management of acute grief. *American Journal of Psychiatry*, 1944, *101*, 141.

Martinson, I.M., Armstrong, G.D., Geis, D.P., Anglim, M.A., Granseth, E.A., MacInnis, H., Kersey, J.H., & Nesbit, M.E. Home care for children dying of cancer. *Pediatrics*, 1978, *62*(1), 106-113.

Miles, M.S. *The grief of parents*. Kansas City, MO: Private publication, 1978.

Morrissey, J.R. Death anxiety in children with a fatal illness. *American Journal of Psychotherapy*, 1964, *18*(4), 606-615.

Nagy, M.H. The child's view of death. *Journal of Genetic Psychology*, 1948, *73*, 3-27.

Schiff, H.S. *The bereaved parent*. New York: Penguin Books, 1977.

Travis, G. *Chronic illness in children*. Stanford, CA: Stanford University Press, 1976.

Veatch, R.M. *Death, dying and the biological revolution*. New Haven, CT: Yale University Press, 1976.

Wolfenstein, M., & Kliman, G. (Eds.). *Children and the death of a president*. Garden City, NY: Doubleday, 1965.

The Educator: Multiple Roles

OVERVIEW

Part III will examine the various functions of teachers of chronically ill children. In this section, the teacher moves into center stage, and the various roles assumed, their interrelationship, and the teacher's response to them form the core of the text. This shift away from the child is only temporary, part of the process of developing a corps of teachers and health professionals whose central function is to provide an optimal educational experience for the child with chronic illness. For in an educational context, the teacher, in fact, plays a central interactive role in relation to the child, family, school, community, and health team. (See Figure III-1.) The next chapters explore the teachers as evaluator, referral agent, coordinator, team member, advocate, friend, and counselor to the child and family. Through an understanding of these various roles, the functions of the educator will be clearer, and the tasks less stressful.

Figure III-1 The Many Roles of a Teacher

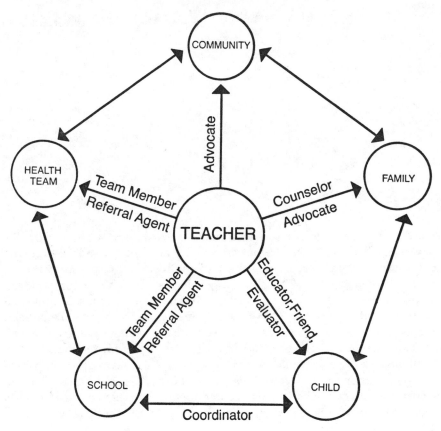

Chapter 10

The Educator as a
Team Member

OVERVIEW

The role of teacher in an educational setting has been well defined over the years. Standardized teacher education and training programs exist nationally, and state certifications are required to verify that established qualifications are met. While there may be current controversy over the issue of qualifications versus competencies, few would disagree that the role of teacher carries with it certain agreed-upon functions, settings, and responsibilities. As was noted earlier, specialized training and its concomitant certification are generally not required for home/hospital teachers, and their roles, responsibilities, and functions are less clearly defined and recognized. Of special concern is the home/hospital teacher's role as a member of a health care or rehabilitation team. Teacher training is often aimed at the teacher-pupil dyad, with some more recent emphasis on the teacher-pupil-parent relationship. Little focus has been placed upon the teacher's role as a member of an interdisciplinary team, yet this is a crucial role for teachers of chronically ill children.

Why is the health care team necessary? Why can't individual professionals perform their functions competently but separate from others? In fact, such separation of services is the reality in most settings, with little communication between specialists.

In addition, resources within the general community—schools, government agencies, and social service agencies—operate haphazardly in relation to one another and are rarely coordinated with the health team caring for a chronically ill child. As noted by the White House Conference on Children in 1970, such practices "fractionalize families to death" and provide fragmented, discontinuous services. DeBuskey (1970) also decries such fragmentation and calls for "orchestrated care" for the chronically ill child. It is generally agreed that the interdisciplinary health care team, when it functions effectively, is able to "bring together diverse skills and expertise to provide more effective better coordinated, better quality service for client" (Ducanis & Golin, 1979, p. 1).

Adequate care of a child with kidney disease and renal failure requires that the family resources be evaluated to determine the need for future financial and emotional supports; that the educational system be involved in alternate educational programming if the child is on a dialysis unit; that the dietitian has adequately reviewed the food and liquid intake requirements with patient and family. Monitoring maintenance of treatment and compliance and being alert to problems is greatly enhanced by effective communication by a team working together for the good of the patient. Teams can also function to identify needed services and assign responsibility to a particular team member to follow through with the identified goals, thus avoiding overlap of function or gaps in service.

If one holds that the child is a dynamic, interacting, integrated system, the team approach becomes a logical extension of that belief. Why, then, is the interdisciplinary team approach so difficult to achieve? A number of obstacles have been identified that may shed light on this question. They include lack of awareness of other professionals' specific competencies and roles; fear of encroachment by other professionals into territory seen as "owned" by a particular profession (e.g., a belief that only social workers deal with families or that only educators "teach" information); language barriers, especially in the field of medicine; and the rules and regulations imposed upon various professionals by the institutions that employ them.

REHABILITATION TEAM MEMBERS: ROLES

In order to help the educator deal more effectively with the professionals who serve as members of the rehabilitation team, reciprocal understanding of roles is necessary. This means that the educator working with the chronically ill child needs to be familiar with a variety of related professional roles, such as medicine, nursing, physical therapy, psychology, and child life. Descriptions of a selected list of such professions will be found at the end of this chapter.

Concomitant with the teacher's lack of knowledge of the roles of other health specialists are the health professionals' misperceptions of the roles that a teacher can and ought to play in the education of the chronically ill child. Health professionals often view teachers in their narrow role, related only to the classroom and the teaching of a structured curriculum. Yet increasingly, teachers are taking on the responsibilities of evaluator, assessing the child's abilities within the often changing context of their illness; referral agent, recognizing and referring for further evaluation many problems that occur as a result of illness or its treatment; and coordinator of services, especially in cases of long-term illness in which there are no centralized health care teams.

Teachers may be in a unique role in respect to children and their parents in that they have an opportunity to observe the children for extended periods of time, in relation to their classmates. "Further," as Mullins, (1979) sensitively points out, "they share with the child and parents many positive, enjoyable experiences that leave a residue of goodwill impossible for the professional who only sees the child in a context of pain, sickness, or anxiety" (p. 36).

In order for teachers of chronically ill children to be effective team members, they need both to recognize the expanded roles that they have come to play and to learn ways to communicate this information to the members of the health care team. This may be a difficult task, but it is one worth attempting in light of the obvious benefits to the children and their parents.

COMMUNICATION SKILLS

Communication is a term used frequently today to identify problems in the human relations arena. One hears a teacher's complaint that "the administration doesn't communicate with us enough" or the often repeated lament from nurses that "we take care of the patients eight hours a day, but no one tells us anything." Workshops and seminars are sponsored, with titles such as "How to Communicate More Effectively" or "You and Your Boss (or Employee): Are You Listening to Each Other?" Numerous books have been written on the subject. Clearly, this problem is of concern to many. Lack of communication often adds to the problems facing a team of health care professionals in caring for the chronically ill child.

While it is not within the scope of this book to provide a detailed investigation of the various communication models developed to understand this complex process, a few key issues that have direct relevance to the teacher's role as a team member will be explored and ways to aid communication will be identified. For a more detailed examination, the reader is referred to D.R. Klinzing and D.G. Klinzing (1977), *The Hospitalized Child*: *Communication Techniques for Health Personnel* and W. Schram (Ed.) (1963), *The Science of Human Communication*. The following summary has been adapted from Klinzing and Klinzing (1977).

Communication is a process, one that is dynamic and that involves the interaction of a number of variables. The first of these is the *speaker*. In order to be effective, the speaker must use appropriate ways to communicate. The credibility of the speaker and others' perceptions of the speaker's credibility can have a great effect on how the speaker's message is received. That *message*, which may be a mix of verbal and nonverbal communication, needs to be consistent.

A nurse who tells the teacher that the child's books will be put away in a safe place and then shrugs her shoulders, shakes her head, and rolls her eyes as if unable or unwilling to implement this may not inspire confidence in her message. Similarly, a teacher who is fearful and apprehensive around hospital equipment will not put the child at ease during a lesson, even if the teacher is explaining the work carefully. As A. Mehrabian (1971) notes, nonverbal signals may carry as much as 90 percent of the meaning of the message.

The way a message is sent also affects its potency as communication. Most people use voice and the written word to communicate, yet touch can be a helpful and supportive channel, especially when dealing with frightened children or anxious parents.

The *listener* is a vital component in the communication process. The listener can choose to listen or to ignore the speaker or to attend to only a portion of the message. Listeners often react to messages both verbally and nonverbally, thus affecting the communication process. These responses or feedback can be used to evaluate the communication process.

A number of factors can interfere with the communication process. Language barriers may seriously interfere with communication, especially among professionals who have various types of technical training or who are used to certain expressions. Examples abound in the hospital setting. The nurses, talking about a child who is dying, state that "he's going bad." The child's roommate, overhearing, is fearful of the implications of his own "bad" behavior. The physician talks to the teacher and parents about the child's condition but without regard for their lack of familiarity with medical jargon. Days later, the teacher still has no understanding of the child's condition or its implications and often feels embarrassed about requesting clarification. After all, the information has been communicated already, hasn't it?

Occasionally professionals use such language barriers as a way to increase their status and power among the team members, albeit unconsciously. The use of technical words can often intimidate a colleague from a different profession, thus affording the speaker a measure of control over the team's functioning. After all, how can you disagree with the doctor's decision not to discharge the patient, if you don't fully understand the doctor's reasons for the decision?

Status and power are often barriers to communication themselves. Nurses often fall into the trap of "ownership" of the ward or unit and may feel resentful of the teacher's or parent's presence or involvement in patient care.

This can seriously interfere with communication and can have the effect of alienating the teachers or parents so that they feel hesitant about spending time in the ward area.

The status conferred upon certain professional groups, such as physicians or psychologists, likewise affects their interaction in a team setting. Professionals with perceived high status may be deferred to by others, and their advice or statements may be taken at face value regardless of their true merit. Those professionals who view themselves as having high status or power may well function in a team setting in an authoritative or patronizing manner, thus intimidating or angering other team members.

The socialization process involved in training professionals also affects their functioning as team members (Levine, 1981). In the process of academic and clinical training, many unexamined assumptions are made, and many values are inculcated. Thus, physicians are trained to act as individuals, making life and death decisions independently, giving orders to others. Teachers are often trained to play the role of the only adult among a group of children, not just teaching, but also acting as group leader and role model. Sharing decisions and relinquishing power may be very difficult for people thus trained.

Sometimes, the teacher's lack of knowledge of the lines of authority or roles in an institution can impede communication. In one setting, the head nurse may be responsible for sharing information about a patient; in another, this may be the responsibility of the primary nurse, nursing supervisor, or physician.

The teacher may ask a passing nurse if a child is able to sit up in bed. Rushed and distracted, the "yes" answer given by the nurse may be against medical advice, and ten minutes later the primary nurse may observe the child sitting and proceed to berate both child and teacher.

In some hospitals, all referrals are coordinated for discharge planning by the social worker; in others, the teacher may be asked or expected to coordinate educational placements. Taking the time to determine the ownership of these functions may avoid unnecessary resentment or duplication of services.

When teachers are asked to share in the rehabilitation team's management plan, they may be expected to play a number of different roles. They may be asked to prepare and give a formal report of the child's academic functioning, or they may be expected only to listen to and give factual information; they may make recommendations and share in interpreting the child's behaviors. Sometimes they are expected to coordinate future services. It is difficult to guess what is expected. Further expectations are rarely voiced explicitly. Teachers may need to determine in advance what roles they are expected to play in order to avoid problems. They may need to develop clear lines of communication between themselves and a key hospital staff member, such as a social worker or child life specialist, in order to clarify their expected roles and functions in the team.

STRESS

Stress can also impede communication, and hospitals are by nature stressful settings. Patients are fearful and anxious, as are their families; nurses are often overworked and under constant pressure. The "life or death" atmosphere that often pervades hospitals adds to each professional's personal tension. Decisions made are often critical to the patient's future prognosis, and staff tend to look for causes when treatment plans fail. Often, in an effort to ease the guilt, blame is placed on others for "failing to do something" or for "doing something wrong."

The teacher, entering such a setting, may feel uncomfortable in the face of the tension, the medical setting, and the illness and pain that abound. No teacher training program ever includes the skills necessary to periodically help a child clear out a mucus-filled tracheotomy, nor does it help to prepare a teacher to view without flinching the open wounds of a burn. Teachers' fears of illness and teachers' reactions to medical settings can play an important part in their relative feelings of comfort or discomfort when assigned to teach in hospitals.

All of these factors can act as barriers to communication and can consequently interfere with coordinated programming for the child. The following guidelines may be helpful in overcoming some of these barriers and in increasing the effectiveness of home/hospital teachers:

- Collect all available pertinent information about the child before making contact with the health team.

- Arrange for a meeting that can take place in a private, nondistracting setting. (Discussing a child's medical history with a nurse who is tube feeding another child or writing in charts is not the optimal way to obtain information.)

- Clearly explain one's role, responsibilities, schedules, and obligations to the child, the parents, and the school system.

- Ask questions! Don't be afraid to appear ignorant or repetitive. Write down what has been told.

- Respect the priorities of the other health professionals and their assigned tasks. If it seems that bath time could be rescheduled to leave time for school, ask why bath time is scheduled for ten o'clock, rather than, "You can always bathe him later; I need to teach at ten." The latter statement assumes that bath time is easily rescheduled and not important, an assumption that may not be true and certainly one that will not be well taken.

- Leave written notes for staff if any follow-up is needed, such as supervising homework. Before leaving notes, ask where they are most likely to be noticed and read. A note placed in the child's nightstand is useless if no one checks the stand regularly.

- Find out the names and schedules of the child's primary therapists and caretakers for future contacts.

- Let the team members know what kinds of information they need to have. For example, they should know if the child begins any treatment that will affect attention span or state of awareness or if discharge is contemplated.

- Arrange for a way to be contacted if a child's schedule is changed, if it affects the teaching day or time. It can be frustrating for the teacher to rush from an appointment to a hospital, only to find that the child is in x-ray for the remainder of the day.

- Arrange for authorizations for release of medical information so that the school system can have access to the team's evaluations.

The home/hospital teacher is often expected to perform evaluations of the child's academic skills and related behaviors and abilities. Coordination with the health team's psychologist, speech pathologist, occupational therapist, and physical therapist becomes essential in performing a comprehensive evaluation. Often, these other professionals have valuable information to share, and they may shed light on reasons for a child's poor or dysfunctional performance on academic tasks. For example, children with severely limited motor ability may be able to comprehend arithmetic problems but may not be able to physically perform the mathematic functions. Children with a severe communication deficit may understand a great deal more than they are able to express verbally; revised tests may need to be developed to more accurately assess their true level of functioning. Such situations have particular relevance in children recovering from head trauma or suffering from a degenerative disease, in whom changes in motor or cognitive function are most common.

The development of an individualized educational plan (IEP) requires the cooperation of team members and can be used as a working, goal-oriented management plan for the team. Exhibit 10-1 gives examples of IEP goals developed for children with various chronic illnesses.

Exhibit 10-1 Examples of IEP Implementation by Related Services

Example 1: 12-year-old girl with severe seizures and moderate mental retardation and motor difficulties as a result of the seizures

Area	Problem	Goals
General health	Seizures	To control seizures through administration and monitoring of medications (medicine)
Gross motor	Ataxia	(1) To increase balance in sitting and walking (physical therapy 3 times weekly) (2) To adapt wheelchair for increased support and balance while sitting (physical therapy in consultation with education)
Psychology	Poor impulse control	To increase attention span and reduce distractibility by developing a behavior management program in consultation with education and nursing

Example 2: 16-year-old boy recovering from severe head trauma, presently at Level VI consciousness: confused, nonagitated

Area	Problem	Goals
General health	Brain trauma	To monitor recovery (medicine)
Gross motor	Right side paresis	To increase movement and strengthen right side by range of motion (physical therapy) Consultation with education to suggest ways to use right hand, supported, for beginning focused schoolwork

The team process, dependent as it is upon clear communication, coordination, sharing, and openness, remains a difficult objective to achieve, yet one that is increasingly necessary. This recognition of the necessity for teams arises as a result of a number of factors. Health costs continue to increase dramatically, and well-run teams can avoid undue duplication of services, thus lowering costs. The increasing number of specializations in health care necessitates centralized coordination of services. Finally, the increasing concern for the psychosocial needs of children in hospitals and health care settings is reflected in the pressures toward coordinated care such as can be provided by a team approach.

THE REHABILITATION TEAM: A WORKING MODEL

For the last three years, the multidisciplinary staff of Mt. Washington Pediatric Hospital has been using a formal team approach in its management of children with chronic illness. Each team consists of a physician, a social worker, a physical therapist, a psychologist, a speech pathologist, a nurse, a child life specialist, and a hospital-based city schoolteacher. The teams meet weekly and develop and review their management plans for each child biweekly. Patient problems are identified and long- and short-term goals are established and reviewed at each meeting. Team notes, summarizing each discipline's involvement with the patient and the ongoing problems and goals, are typed and distributed to the medical chart and all team members. Exhibit 10-2 represents an example of excerpts from notes of a child with diabetes.

As the team concept has evolved, the staff has been able to identify seven primary functions that the teams are performing, and team evaluations based upon these roles are conducted regularly to assess performance. The seven identified functions are:

1. to share assessment information in order to develop a total picture of the child
2. to develop a treatment plan for inpatient care and for discharge and follow-up services
3. to disseminate team information and patient management plans to patient care staff
4. to monitor day-to-day programming—i.e., to carry out the team plan
5. to continually assess team interaction
6. to provide continuing and interdisciplinary education of team members and staff
7. to monitor execution and effectiveness of team plan for discharge

In these teams, the hospital-based city teacher plays a role as an equal team member, sharing information with the team relevant to the child's academic needs and progress and acting as coordinator in finding an appropriate school placement for the child upon discharge. Such coordination can expedite a discharge and can provide for the child's smooth transfer from hospital to community.

Exhibit 10-2 Team Excerpts

A. Admission Discussion

Disciplines

Medicine: 7½-year-old black male admitted for control of juvenile diabetes mellitus. On 2,200 calorie ADA diet and taking 16 units NPH and 5 units R1 at breakfast. *Past Medical History*: Unremarkable. *Physical examination*: Unremarkable.

Psychology: To be evaluated.

Speech: To be evaluated.

Physical
  Therapy: To be evaluated.

Nursing: NPH 16 units and regular insulin 5 units at 8 A.M. q day. Administers insulin well for age. Lethargic upon admission.

Dietary: There is a need for patient and parent education. Suggest in-service training to aid in diabetic diet so adherence to the diet can be maintained.

Social Work: Lives with mother and 6 siblings; admitted to MWPH due to unsuccessful attempts to control his diabetes as an outpatient.

Education: Will contact his home school. Enroll him in hospital school, and assess academic and socialization skills.

Problems	*Goals*

1. Juvenile diabetes mellitus
  A. Teaching
  B. Control
	1. A. Nursing to work with parents and patient.
	  B. Adjusting the insulin dose according to urine testing (medicine).
	  200 calories ADA diet.

C. Poor compliance	C. Meet with mother (S.W., Nursing) and child (Child Life, S.W., and Nursing).
2. Mother's inappropriate reaction to condition	2. Meet with mother (S.W.)
3. Problems with vision	3. Vision screening
4. Assessments	4. To be assessed (All).

B. Team discussion, 4 weeks later

Disciplines

Medicine: Satisfactory control. Needs supervision.

Exhibit 10-2 continued

Nursing:	Tests urine well—needs to be reminded. Needs supervision in insulin administration—improving in preparing insulin. Still hesitant and at times refuses to give own injection. Complies with diet.
Psychology:	Evaluation is ongoing. His overall level of functioning is within the dull normal range. There are indications of emotional conflicts regarding interpersonal relationships and dependency needs. There are signs of depression. Continue with psychotherapy.
Speech:	Was seen for speech and language evaluation. Hearing—within normal limits bilaterally. Language—his overall language abilities were found to be below age level, commensurate with approximately the 5 year, 10 months level. Articulation—needs further evaluation. Consult with Psychology to compare cognitive ability with language level in order to make recommendations for placement.
Physical Therapy:	No active involvement.
Child Life:	No significant change. He attends all activities, but is often depressed and withdrawn.
School:	He still resists coming to school. He works well at times but is inconsistent.

C. Team discussion, 3 months later

Disciplines

Medicine:	9 units NPH, 4 units regular insulin each morning. Satisfactory control.
Child Life:	He is continuing in the recreation school program. Much more outgoing.
Psychology:	Individual time 1–2 sessions per week continues. Plans for psychotherapy after discharge have been arranged.
Physical Therapy:	No active involvement.
Speech:	No active involvement.
Dietary:	Good understanding of his diet but compliance is questionable.
Nursing:	Insulin has stabilized over past week. Still needs supervision giving insulin; occasionally draws up incorrectly. Injects well and uses all sites. Knows diet and will let staff know if he is served wrong foods by error. Tests urine well. Very excited about impending discharge.

Exhibit 10-2 continued

Social Work: He will be discharged home this Thursday. Follow-up will be provided. Homemaker is already in the home.

On-going Problems	Goals
1. Diabetes	1. Medical follow-up at _____ Hospital
2. Poor compliance	2. City Department of Social Services will assign worker to monitor.
3. Poor emotional reaction to illness	3. Arrange for outpatient psychotherapy (S.W. & Psych.)
4. Poor school attendance.	4. Arrange for Baltimore City chronic health impaired program to assign counselor (C.L.).

The team concept described earlier is still evolving, and its continued success depends upon hard work and cooperation, in spite of the many stresses and conflicts that are inherent in medical settings. Unfortunately, the majority of hospital teachers, homebound teachers, and teachers who educate children with chronic illness do not have access to such coordinated efforts. This makes the role of the professional educator complex and often emotionally demanding. The pressures inherent in teaching such a specialized population, often in noneducational settings, can quickly lead to stress and "burnout" for the educator.

STRESS: CARING FOR THE CAREGIVER*

In a study conducted among Baltimore City homebound/hospital teachers (Kleinberg, 1981) the single factor most frequently identified as stress-producing was the excessive amount of paper work involved. Also cited was the identified lack of communication among teachers, parents, and hospital and school staff, and the difficulty in setting up and adhering to schedules.

Some of these sources of stress may be reduced by teacher awareness of their existence and by putting some of the communication skills discussed earlier into practice. But high stress among public educators is a critical issue at this time. C. Kyriacou and S. Sutcliffe (1977) define teacher stress as a

---

*This section on stress and the special educator has been contributed by Deborah Meehling.

"response syndrome of negative affects (such as anger and depression) accompanied by potentially pathogenic physiological changes (such as increased heart rate, or release of adrenocorticotrophic hormone into the blood stream) as a result of the demands made upon the teacher in his role as a teacher" (p. 159). According to a survey conducted by the National Education Association (1967), 78 percent of the respondents believed they were working under moderate to considerable stress. In a recent poll conducted in San Diego County (Wilson, 1979), 90 percent of the teachers contacted reported experiencing moderate to high stress related to their jobs. Another 95 percent of this population indicated the need for stress management courses. Responsibility for the welfare of people, pressures to accomplish more than is possible, isolation in a work setting, low status, and involvement with people who are ill or dependent are all factors that have been identified as sources of stress (DeShong, 1981).

S. Truch (1980) identified two major sources of stress that teachers must face. The first is characterized by events specific to the teaching profession such as student behavior, time management, administrative relationships, and parent/teacher relationships. Stressors of this nature are comprehensively listed in the *Stress Profile for Teachers* (Wilson, 1979), which provides a measure of self-reported teacher stress.

The second source of teacher stress identified by Truch (1980) involves life events outside of teaching. Specific life events contributing to stress are listed and assigned point values in the Life Events Scale developed by T.H. Holmes and R.H. Rahe (1967). Examples of the more potent stressors include death of a spouse, divorce, or birth of a child. This scale is a good predictor of those individuals who might be more vulnerable to stress at a given time in their life.

One cannot ignore that individual differences among teachers have a tremendous effect on perceived stress from various stressors. Personality variables such as locus of control, self-esteem, and chronic level of anxiety certainly shape people's perception of the stressfulness attached to events in or out of their job. Other determinants such as age, sex, and family constellation all enter into the degree to which any one stressor will affect a person.

There is an obvious close association between job dissatisfaction and teacher stress. A major study of job satisfaction and dissatisfaction (Holdaway, 1978) indicates that teachers are most satisfied in areas of perceived control such as selecting teaching methods and structuring lessons. Teachers feel the least satisfaction in an area in which they appear to have little or no control, such as the attitude of society towards education.

For home/hospital teachers, this issue for the relationship between perceived control and personal stress is particularly salient. They usually work in noneducational settings in which teacher control may be even further minimized. Additionally, the child's emotional reactions to the illness or treatments may require that the teacher be unusually flexible in structuring academic tasks.

Manifestations of Stress

Distinctions between sources of stress and the manifestations of stress may be unclear—poor human relations between teachers may be the result of general work overload, and thus be considered manifestations of stress, or they may be sources of stress themselves.

The effects of stress can create serious problems for teachers in the emotional, behavioral, and/or physical domains. Emotional conditions may include depression, irritability, anxiety, yelling, excessive worrying, nightmares, apathy, nervousness, and emotional tension. Behavioral demonstrations of stress may be characterized by increased smoking, alcohol use, drug use, increased proneness to accidents, impulsive behavior, inability to concentrate, increased use of prescription medicines, tranquilizers, aspirin, and so forth. Physiological stress may result in cardiovascular disorders, such as high blood pressure, rapid heartbeat and heart disease, vascular headaches, muscle tension, and ulcers in the gastrointestinal tract. Physical illness, which is often considered a manifestation of stress, can become a source of stress, either directly because of concern over one's health or indirectly because of financial implications. Physical illnesses, emotional disorders, increased absences, and teacher turnover can be considered indicators of teacher stress whether they are the cause or the result.

Stress Management and Reduction

Recent research in the area of teacher stress clearly indicates the need for stress management and stress reduction techniques. No simple solutions have been discovered, but several researchers provide direction for stress management. S. Truch (1980) developed a program entitled R.E.A.D. for personal stress management. These initials stand for:

- R–deep relaxation
- E–regular exercise
- A–attitude and awareness
- D–diet

Specific guidelines for implementing this program are available in Truch's text, *Teacher Burnout and What To Do About It* (1980).

D.A. Girdano and G.S. Everly (1979) provide a comprehensive program for stress management and reduction that is designed for any individual who experiences personal physical or social maladaptation to stress. They first address social engineering, which refers to the willful altering of lifestyle and/or general environment to modify exposure to stressors. Examples include setting up goal alternatives and improving time management. The method of personality intervention refers to an altering of values, attitudes, and behavior patterns. Strategies are presented to enhance self-esteem, modify patterns of Type A behavior (behavior identified as relating to high stress), and reduce anxious reactivity. This text also provides descriptions and examples of more intense intervention techniques such as meditation, biofeedback, and relaxation training. Methods for implementation, activity worksheets, and self-assessment forms are also included.

Teacher stress is a complex subject. The sources of stress are many and stem from historical sources, current training procedures, social sources, and expectations about the role of the teacher. Teaching children with illnesses, in hospital settings, adds to this stress. Because solutions to teacher stress are not found in any one simple method, a multifaceted approach to stress management, including physical, behavioral, and social concerns, is needed. Managing personal and teaching stressors effectively is important in order to achieve more potential both as a teacher and as a human being. In order for teachers to effectively care for their students, they must first learn to care for themselves and to develop a network of supports for themselves so that they can open their arms, reach out, and help their students.

REHABILITATION TEAM MEMBERS: ROLE DESCRIPTIONS*

Profession: Medicine
Usual degree: Graduate of an accredited medical school, followed by postgraduate training of 0-5 years, depending upon the specialty. This training is referred to as a residency. Separate specialty boards are organized to certify physicians in a variety of settings.
Usual setting: Hospitals, health departments, schools, private practice
Among the specialties in medicine are the following:
Surgery
A general surgeon uses operative procedures to perform diagnosis/treatment. Although they may often use nonsurgical techniques to develop a diagnosis, surgeons are qualified to perform operations.

*The information for these descriptions was obtained from a survey of the various department heads at Mt. Washington Pediatric Hospital and from the following references: American Hospital Association: *Job Descriptions and Organizational Analysis for Hospitals and Related Health Services.* Washington, DC: U.S. Department of Labor, U.S. Government Printing Office, 1970; and *A Guide to Health Facilities, Personnel and Management*, R.N. Sloane and B.L. Sloane. St. Louis: C.V. Mosby Company, 1971.

Surgeons may focus on a class of patients, such as classified by age, as in pediatric neurosurgeons. Surgeons may evaluate the rehabilitation potential of a patient without recommending any operative procedure. In many instances of serious congenital deformities, such as spina bifida, surgeons from a number of specialties may follow the child for long periods of time, constantly reevaluating the need for surgery.

Neurology

This specialty studies the diseases of the nervous system. Often, neurologists work closely with neurosurgeons to follow patients with serious nervous system disorders.

Pediatrics

The pediatrician provides for the total care of children from birth through adolescence. Recently, as noted by Mullins (1979), it has been suggested that the field of adolescent medicine be established.

Physical medicine

This specialty, whose practitioners are known as *physiatrists*, involves the study of the muscles and the nerves. Heat, cold, light, electricity, hydrotherapy, exercise, and manipulation are among the physical means used for diagnosis and treatment. Physicians with this specialty usually work very closely with physical therapists and orthopedic specialists.

Dermatology

This specialty is concerned with the varieties of skin disease and its treatment.

Oncology

This specialty comprises physicians who study tumors, or new growths, and use the full range of treatments (surgery, medicine, and radiology) in their work.

Psychiatry

These specialists treat both organic and functional disorders of the mind. They work closely with psychologists, social workers, and others who share a counseling function. Psychiatrists are medically trained and are able to prescribe drugs as well as use other forms of treatment, such as individual or group therapy.

Pathology

These specialists perform visual, chemical, and microscopic examinations of tissues or body secretions to ascertain the presence of disease and its nature. Pathologists usually work within a clinical laboratory.

Radiology

Physicians trained in this area use radiation, fluoroscopes, and radiographic x-ray equipment to diagnose and treat disease. This specialty has grown in importance with the increased use of radiation therapy for treatment in cancer and the more sophisticated use of radiation technology in diagnosis (for example, the CAT scan).

Internal medicine

These are physicians who tend to treat patients with nonsurgical methods. Like the general practitioner, the internist usually sees patients on a long-term basis and may treat more than one body system. The training is more extensive, however, and internists may develop subspecialties in areas such as cardiology (heart), hematology (blood), allergies, gastroenterology (intestines, stomach, liver, and gall bladder), chest diseases (especially concerning the lungs), and endocrinology (glands and hormones).

Usual battery of tests and assessments:

History and physical examination, followed by chemical and cytologic (cell) examination of various body fluids and tissues, x-rays, EEG (electroencephalogram), and other medical or laboratory evaluations.

Usual treatment modalities: Individual therapy

Profession: Nursing

Usual degree: A registered nurse (R.N.) must be a graduate of an accredited school of nursing and have passed a state board qualifying examination. Nurses may have either an A.A. (associate arts) degree, or a B.A. (baccalaureate). A licensed practical nurse (L.P.N.) must be a high school graduate with 9–15 months study in a state-approved program and must be state-board certified. L.P.N.s must work under the supervision of a registered nurse or physician.

Usual settings: Hospitals, health care settings, schools, as members of visiting nurse associations, public health clinics, nursing homes

Usual battery of tests and assessments:

History, vital signs (such as temperature, blood pressure, pulse), observations

Usual treatment modalities:

Individual therapy or care, under the orders of a physician. Nurses cannot prescribe drugs or give medications without written physician's orders.

Nursing assistants may function in hospitals as aides, but they are not licensed or registered, cannot give medications, and must be supervised by a registered nurse. Often, they perform essential physical care routines.

Profession: Occupational therapy (OT)

Usual degree: Bachelor's degree from an accredited occupational therapy program, 6–9 months clinical experience in a variety of health care settings. O.T.s must pass a national examination as well.

Usual settings: Hospitals, rehabilitation centers, schools, health departments, residential settings

Usual battery of tests and assessments:
Fine motor evaluations, activities of daily living, assessments of oral-motor areas, prevocational skills, sensorimotor integration

Usual type of treatment modalities: Developmental therapy; functional training in skills such as dressing, feeding, hand coordination; adaptation of equipment; individual and group recreational programs to foster recovery.

Profession: Rehabilitation counseling

Usual degree: B.A. from an accredited rehabilitation program. Currently, general mental health counselors may also provide rehabilitation counseling.

Usual settings: Hospitals, rehabilitation centers, health clinics, vocational rehabilitation centers

Usual battery of tests and assessments:
May use interviews, observations, variety of vocational and prevocational assessment scales

Usual type of treatment modalities:
Individual or group counseling

Profession: Recreational therapy

Usual degree: B.S. in recreational therapy, with clinical field placement

Usual settings: Hospitals, specialized schools or residential settings, recreation and parks facilities, nursing homes

Usual assessments:
Interviews, observations of recreational and leisure skills

Usual treatment modalities: Group programming to provide adaptive recreational experiences, leisure activity pursuits, crafts, and socialization skills

Profession: Child life

Usual degree: B.S. in a field related to child development, psychology, education, or child life. This profession is relatively young, and only a few colleges nationally offer a child life curriculum. Field experience is usually substituted for a specific core curriculum.

Usual settings: Hospitals, outpatient clinics

Usual assessments: Observations, developmental evaluations of child's emotional, cognitive, educational, and socialization skills (this may be done in conjunction with other health professionals)

Usual treatment modalities: Individual or group programming for hospitalized children in playrooms or at bedside. Programs can include presurgical or preadmittance tours, preparation for treatments, play as therapy, and the provision of normal or adaptive social, educational, and recreational programs.

In many settings, the roles of child life, occupational therapists, and recreational therapists are overlapping, and responsibilities are either shared or designated.

Profession: Physical therapy

Usual degree: Presently B.S. (150 credits) with 2 years undergraduate and 3 years professional experience, but by 1990 will require M.S. for entry level, plus 3–4 years internship

Usual settings: Hospitals (acute, chronic, and rehab), private practice, schools, industry, health departments, special centers (trauma and burn), residential centers (adult and pediatric), neonatal ICU

Usual battery of tests and assessments:

Gross motor/fine motor reflexes; sensation; range of motion (ROM); postural analysis; muscle tone and strength, oral motor; soft signs; activities of daily living; adaptive/assertive and orthotic/prosthetic tests; pulmonary function

Usual types of treatment modalities:

Developmental therapy; postural drainage and breathing exercises; muscle strengthening and joint ROM; automatic movement/perceptual motor training; functional training (ADL); design and fabrication of adapted equipment; training in application, care, and use of orthotic/prosthetic devices; oral-motor function in motor-impaired child

Profession: Psychology

Usual degree: M.A., minimum; Ph.D. generally required.

Usual settings: Private office, clinical setting, hospitals, mental health clinics, colleges

Usual battery of tests and assessments:

These vary with age of child and reason for referral. Assessments include development, intellectual, personality. Techniques include use of Bayley scales, Cattell, observation, Wechsler scales, Stanford-Binet, projective techniques.

Usual types of treatment modalities:

Individual and group counseling and psychotherapy, use of behavioral therapies, consultation for management through team approach (multidisciplinary)

Profession: Clinical social work

Usual degree: Masters in social work with a major in clinical social work, and clinical experience. Social workers must pass an examination to become registered.

Usual settings: Hospitals, family service agencies, department of social services, mental health settings, schools, residential facilities

Usual battery of tests and assessments:

Assessment is mainly done by interview. There is some use of marriage inventories, etc.

Usual types of treatment modalities: Individual therapy, including children and adults, couple therapy, family therapy, group therapy

Profession: Clinical dietetics

Usual degree: B.S. with internship or B.S. with Masters or B.S. in C.U.P. program. B.S. can be in home economics, food and nutrition, or human ecology. A registration exam is usually required.

Usual settings: Hospitals, nursing home, restaurants, private consultation, schools, colleges, and consultant to many areas

Usual battery of tests and assessments:

Diet history as recalled by patient; Anthropometric measurement (height, weight, head circumference); lab testing

Usual types of treatment modalities:

Usually one-to-one instruction; classes for groups, such as diabetic class, heart class, etc.

Profession: Speech pathology

Usual degree: Masters degree in speech pathology from an accredited program, plus 9 months practical supervised experience and the satisfactory completion of a qualifying examination

Usual settings: Hospitals, schools, clinical service centers, health departments, private practice

Usual diagnostic tests and assessments: Developmental history; standardized articulation tests; standardized tests to assess communication skills; aphasia, voice disorders; oral-motor assessments

Usual treatment modalities: Individual therapy, group therapy in small groups

Profession: Audiologist

Usual degree: Masters degree in audiology, 9 months supervision in a clinical setting, plus passage of a qualifying examination

Usual settings: Hospitals, schools, clinics, health departments, private practice

Usual diagnostic tests: Tests of auditory sensitivity, behavioral conditioning techniques, behavioral observation procedures, electrophysiological technique, tests of auditory discrimination ability

Usual treatment modalities: Audiology evaluation, audiology selection and evaluation of hearing aids, audiology habilitation (individual or group)

SUMMARY

This chapter has examined the role of the educator as a team member, identifying the ever increasing number of functions that the teacher of chronically ill children is expected to perform. It would seem from these various and varying roles—teacher, coordinator, referral agent, evaluator, clerk, parent confidante, child advocate—that what is called for is a superperson, one who, in DeShong's (1981) words, has "magic coping skills" (p. 5). Yet teachers are human and vulnerable to stress; hence, they need support and care if they are to give support and care in return. Recognizing the demands that these roles entail, this chapter briefly reviewed stress, its effects, and some techniques for its management.

REFERENCES

Debuskey, M. (Ed.). *The chronically ill child and his family.* Springfield, IL: Charles C Thomas, 1970.

DeShong, B.R. *The special educator: Stress and survival.* Rockville, MD: Aspen Systems Corp., 1981.

Ducanis, A.J., & Golin, A.K. *The interdisciplinary health care team.* Rockville, MD: Aspen Systems Corp., 1979.

Girdano, D.A., & Everly, G.S. *Controlling stress and tension: A holistic approach.* Englewood Cliffs, NJ: Prentice-Hall, 1979.

Holdaway, E.A. Teacher satisfaction: An Alberta report. Edmonton, Alberta: University of Alberta, Department of Educational Administration, 1978.

Holmes, T.H., & Rahe, R.H. The social readjustment rating scale. *Journal of Psychosomatic Research,* 1967, *11*, 213–218.

Klinzing, D.R., & Klinzing, D.G. The hospitalized child: Communication techniques for health personnel. Englewood Cliffs, NJ: Prentice-Hall, 1977.

Kyriacou, C., & Sutcliffe, S. Teacher stress: A review. *Educational Review,* 1977, *29*(4), 299–306.

Levine, L. Symposium, ACCH, 1981.

Mehrabian, A. *Silent messages.* Belmont, CA: Wadsworth, 1971.

Mullins, J.B. *A teacher's guide to management of physically handicapped students.* Springfield, IL: Charles C Thomas, 1979.

National Education Association. Teacher's problems. *Research Bulletin,* 1967, *45*, 116–117.

Schram, W. (Ed.). The science of human communication. New York: Basic Books, 1963.

Truch, S. *Teacher burnout and what to do about it.* Novato, CA: Academic Therapy Publications, Inc., 1980.

White House Conference on Children. Washington, DC: U.S. Government Printing Office, 1970.

Wilson, C. Stress profile for teachers. Survey conducted in San Diego County, San Diego, California, Department of Education, 1979.

Chapter 11

Changing Attitudes:
Teacher as Advocate

OVERVIEW

Throughout this book, an attempt has been made to provide teachers with helpful tools in their efforts to educate chronically ill children. However, educators' increased understanding of medical conditions and educational strategies alone are not sufficient to assure this population appropriate, equal educational opportunity. Chronically ill children are a uniquely vulnerable population. Weakened by their various illnesses and their treatments, chronically ill children are often further handicapped by fragmented educational services and by systems that are unable or unwilling to adapt to their needs. Families that are burdened emotionally, financially, and physically are often unable to assume the added task of advocating for their children within the educational system. Given such a set of circumstances, the role of teachers who serve chronically ill children must necessarily expand to include advocacy for the rights of such children. As F.J. Weintraub and M.A. McCaffrey (1976) note:

> The professional who works with the vulnerable child must be an advocate for the child thus reducing the vulnerability. Failing to assume responsibility, the professional can only play the role of participant in whatever injustice may befall the child and assume any corresponding liability. There is no passive role possible for the professional who serves exceptional children. (p. 333)

This often places teachers in a difficult situation in which the needs of the child and the demands of the educational system are at odds with each other (Weintraub & McCaffrey, 1976). When the constraints of the health system are added to this picture, the pressures upon teachers increase even more. In

265

such circumstances, the reluctance of teachers to "get involved," to "make waves" is understandable, although unfortunate.

The very term, *advocacy*, evokes strong reactions and has come to take on many meanings. For some, advocacy has come to mean taking strong, vocal, public stands in support of the rights of children with special needs. For others, advocacy is viewed as a way of providing support to parents and children through a continuous and cooperative mediating process between the family and the institution or health system (McLouglin, McLouglin, & Stewart, 1979).

Common to all the descriptions of advocacy roles is the recognized need for those professionals who are knowledgeable about the issues to take some role in effecting change for the better. The following section takes the position that the role of advocate is a vital component of a teacher's professional duties and suggests ways to provide such essential support to the child and family without threatening the educational system. Viewed in this way, advocacy can be seen as another component of the teacher's array of educational strategies. Four aspects of advocacy will be explored. They include: (1) gaining the recognition of the special needs of the chronically ill child and obtaining appropriate help for the child so that education can occur in the least restrictive setting; (2) helping to change attitudes of classmates toward the chronically ill child; (3) overcoming personal biases and those of colleagues that may interfere with the appropriate education of the child; and (4) providing general community education around the issues of illness and hospitalization.

FACILITATING SCHOOL REENTRY

Children with chronic illnesses often have accompanying learning difficulties. They may be those associated with the illness directly, such as brain damage due to head trauma. They may be the result of treatments given or time lost from regular school programs, or they may be unrelated problems. Whatever the cause, children with chronic illnesses may need to be screened and evaluated for special education services. The erratic nature of their school attendance often causes these children to "fall through the cracks" in the educational system, thus further impeding their academic progress. The home/hospital teacher may need to play the role of advocate, monitoring the child's school progress and requesting screening for special services if needed.

At times, children are placed on home teaching and remain on the home teaching rolls for extended periods, regardless of their improved medical status. Many factors contribute to this delay, and each needs to be recognized and addressed by the homebound teacher. Parents or children may be fearful of the risks if they return to school and may consequently slow down the screening or reentry process.

Irene, a 14-year-old girl with recurrent bouts of sickle cell anemia, became increasingly fearful of social interactions outside the hospital or home and began refusing to attend school on days when she was physically well. Her mother had difficulty rejecting any of her demands and requested home teaching. The home teacher became increasingly frustrated by Irene's lack of motivation to return to school. Often, Irene would exaggerate her pain or weakness in order to avoid any suggestion by the home teacher that she was now well enough to attend school. To resolve this dilemma, the home teacher set up a conference with the girl's physician and asked that a hospital social worker be invited as well. At this conference, the home teacher presented a detailed appraisal of Irene's reasons for avoiding school and recommended that Irene receive counseling services. Irene's physician was persuaded by the presentation and concurred with the recommendation. Counseling was initiated. The home teacher then arranged for Irene to have a few classmates visit her at home with school projects that required group efforts. Gradually, Irene gained enough confidence in her social skills and was able to return to school with few absences.

The key role played here by the home teacher as advocate and coordinator enabled Irene to reenter school and allowed the home teacher to direct her teaching time to other children who were physically unable to attend school.

Waiting lists for screening and placement may further impede the reentry process. Often, a vicious cycle is set in motion when a long awaited placement is found, only to have the child relapse, return to the hospital, and lose the placement to another child.

Such was the case with Billy, an 8-year-old boy with severe asthma and a moderate language deficit. Academically, he required a special school placement in a self-contained class that focused on the remediation of language disorders. There were not enough classes in the city to accommodate all the children with this need, however, and Billy's place was not held for him during an extensive hospitalization in early October. The hospital school teacher conferred with Billy's mother, and both agreed to appeal this decision and to request a placement for Billy that would be held open for the whole school year. The hospital teacher obtained documentation of Billy's need for language services from the hospital psychologist and speech pathologist and a medical report on Billy's asthmatic condition from the hospital physician. Both strongly supported the teacher's request for placement. A placement was opened for Billy as a result of such advocacy, and Billy was able to attend school with only a few absences for the remainder of the school year. This was made possible by further coordination of services. The physician arranged to have Billy and his mother participate in an asthma training program to help him control most of his attacks without emergency room care. He also provided a packet of information to the teacher to enable her to recognize Billy's early wheezing and arrange for him to practice his special breathing and exercise techniques in the health suite.

Files transferred between school, hospital school, and home/hospital services offices may be misplaced, and the child may thus be in limbo, receiving no services, lost to the system. Although it is difficult to prevent such an occurrence, a phone call made to the school or program that a child is being transferred to will serve to alert the staff to look for the child's records. Records should always be sent to a specific person, rather than merely the building address, so that the teacher can call and check up on their safe arrival.

Sometimes, broken wheelchairs or homes inaccessible to bus service are the sources of delay. The home teacher may need to play the role of coordinator to facilitate the delivery of these noneducational but essential services. A referral to the local social service department may be necessary to help the family find appropriate housing or financing for medical support services.

A child with low energy levels may benefit from the peer interaction and academic programs in a school setting if the teacher can arrange for a shortened school day or a private place for the child to rest for periods in school. The benefits to the child may well be worth the added effort it takes to make such arrangements. What is required is a concerned, dedicated teacher willing to advocate for the child, a lot of perseverance, and the knowledge that such efforts do make a substantive difference.

Advocating for a child on the hospital or homebound rolls can be time-consuming and frustrating to the teacher. A carefully worked out plan may be undermined by a parent who is not in agreement with its goals or by the sudden recurrence of a chronic illness. Such setbacks often create a mood of helplessness and failure on the teacher's part. It is at these times that the hospital/homebound teacher needs the support of a peer group.

Too often, as F. Connor (1964) notes, "the home/hospital teacher is deemed the school district's expert and is expected to work, quite unsupported at maximum efficiency with neverfaltering high morale" (p. 23). Regular meetings held for a school district's homebound/hospital teachers can serve to provide them with fresh ideas and suggestions for difficult problems. Such meetings can also provide an opportunity for teachers to develop new skills in advocating for change.

For the regular classroom teacher, advocacy may involve the role of evaluator and referral agent for the chronically ill child. The sensitive teacher may be able to recognize the early signs of a learning disability or the beginnings of a severe psychological reaction brought on by the child's response to the trauma of illness or treatment. Early warning signs such as abrupt behavior changes, a sudden drop in test scores, withdrawal, or depression can be identified by the alert teacher. A parent conference or a phone call to the child's physician may expedite a referral for treatment for the child.

CHANGING PEER ATTITUDES

The successful reentry of a chronically ill child into a school program often depends upon the support and cooperation of the child's schoolmates. Social isolation and lack of peer interaction remain as serious negative consequences of extended home teaching. The resulting fear and hesitancy on the part of chronically ill children to reengage socially is often reinforced by peers who either isolate them or tease them regarding their disability. By developing strategies that can sensitize classmates and thus change their attitudes, the classroom teacher can play a key role in the successful reintegration of the chronically ill child into the regular class setting.

Negative reactions to chronically ill children have their roots in a number of sources. Lack of knowledge as to the causes of illness often leads to misconceptions and fear. Children and adolescents may mistakenly assume that many diseases are contagious, especially diseases that cause coughing or rashes. Epilepsy has long been erroneously associated with mental retardation or "craziness," and its victims may consequently be avoided or teased.

The strong pressure exerted by peers to look, act, and perform alike further alienates chronically ill children, especially if their disabilities are visible. Differentness in any form is suspect, and weakness is often ridiculed. This creates a dilemma for children with conditions that are debilitating or that are exacerbated by strenuous exercise. Refusal to participate leads to teasing or isolation, while participation often leads to further illness. Such pressure to conform often comes from the peer group's uncertainties as to their own abilities. In their efforts to match themselves against their ideal image, their tolerance for differentness in others is greatly reduced.

There is also a cultural bias against illness or debility. In a society that glorifies beauty, health, and physical fitness, illness is often associated with weakness. There is often a "lack of sympathy for the ill: an unspoken assumption that a correct lifestyle would confer immunity from health problems" (Beuf, 1979, p. 114). For children, some of this bias may stem from an unspoken fear of being a victim of the disease themselves. This is often reflected in the questions school-age children ask when discussing various diseases. Typical are comments such as "Can I get it too?"; "Does it hurt?"; "How do you know if you have it?"; "What does it feel like?"; and "Could you die?"

The classroom teacher needs to address these concerns directly in order to effect attitude change. This can be done by increasing students' general knowledge about disease, illness, and its effects and by helping them to explore and clarify their attitudes toward illness. In the following section, some ideas and suggestions will be presented. They are by no means inclusive but are meant to be used as examples of possible learning activities. Hopefully, they will stimulate the reader to expand and develop a whole range of fresh curriculum ideas.

Knowledge of Disease and Illness

General knowledge can come from many sources. For preschoolers or young school-age children, hands-on experiences offer the most fruitful avenue for increasing their knowledge base. Play with dolls that can be casted or fitted with tracheotomies allows for open discussion about the reasons such treatments are needed. Preparation for the reentry of a classmate with a similar condition often allows the teacher to answer many questions before the child's actual arrival. Crutches, wheelchairs, and jobst garments can be made available as well. Children can take turns using these devices and begin to understand the difficulties that face a child who must use crutches or a wheelchair in order to get around. Unusual casts or prosthetic devices may at first frighten the young child. In such instances, staff from the hospital may be able to visit the class, bringing along a model of the appliance. The class can freely examine it, asking questions and expressing fears before the affected child returns to school. In one example, a young first grader was entering a new class with a Hoffman device in place around his leg. This device consists of a metal frame with pins that enter the leg and bone, thus holding the bone in place. Although the pins do not hurt after insertion, their placement and appearance can be quite frightening to a child. The social worker assigned to the hospital's orthopedic unit visited the class with a sample Hoffman device in place, in a plastic model of a leg. She passed around the appliance, explaining its purpose and answering all questions. After such initial exposure, the class reaction to the young patient was warm and welcoming. They showed only mild curiosity about the device, rather than fear or disgust.

Book corners with appropriate reading matter can be used effectively as discussion-starters for many children. Commercially available videotapes that discuss different illnesses are also good introductions to class discussions. Family Communication's Mr. Rogers Tapes and Susan Linn's puppet tapes are two excellent sources of commercial packages (Family Communications, 1976; Linn, 1980).

Older school-age children may enjoy building models representing human anatomy, thus discovering firsthand how the heart and respiratory system operate or what the consequences could be when the spinal column is injured or severed.

Explanations of the effects of diabetes using models or drawings can help children to understand why their classmate cannot eat candy and cake. Likewise, explanations about seizures may make children more understanding and less likely to be frightened by an epileptic classmate.

Textbook materials can be revised, and diseases can be studied as part of general curriculums of health, biology, or science. Guest speakers can be invited into class to share information about the latest research in the field, or classes can make field trips to science centers or research facilities.

Preparing a class for the reentry of a chronically ill child should be done with the cooperation of the child, the child's parents, and the health team. The child and family must give their permission before confidential information can be shared with the class. Often, they can be encouraged to participate in class preparation. This allows them some measure of control over the content and form of the preparatory materials and provides the ill child with an opportunity to be a part of the reentry process. Photographs of the child, especially if the illness or accident resulted in an alteration of appearance, can be helpful. Tape recordings of messages from ill children, explaining their disease and introducing or reintroducing themselves to the class, can act as a social icebreaker.

Exploring Attitudes

Increasing a classmate's fund of information about disease can be invaluable in helping the chronically ill child readjust to a class setting. Equally vital is an exploration of the attitudes held by classmates. The teacher needs to provide an opportunity for classmates to recognize their own attitudes toward disease and illness in order to establish a climate of acceptance or support in the classroom. Simply being told the facts about a disease and encouraged to "be nice" to the ill child may not be sufficient motivation for change on the part of a classmate. On a practical level, a class could be encouraged to figure out the consequences of different diseases and urged to find solutions for problems encountered. Instead of chronically ill children being seen as different or as a burden, their problems are thus taken on by the whole class. The class begins to be a part of the process and becomes invested in finding solutions. The chronically ill child in such a setting is likely to be more readily accepted into the group. Classes encouraged in this manner often come up with imaginative solutions. One class discussed alternate party ideas so that their diabetic classmate would not be excluded from the routine cake and ice cream parties. Their solution was to set up a party fund and serve diet soda, regular soda, fruit, and cheese at all parties. In another class an imaginative math project developed out of the need to make the class barrier-free for a child in a wheelchair. The class began by measuring their own aisles and doorways and rearranging furniture to make their classroom barrier-free. They then decided to explore their whole school, checking it out for architectural barriers. This project expanded in the context of studying their community. Along with an examination of the goods and services provided by neighborhood stores and the careers of neighborhood workers, they began to evaluate their community in terms of its accessibility to wheelchairs. Armed with rulers and determination, this group of third graders became active advocates for the physically handicapped.

Other problems have been met with equally creative solutions. One class set up a "cough corner" for a peer with cystic fibrosis; another discussed job assignments to help a friend go through the cafeteria line with crutches. Classes can be assigned to figure out alternative ways for children with a physical handicap to do their regular classwork.

This elementary form of task analysis not only helps the physically handicapped child, but it is a valuable educational tool for the class. It encourages problem solving rather than simple memory and recall and such learning sets can be carried over into other learning experiences.

On a more general level, empathy can be increased by means of role play sessions, in which the class takes on temporarily the disability under discussion. "Trust walks" with blindfolds to simulate vision loss or ear plugs for hearing loss help a child to understand the pitfalls of sensory deprivation better than any text or film. For less obvious disabilities, the class can be assigned to research a disease and then write an essay on how such a disease could affect their daily life. Using a child who has the disease as an "expert consultant" increases social acceptance and helps to break down barriers. In conditions such as epilepsy, where public misconceptions are rampant, a class may take on the task of inventing a public relations campaign. Posters, television or radio ads, and newspaper articles can all be developed by the class as part of their own education project. Such projects can cross many subject areas. Research into famous people with similar disabilities can be a part of a history or social science curriculum; art or writing courses can incorporate this material; science activities can center around the physiology of the brain, or the effects of certain drugs and medications on the body. Research around fire, fire prevention, and the effects of burns can increase a class's empathy for a severely burned peer and help them to overcome the feelings of shock upon seeing the severe distortions caused by the aftereffects of burns.

These and other ideas can be generated by the teacher or class in preparation for the reentry of a disabled student. Students whose illness necessitates frequent absences face the added problem of cyclical reentry and have to face the difficulties of adjustment and acceptance over and over again. These children are forever out of step with the class, unsure of the nature of the work assigned, unfamiliar with a new subject just introduced. Self-paced education packets, when available, are helpful in overcoming much of this problem. Children can take up where they left off and can often do their work at home or in the hospital. When group-paced programs are unavoidable, scheduled absences can be planned for with long-term projects. If a child is absent regularly for outpatient therapy, clinic appointments, or dialysis, the teacher may be able to restructure lesson plans so that no tests are administered on that day and no new material is introduced. At times, team projects can be planned so that children who are sick can do their part at home, and teams can take up the slack for missed work. A child should have a friend assigned to take home schoolwork and return finished work the next day. Although many children may volunteer to help in this way, the teacher needs to coordinate the plan. Children often forget to stop by their friend's class for work at the end of the day. The teacher needs to develop a mechanism for getting the work to the friend to avoid the inevitable guilt on the friend's part and annoyance on the part of the sick child.

OVERCOMING TEACHER BIAS

If classroom teachers are to be successful in changing the attitudes of classmates toward a chronically ill child, they must first identify their own biases and negative attitudes. A number of concerns raised by teachers when faced with having a chronically ill child in class are realistic, while others are based less on the problem and more on the teacher's fears or biases.

Teachers are often expected to meet the needs of 25 or 30 or more children simultaneously. With so many pressing demands, it becomes difficult to think about one child's schedule for medicines, another's need for supervision for periodic self-catheterization. Fear of a child's sudden seizure or weakness adds to the teacher's distractions. There may also be the fear of doing the wrong thing and thereby hurting a child, as in lifting a child with brittle bones, or supervising a hemophiliac in a rowdy class or at recess. "I'm not a doctor or nurse; I wasn't trained to differentiate wheezing from heavy breathing, or recognize the beginnings of insulin shock or diabetic coma." Such concerns are often legitimate. Often, however, the underlying fears are not just related to concerns for the child's safety but represent concern regarding legal liability. In the increasingly complex litigious society of the 20th century, the specter of malpractice suits is being raised in relation to teachers. Unfortunately, the educator's response to such issues is often fear and defensiveness, a wish to avoid potential legal problems instead of becoming more aware of the issues and the teacher's legal rights and responsibilities (Weintraub & McCaffrey, 1976). Many teachers are presently protected by some form of liability insurance. For example, members of the National Education Association (NEA) receive the protection of an educator's employment liability policy as part of their membership (Axelrod & Bailey, 1979).

The issue of the legality of giving medication to children is the most common one that faces regular and special educators. There are legal and ethical issues involved in dispensing medications, and guidelines are often fuzzy or nonexistent (Haslam & Valetutti, 1975).

Most liability policies do not include protection when administering medications in nonemergency situations, and teachers are realistically hesitant. The reasons for concern raised in regard to teacher administration of medicines include: (1) local and/or state statutes that may prohibit the administration of medication by non-nursing staff; (2) the possibility of teacher error in giving a wrong dosage or forgetting to administer a dosage on time; (3) the child who may react to a drug adversely (Axelrod & Bailey, 1979). S. Axelrod and S.L. Bailey (1979) recommend a set of guidelines that they identify as representing a "minimal level of prudence" (p. 548). They strongly recommend that the teacher obtain legal advice or a statement regarding liability coverage. The guidelines outlined recommend:*

1. A copy of the doctor's prescription should be on file containing at least the date of prescription, name and dosage of drug, specific time to be administered, and prescription expiration if applicable.
2. A statement of the purpose for administering the drug should be on file.
3. The file should contain a form from the parent(s) requesting that medication be given during school hours for a specified duration of time. The form should be renewed at least annually or sooner, especially if major changes occur (e.g., class placement).
4. Medication should be sent to the school only via a responsible adult. Drugs should never be accepted if sent to school via the child.
5. Medication should be fresh, clearly identified, labeled with the child's name and dosage, and kept in a secure location.
6. Medicine that is not going to be immediately administered should not be kept in the classroom (e.g., a week's worth of medication should not be stockpiled in the teacher's desk).
7. Whenever medication is administered a precise record should be kept of the child's name, medication's name, dosage administered, exact time given, and signature of the person administering the drug. (p. 549)

---

*Source: Reprinted from "Drug treatment for hyperactivity: Controversies, alternatives, and guidelines" by S. Axelrod and S. Bailey with permission of Council for Exceptional Children, © 1979.

Teachers should be aware of their school district's policies regarding medications and help families work out solutions to problems regarding the dispensing of medicine during school hours. The difficulty in dispensing proper medication in a legal way should not be the cause for denying a child school placement.

It is easy to refuse admittance to an ill child on the basis of concerns over the child's safety or health, the teacher's excessive workload, or legal red tape. Too often, the teacher or administrator fails to see the child, looking only at the handicap. As Lubin notes (1975), "to see the child behind the handicap, we must first become aware of the feelings aroused by the handicap" (p. 268). The home-hospital teacher or health professional may feel anger at a teacher or administrator who refuses admittance to a chronically ill child, citing potential hazards for the child of poor supervision, the lack of a barrier-free environment, or the negative reactions of the other children. Many of the reasons cited may be smokescreens for the staff's fear of dealing with a handicapped child and are often based upon the same misconceptions, fears, and stereotypes present in the students. At times, these biases can interfere with the ability of the teacher or administrator to find solutions to the legitimate concerns raised. An advocate who reacts with anger or annoyance at such responses often fails to make headway and may even harden the negative reactions voiced by the teachers or administrators, who then fall back onto bureaucratic dogma to reinforce their stance. A sensitive advocate needs to (1) recognize the fear behind the voiced concerns, (2) help the classroom teacher or administrator to sort out realistic problems from imagined ones by sharing facts and information about the condition, and (3) help to develop a step-by-step approach to solving the realistic problems that act as barriers to the child's reintegration into school. Some guidelines to follow include:

1. Setting up a meeting to include all those professionals who are or will be involved with the child. The classroom teacher as well as the school principal should be present, to avoid the possibility that the principal will accept responsibility for a task that the teacher cannot perform and to ensure that all parties have voiced their concerns openly. School nurses should be present if any task is to be assigned to them.
2. Listing all possible problems to be addressed. This provides an opportunity for the school staff to vent feelings and may bring to light concerns or problems that may not have occurred to the home teacher or health professional.
3. Dealing with one problem at a time. Each problem needs to be looked at separately, with tasks assigned to a specific person or persons. The nurse-educator from the hospital or clinic may need to be present to explain a treatment procedure or review a special diet or limitations.

4. Relaying all information verbally and in writing. This could include general information regarding the child's condition as well as specific care instructions.
5. Providing a starter set of any special treatment equipment needed, such as gauze pads, lifesavers, disposable bags, and so forth. School systems are always financially squeezed, and the hospital and/or family needs to provide any equipment required, at least until the school can obtain its own supplies. Providing an extra set of clothes or underwear for a child who may be incontinent is always helpful.
6. Providing backup systems and resources for the school, to avoid any crises due to unexpected problems.
7. Agreeing to a trial period, with a 30- and 60-day review date to meet and tie up any loose ends.

With good, effective communication skills and the ability to work as a team member, the advocate can often ensure the successful reentry of the child.

GENERAL COMMUNITY EDUCATION

The previous section suggested ways for the teacher to help support a chronically ill child by preparing the child's classmates and teachers, as well as reorganizing the physical environment to accommodate the child's special needs. Such preparation is essential to create a welcome, safe, and supportive setting for the chronically ill child.

But children's knowledge of hospitals and illness need not be predicated upon their own or their classmates' hospitalization or illness. In fact, hospitals can be stimulating and exciting centers of learning for children of different ages. As Elizabeth Crocker (1975) notes:

> Hospitals are fascinating places where lots of interesting things happen. They're much more than doctors and nurses and pain. However, because one rarely has contact with a hospital outside a patient/visitor context, one doesn't have the opportunity to look at hospitals in a broad and objective light and see the complete picture of all that hospitals are. Not having the chance to experience hospitals in a non-threatening way or in a context other than patient/ visitor can lead to the development of fears, myths, misconceptions and unnecessary anxieties about the hospitals. (p. 3)

The inclusion of the hospital as a course of study for school groups is becoming more prevalent today. In the following section, Elizabeth Crocker*

Source: Reprinted with permission from *Hospitals Are for Learning* by Elizabeth Crocker with permission of Atlantic Institute of Education, © 1976.

details a rationale for this curriculum and explores three alternative approaches to field trips on the following pages.

WHY HOSPITALS? A RATIONALE

Five good reasons why schools should include 'hospitals' in their curriculum and/or programs of study:

1. Children often harbour both fears and misconceptions about illness and hospitals; a school field trip would enable them to deal with their ideas in a non-threatening situation. A school field trip is a 'safer' time to ask questions than when one is being admitted as a patient.
2. Thousands of children are hospitalized each year; ideally, children should be prepared for such an experience in terms of having at least some familiarity with what hospitals are and what goes on in them. While an individualized pre-admission tour for an anticipated hospitalization may be the ideal form of preparation, it remains true that a percentage of pediatric admissions are as a result of emergency situations. A field trip to a hospital allows for some familiarization in the event of a future admission.
3. "The hospital" is a topic that co-relates with all subject areas and, as such, is ideally suited to an integrated curriculum approach in the classroom. Learning about hospitals and health care provides a practical dimension to the study of science, language arts, mathematics.... An elaboration of this point is provided in a later section.
4. Field trips are both informative and enjoyable and provide students with real experiences to complement and extend text book and classroom experiences.
5. Hospitals are in themselves interesting places. Unless you are a patient or are employed in a hospital, the chances are good that this community education resource is overlooked.

HOSPITAL FIELD TRIPS

The success of any field experience is good planning and organization. A visit to a hospital is no exception. Joint discussions between you and the appropriate hospital personnel are a priority in the planning stages. Although the actual details and organization of any hospital field trip will be largely up to the particular hospital involved, the following alternative approaches to looking at a hospital and its multiple services might help determine one or more focal points.

WHAT TO SEE AND DO WHEN YOU GET THERE: THREE ALTERNATIVES

A. Hospital Routines—The Child's Point of View

When a child is admitted to a hospital, it happens either through Emergency or through elective (when you know in advance) admission. Children could visit both Emergency and the Admitting Department and learn what happens, why certain questions are asked, and whether it makes any difference if you have a cold when you come to hospital to have your tonsils out.

On a hospital unit, children could learn many other things about what it would mean to be in hospital including:

- What kind of bed would they sleep in?
- Would they have to wear different clothes?
- Could they call for a nurse without leaving their beds?
- When are temperatures taken and how and why?
- What do "pulse" and "blood pressure" mean and how and why are they determined?
- Would they get weighed in pounds or kilograms?
- What are bed pans and urinals and why are they used?
- Would someone in the hospital take blood from their fingers or arms— why would medical people want it and what would the lab technicians do with it?
- Who are all the people who work on the hospital unit?
- Where do meals come from and would they eat in bed?

Some of these questions would suggest visits to other areas of the hospital like the labs, kitchen, and laundry room. Apart from the things that might actually 'happen' to children on a unit, they would probably be interested in knowing some other general things that would touch on their regular worlds if they were hospitalized.

- Could their parents stay with them? Or at least visit them every day?
- Could friends and brothers and sisters visit?
- Could people send them letters?
- Could they make phone calls?
- Would they be able to play and/or do some school work if they wanted?

The children might also want to know what would happen if they were going to have an operation. They could learn what "N.P.O." is and see a stretcher bed, which is different from other beds.

B. Hospital Services and Functions—From A to Z (Almost)

A hospital has many more departments than most people ever think of, and as would be expected, larger hospitals have a greater variety than smaller ones. Although certain departments may be more interesting in terms of activities or facilities to children than others, it is useful for students to realize that a lot goes together to make a hospital work properly. Brief descriptions or explanations of 16 different hospital departments follow:

Audio-visual

Some hospitals have audio-visual departments where slides, video-tapes, medical illustrations, and audio-tapes can be made for medical staff. These audio-visual materials would normally be used for teaching purposes—e.g., so that medical and nursing students can see pictures of different conditions, see video-tapes of operations, and hear audio-tapes of special lectures.

Central Dispatch and Bulk Storage

A central dispatch and bulk storage department is one which houses and systematically distributes the various supplies that are required to make a hospital run. A practical problem, especially if it's a large hospital, students could consider for central dispatch is how much toilet paper should a hospital buy at one time and how often should bathrooms be checked to ensure a constant supply?

Dietary

This department includes the kitchen and all its staff as well as the dietitians who determine special menus for patients on various special diets. The dietitians might explain why they suggest certain foods for certain people and explain how they calculate things like calories and vitamins.

The kitchen staff could show off their facilities and huge (depending on the size of the hospital) pieces of equipment—for example, mixing bowls big enough to make pudding for over 100 people; a refrigerator that is a room; machines that wash hundreds of dishes every day; carts that carry meals to patients; oversized cake pans, large ovens, and huge tins of tomato juice.

EEG and EKG

These are two departments with big names. The EKG department has a machine (an electrocardiograph) which records information about heartbeats and traces this information on a special piece of paper (electrocardiogram). This is a painless procedure and is done to determine whether there are any problems with a person's heart action. The EEG department is where an apparatus (an electroencephalograph) traces changes in electric potential in the brain. This, too, is a relatively painless procedure. Both procedures are quite interesting, and children are usually intrigued by the respective tracings.

Emergency/Poison Control Center

The emergency department is often one of the busiest places in a hospital. Some hospitals also have a poison control center as part of the emergency department. Children could learn why and when some people go to emergency departments rather than to their regular doctors and could talk about things that may both cause and prevent emergencies. An especially exciting thing to do in this department would be to see the inside of an ambulance and to talk to an ambulance driver.

Hospital Wards or Units

Other than in very small hospitals, patients stay in different wards or units of the hospital. These units are usually organized to reflect general medical categories; hospitals may have some or all of the following units: surgical (patients who have had or will have an operation); medical (patients who require care and treatment but do not require surgery); pediatrics (patients who are children—usually about 14 years of age and younger); neo-natal (new-born babies); maternity (women who have just had or are about to have a baby); orthopaedics (patients who require some corrective or preventative surgery for a disease or deformity of a bone or joint); intensive care (as the name implies, patients who require additional and/or constant care and surveillance); psychiatry (patients who are receiving care, treatment, and support for conditions or problems that have led to mental illness). Very large hospitals may have more categories of units than listed here; students could make up a list of a hospital's units and find out why the hospital has the ones it has. In terms of a tour, the two units that would probably be of particular interest to children would be the pediatric unit and the neo-natal unit. On the pediatric unit, the students could explore all the questions previously outlined in (a) and on the neo-natal unit, children could see and learn about newborn babies (a common fascination especially with young children).

Housekeeping

This is an important department but one that is often not thought of; people normally associate hospitals with doctors and nurses and possibly forget the significant question—who keeps the building clean? Housekeeping in a hospital is not quite as simple as housekeeping at home; children could see the equipment used that helps make the job easier and could learn why and how objects and rooms in a hospital are sometimes sterilized.

Laboratories

The lab area of a hospital is one of particular interest and relevance to children. This is the place where, if they were ever patients and had to have blood or urine collected, the samples of blood or urine would be tested and analyzed. However, hospital labs do far more than test blood and urine. Children could look through microscopes and see tissue cultures and blood samples and learn about what kinds of tests are done to determine or examine different things. Some hospitals also have research laboratories which also might be of interest particularly to older children.

Laundry

A hospital laundry is almost always an extremely busy and interesting place. Sheets, clothes, and other things in a hospital are washed frequently and this requires big and efficient machines for washing, drying, and ironing. For example, imagine a single washing machine that takes a clean, crumpled, and damp sheet and has it pressed and folded in 5 seconds!

Mail Room

Although there's not a great deal to see in a hospital mail room, children might like to know what happens to letters and parcels, and how they get sorted by the patient's name and ward.

Maintenance and Engineering

As much as possible hospitals like to have people on staff and workshop facilities in the building so that things can be made and/or repaired quickly. Consequently most hospitals have one or more departments related to the general maintenance and repair of the hospital building and its machines and other equipment. Children might not be aware of the variety of machines and general equipment that is used in a hospital. For example, what happens if the EKG machine doesn't work, if there's a power failure, if the sliding doors don't slide, or if the elevator gets stuck? Through this department, they could again develop an appreciation for all the component parts that go together to make a hospital function smoothly.

Medical Records

Whenever someone is hospitalized, information about that person, the illness, the treatment given and the rate of recovery is kept in the form of medical records. Even when a patient goes home, these records are kept. Some hospitals have begun to use a system of keeping the information contained in the medical record on film. Some children might be interested in knowing how and where the information is filed.

Outpatients

With the changing emphasis in delivery of medical care, the tendency is to try to look after people as outpatients rather than have them come into the hospital overnight. Sometimes even 'day surgery' is done via the outpatient department. The general clinic area often includes many associated clinics geared to people with specific problems that require treatment or check-ups. Children could consider what kind of waiting room (or rooms) a hospital should have for outpatients and whether it should have toys, magazines, phones, etc.

Pharmacy

Hospitals have their own 'drug stores' where major supplies of drugs and medicines are kept and where special prescriptions for patients are filled or made or mixed. Children could see the broad array of pharmaceutical substances, learn why some things are kept in refrigerators, why some medicines are pills and others liquid or capsules, and see the tiny weights and measures that are used to be exact about very small amounts.

Physiotherapy and Occupational Therapy

These two departments are often combined in hospitals, or at least located near one another. Small hospitals are more likely to have physiotherapy than occupational therapy; children might want to find out why. Both departments are geared to helping people do things and improve their skills—everything from learning how to walk again to how to feed oneself, get dressed or dial a telephone. These departments have a variety of equipment and facilities for helping patients, and children would likely be interested in things like whirlpool tubs, walking ramps, and hand attachments.

Radiology

This is the x-ray department and many children may have had experience having x-rays taken. This area is full of fascinating things—x-rays that have been taken, x-ray machines that move, people wearing heavy aprons, and x-ray tables. Children could learn about the different positions for x-raying differents parts of the body.

Other

The foregoing list of hospital departments is not definitive. The size of the hospital you visit will have a bearing on the number of departments. Some examples of other departments are as follows: dentistry, public relations, staff health, medical library, social services, volunteers, pathology, respiratory technology, purchasing, and psychology. Sometimes, too, there are variations in terminology from hospital to hospital—for example, a hospital might call their Laundry Department the Linen Department, or refer to the Kitchen as Food Services.

C. Hospital Careers—The Specialized Staff

The third approach to looking at a hospital is to look at the many people who work there and at the jobs they do. Rather than provide a description and definition of everyone's job, the following simply lists the various categories of hospital staff. A project possibly connected with a field trip could be to find out what all these people do. The list does not pretend to be exhaustive; teachers and students (not to mention hospital workers) may be able to add many more.

- accountants
- administrators
- ambulance drivers
- biomedical engineers
- child care workers
- cooks (and other kitchen staff)
- dentists (and dental surgeons)
- dietitians
- doctors (there are many doctors with specialties such as anesthetists, allergists, cardiologists, dermatologists, general practitioners, gynecologists, nephrologists, neurologists, neurosurgeons, obstetricians, opthalmologists, orthopedic surgeons, pathologists, pediatricians, plastic surgeons, psychiatrists, radiologists, urologists)
- housekeeping staff
- interns

- laundry staff
- maintenance staff (carpenters, electricians, etc.)
- medical illustrators and photographers
- medical librarians
- medical secretaries
- microbiologists
- nurses (there are variations of this category, too: registered nurse—RN; certified nursing assistant—CNA; student nurse; head nurse; nurse clinician; nursing supervisor, etc.)
- pharmacists
- residents
- security personnel or commissionaires
- social workers
- teachers
- technologists in various fields (audio-visual, research, radiology, laboratory, respiratory)
- therapists in various fields (occupational, physical, recreational, inhalation)
- volunteers

SUMMARY

In the preceding sections, the role of the teacher as advocate was advanced, and four aspects of advocacy were explored. From the specific aim of helping the child reenter school by providing a supportive setting free of environmental, social, or academic barriers, to the more general goal of increasing the student's awareness of the hospital and illness as components of their lives, this chapter takes the position of recommending advocacy as a legitimate function of the teacher.

It is hoped that this book, as a whole, can serve as a handbook for the teacher. Its goals are to help the teacher (1) identify the problems encountered by chronically ill children and their families, (2) gain increased practical knowledge of the various chronic illnesses, and (3) recognize and address individual biases and fears in relation to this special population.

If it serves these purposes, perhaps the many hats the teacher is expected to wear simultaneously—educator, evaluator, referral agent, coordinator, team member, advocate, and friend—will all fit more comfortably.

REFERENCES

Axelrod, S., & Bailey, S.L. Drug treatment for hyperactivity: Controversies, alternatives, and guidelines. *Exceptional Children*, 1979, *45*(7), 544-550.

Beuf, A. *Biting off the bracelet*. Philadelphia: University of Pennsylvania Press, 1979.

Connor, F. *Education of the homebound/hospitalized child*. New York: Columbia University, Teachers College, 1964.

Family Communications, Inc. Going to the hospital (videotape). Pittsburgh: Family Communications, Inc., 1976.

Haslam, R.H.A., & Valletutti, P.J. *Medical problems in the classroom*. Baltimore, MD: University Park Press, 1975.

Linn, S. *The children's medical series with Susan Linn and her puppets*. Newton, MA: Family Information Systems, Inc., 1980.

Lubin, G.I. Emotional implications. In R.M. Peterson & J.O. Cleveland (Eds.), *Medical problems in the classroom*. Springfield, IL: Charles C Thomas, 1975.

McLouglin, J.A., McLouglin, R., & Stewart, W. Advocacy for parents of the handicapped: A professional responsibility and challenge. *Learning Disability Quarterly*, 1979, *2*(3), 52.

Weintraub, F.J. & McCaffrey, M.A. Professional rights and responsibilities. In F.J. Weintraub et al. (Eds.), Public policy and the education of exceptional children, Reston, VA: Council for Exceptional Children, 1976.

Psychosocial Policy Guidelines for Administration of Pediatric Health Care Facilities*

I. EQUALITY AND RESPECT

A. Equal Treatment

What the Health Care Setting Must Do

The health care setting should ensure that each child and family are treated equally, with dignity and respect, and with an appreciation for the family's life style, customs, language, culture, and diet. Regardless of the type of facility (whether or not it is specifically a pediatric hospital, general hospital with a pediatric department, or hospital with no pediatric department) each child should have every opportunity for care which is appropriate to his/her age group, including staff trained to work with children.

Explanation

Without exception, all children are entitled to the best available care regardless of their own or their family's race, color, language, physical or mental status, religion, national origin, political opinion, socioeconomic status or sex.

Source: Reprinted with permission from *Psychosocial Policy Guidelines for Administration of Pediatric Health Care Facilities* by Lyn Gordon, Susan Kleinberg, Mary McCarthy, and Constance Battle, Metropolitan Washington Affiliate Association for the Care of Children's Health, © 1980.

Specific Recommendations

The health care setting should:

1. instruct all staff that respectful treatment is to be accorded each child and family.
2. assign children to appropriate units within the hospital so that adequate care for the child's particular age group and diagnosis can be provided. Children of similar ages and abilities should be grouped together. At no time should a child share a room with an adult.
3. provide a translator when there is a language barrier.
4. provide a diet which is in keeping with the customs of the family, insofar as this is possible.

B. Confidentiality

What the Health Care Setting Must Do

The health care setting should provide for the child's (and his/her family's) right to confidentiality throughout the entire care process and afterwards.

Explanation

The child and the family need to know that they are protected from embarrassment and distress which could be caused by public knowledge of their intimate personal affairs. Only when they feel that their privacy is guarded will they feel free to cooperate fully and honestly in the course of treatment.

Each member of the health care team must preserve confidentiality in all matters, both in the keeping of medical records, and in discussions regarding the child, his/her family, history, diagnosis, and treatment. This policy must apply in all situations, including the provisions of birth control services, treatment for venereal diseases, care relating to conditions of pregnancy, seeking and obtaining of psychiatric care and counseling, and care for substance abuse (drugs, alcohol, etc.)

Specific Recommendations

The health care setting should:

1. limit access to a child's records to authorized personnel only.
2. limit discussions regarding patient care and treatment to those persons who need to be so informed.
3. when appropriate, code medical charges confidentially for billing purposes.

C. Acknowledgment of the Child

What the Health Care Setting Must Do

The health care setting should ensure that by their language and behavior all members of the staff acknowledge the child as a person, not as an inanimate object, not as a disease or condition. The individuality of each child must be respected.

Explanation

All children are entitled to the full dignity and respect they deserve by virtue of their humanity and intrinsic personal worth. Their treatment in any setting should reflect a true concern for their physical and emotional comfort.

Specific Recommendations

The health care setting should:

1. instruct all staff to treat the child with courtesy, including greeting the child by name, introducing unfamiliar staff, and talking to the child directly rather than using the third person.
2. ensure that the child is either included in any discussion (consultation, rounds, etc.) or that the discussion is delayed until a time when the child is not present.

D. Rounds at the Child's Bedside

What the Health Care Setting Must Do

The health care setting should ensure that medical and other personnel will limit their discussion in the presence of the child to conversation which is beneficial and instructive for the child, and which is geared to his/her cognitive, emotional, social, and language development.

Explanation

Rounds at the bedside must not include discussion for the education of medical and/or other personnel unless it is thoroughly appropriate that the child hear the proceedings. Too frequently, the child is treated as an object or disease with no thoughts and feelings of his/her own. The child is left no recourse but to imagine or fantasize about the meaning of the conversation at his/her own developmental level. This can result in frightening misperceptions about a child's condition and treatment.

Specific Recommendations

The health care setting should:

1. instruct all staff that conversation occurring at the child's bedside, or anywhere within the child's hearing, be directed to the child and geared to his/her level of comprehension. All such discussion should be appropriate for the child to hear.
2. ensure that discussion or conversation which must occur among professionals will take place out of the child's hearing.
3. provide follow-up conversation with a child who demonstrates a misunderstanding of his/her condition or treatment.

E. Protection of Privacy

What the Health Care Setting Must Do

The health care setting should ensure that the privacy and delicate feelings of each child about his/her body are protected at all times.

Explanation

Every child is a human being and has the right to be treated with dignity and respect, as well as the right to refuse being put on display and potentially embarrassed in front of others regardless of the rationalizations of the medical personnel. Most children will not be able to refuse invasions of their privacy.

Specific Recommendations

The health care setting should:

1. make sure that no staff member will conduct treatments, procedures, or physical examinations in playrooms, hallways, or other public places.
2. provide treatment rooms accessible to the child's unit.
3. make sure that curtains or screens are placed around a child's bed when a treatment, procedure, or physical examination is conducted in multiple-bed rooms.

F. Informing the Child

What the Health Care Setting Must Do

The health care setting should provide adequate and appropriate explanations to the child so that he/she fully understands the reasons for and specific details regarding the health care to be provided.

Explanation

In order to cope with illness, medical procedures, and hospitalization in general, a child needs to know what is being done to him/her now and what treatment plans for the future include. This approach will limit misunderstandings, fears, and fantasies which might seriously impede recovery or cause secondary emotional or psychological trauma.

Specific Recommendations

The health care setting should:

1. instruct the interdisciplinary team to inform the child in simple, developmentally appropriate language why he/she is in the health care facility and what the treatment will entail.
2. assign a team member to ascertain that the child has correctly understood the explanation that he/she has been given.
3. encourage the child to express his/her perceptions and fantasies.
4. instruct a team member to correct a child's misperceptions if necessary.

II. FAMILY INVOLVEMENT

A. Maintaining Family Ties

What the Health Care Setting Must Do

The health care setting should provide the opportunity for families to maintain close and continuous relationships when a child requires hospitalization.

Explanation

Separation and illness create anxiety and stress for children. Young children may feel abandoned by their parents, and may view the separation as permanent. This stress can be minimized by encouraging the presence of family members in order to provide emotional support and approximate familiar patterns and routines of care. Parents, however, may be stressed or overemotional when their child is hospitalized. Memories of their own hospitalization as children and other separation experiences may make them incapable of providing emotional care or even routine physical care for their child. Staffing patterns should be adequate to provide appropriate patient care whether the parents are present or not. Thus the hospital must not view a child's parents as ancillary staff.

Specific Recommendations

The health care setting should:

1. recognize the primary role of the parents as caregivers, and make formal arrangements which allow them to assume as much or as little care for the child as they feel comfortable with, and as is consonant with sound medical practice.
2. post visiting hours, indicating that parents are allowed to visit around-the-clock.
3. encourage parents to remain with the child as much as possible, and provide rooming-in facilities whenever feasible. Where rooming-in is not possible, be flexible in providing some other temporary sleeping arrangements within the hospital.
4. plan hospital stays for children to be as short as possible. In order to avoid undue separation, outpatient procedures should be the first choice whenever possible.
5. set specific policies to facilitate sibling visiting privileges.
6. ensure the free exchange of information: a) from family to staff, regarding the child's usual behavior patterns and coping mechanisms; and b) from staff to family regarding the child's condition and adaptation to the condition and/or health care setting.
7. obtain information about family cultural, religious, or personal routines, and be flexible in accommodating these differences whenever possible.
8. provide written information for distribution to parents covering all hospital policies and procedures pertaining to children (i.e., accompanying a child to a procedure, rights of patients and parents).

B. Supporting and Preparing Families

What the Health Care Setting Must Do

The health care setting should provide support and preparation for parents which will enable them, in turn, to support their child.

Explanation

The confusion and anxiety of parents in stressful situations is often transmitted to the child, increasing his/her own anxiety. Support for and preparation of parents can aid them in providing emotional strength for the child.

Specific Recommendations

The health care setting should:

1. explain all procedures to parents, and allow them the privacy and time to assimilate medical information.
2. reinforce oral explanations with printed teaching materials.
3. offer counseling to parents, which allows them time to work through their own feelings.
4. offer parent support groups to help families cope with stress of illness and hospitalization.

III. PREPARATION OF THE CHILD AND FAMILY FOR THE HEALTH CARE EXPERIENCE

A. Routine Education of Families in the Community

What the Health Care Setting Must Do

The health care setting should ensure that children and families in the community are given varied opportunities to learn about health care facilities and practices before there is any indication that they will need to use them.

Explanation

A child who is sick or hurt is less likely to cope well with the unfamiliar environment and potentially painful experiences of hospitalization or clinic visits. Similarly, the families of such children tend to be anxious and upset. It is important that as many children and families as possible have advance knowledge of what various health care settings are like, and what occurs routinely during a hospital admission or clinic visit.

Specific Recommendations

The health care setting should:

1. develop out-reach programs which include visits to pre-schools, kindergartens, and other child groups to present interesting and relatively non-threatening aspects of hospitals and health care.
2. initiate tours for school groups, during which children and adolescents can visit the health care facility and become familiar with the sights, smells, and sounds which they encounter there. Tours might be incor-

porated into a class curriculum or theme such as "Community Helpers" or "Careers."
3. send staff to participate in the meetings of PTAs and other parent groups, explaining common childhood and adolescent health problems, typical reactions of children to these problems and the importance of attention to the psychosocial and emotional aspects of health care for children.

B. Adequate Explanation

What the Health Care Setting Must Do

The health care setting should ensure that children and their parents are informed, understand, and have the opportunity to review and discuss experiences of separation, diagnosis, and treatment. These experiences are potentially stressful to any and all members of the family.

Explanation

A child needs to be protected from overwhelming anxiety resulting from fear of the unknown. A child obtains some sense of control from knowing what is to come and having sufficient time to prepare for it. This need for adequate preparation is especially important for any child who is handicapped in his/her capacity to understand, by virtue of serious illness, or emotional, cognitive, or social deprivation. It is equally important for young children (under five years of age) because of their fragmentary understanding of the concepts of time, health, and illness.

Specific Recommendations

The health care setting should:

1. provide the child with an opportunity for a pre-admission visit to: a) meet the staff; b) become familiar with the hospital environment; c) have the opportunity to ask questions and discuss what he/she has seen.
2. instruct staff to meet the child and family and provide such a tour soon after admission, if a pre-admission tour is not possible.
3. direct staff to ensure that the child and family learn the names of those who are responsible for his/her direct care, in particular, which physician is responsible for the care. For the child who can read, his/her family, and all hospital staff and volunteers, a card should be taped to the bedstand with the first and last names of the child's hospital caretakers.

4. provide an explanation of communication channels as soon as possible after admission.
5. develop a routine procedure for informing a child and his/her parents concerning the diagnosis, prognosis, and treatment, in language which is readily understandable.
6. make specific provisions for special circumstances in which impediments to communication exist (i.e., limited understanding of child or family, language barriers, hearing impairment, chaotic or unstable family).
7. provide a specific opportunity each day for the child and family to ask pertinent questions concerning the diagnosis and treatment, tests and procedures performed.

C. Acceptance

What the Health Care Setting Must Do

The health care setting should ensure that children and their families are given the time and assistance they require to come to an appropriate acceptance of the diagnosis, prognosis, treatment, and sequelae associated with the condition of disease which they face.

Explanation

Manageable anticipatory anxiety facilitates a more complete working through of thoughts and feelings, which ultimately leads to a better acceptance of the procedures or consequences. In any life change, such as loss or diminution of function, a mourning or grieving process must take place. A child needs sufficient time and assistance for this process. He/she deserves the developmental challenge of facing a new experience, of learning about it, and of adjusting to it. Parents may need additional support and possibly formal counseling during this process.

Specific Recommendations

The health care setting should:

1. provide each child with an appropriate length of time to prepare himself/herself for any particular procedure to the fullest extent that it is medically feasible and in accordance with the child's developmental age and individual coping skills. A sufficient period should be allowed as well for a child to work through life changes which will result either from the disease or condition itself or from the treatment.

2. develop a staff structure and pattern which gives serious attention to providing: a) basic, general emotional support from all hospital staff; b) indirect intervention by helping the parents support the child; c) explanations, guidance, and instruction in practical techniques of coping with specific life changes on a day-to-day basis from nurses or the appropriate therapist; d) direct intervention by a mental health professional, using play therapy, art and literature, or, for older children, the more conventional types of therapy.

IV. PARTICIPATION BY THE CHILD AND FAMILY IN DISCUSSION AND DECISION-MAKING

What the Health Care Setting Must Do

The health care setting should ensure that the child and his/her parents have opportunities to participate in decision making, in collaboration with health care professionals.

Explanation

A child has the need to participate in the discussion and consideration of medical or surgical treatment, and to consider the refusal to consent in those instances where the prognosis is clearly poor, and/or the treatments would interfere with other objectives more important to the child and family, such as "peaceful final days." Every child has the right to have his/her wishes and preferences given serious consideration when decisions are being made regarding course of treatment, including discontinuation of treatment for a terminally ill child. A child's sense of self-determination and feelings of control are enhanced when he/she has input into the decision-making process. Not only does this participation serve the practical purpose of increasing the child's cooperation, and possibly putting him/her into a frame of mind where maximum benefits from treatments can occur, but it is in accord with a general policy of respecting the right of any person to have a say (for adults, 'informed consent') in what will happen in his/her life.

Specific Recommendations

The health care setting should:

1. encourage staff to develop a written philosophy of patient and parent participation which acknowledges their right to participate as well as the beneficial outcome of such mutual collaboration.

2. assess the extent to which a child can participate in planning for his/her health care based upon the child's age, emotional maturity, and most of all, on the cognitive ability to perceive and understand clearly the following: a) alternatives b) chance which the therapy has of being successful; c) degree to which it is thought that the child will be returned to normal or near normal functioning; and d) potential pain, discomfort, or traumatic side effects.
3. develop a comprehensive interdisciplinary discharge plan which takes into account family needs and preferences.

V. ENVIRONMENT AND DAILY STRUCTURE

A. Provision of Developmentally Appropriate Opportunities

What the Health Care Setting Must Do

The health care setting should provide every child with the opportunity to participate in developmentally appropriate educational, recreational, and social activities, such as those offered by child life specialists and hospital teachers.

Explanation

Children in hospitals and out-patient clinics need to have their emotional, social, educational, and recreational needs addressed in order to maintain normal routines, facilitate development, and alleviate anxiety and stress. Child life programs, staffed by skilled, sensitive child care professionals, are an essential component of health care because they provide children, through play, with the chance to impose control and demonstrate mastery in at least one aspect of their lives. Educational programs which cater to individual needs are also extremely important to help hospitalized children maintain and improve their academic skills, so as not to fall behind in their regular schoolwork.

Specific Recommendations

The health care setting should:

1. provide professional child life specialists in ratios sufficient to ensure adequate developmental programming and emotional support.
2. provide the services of licensed teachers (either directly through hospital employment, or by an arrangement with the local school system) who will continue a child's education, helping him or her to

maintain and improve important academic skills, so as not to fall far behind in regular schoolwork.

3. appoint a child/family advocate, either a nurse or physician, to oversee the quality of care of children in hospitals which have no specific designated pediatric beds.

4. set aside adequate space for activities, separate from other areas, and appropriately designed for the population served.

5. allot an appropriate budget to provide suitable educational and recreational materials and equipment.

6. train all staff and volunteers in an ongoing fashion to ensure their continuing educational development. Child life specialists should offer consultation to other departments so that emotional care will be consistent and continuous.

B. Provision of 'Safe' Times

What the Health Care Setting Must Do

The health care setting should provide specific 'safe' times for each child on a daily basis, time which will be free of any unexpected or painful experiences.

Explanation

Children in hospitals are required to undergo treatments and therapy which are often painful and/or frightening. These are usually scheduled to meet the varying needs of staff, and often result in the inability of the child to control any aspect of his/her schedule or environment. Specific free time, scheduled daily, allows a child some control, and the freedom from fear of unexpected pain.

Specific Recommendations

The health care setting should:

1. schedule a time each day to allow a child some 'safe' time. This should be noted on the nursing care plan and respected by all staff.

2. instruct staff that painful treatment not be given to the child without warning and explanation, and should never be given in playrooms, lounges, or other public areas.

C. Appropriate Physical Environment

What the Health Care Setting Must Do

The health care setting should provide an environment for every child which is planned and scaled to his/her needs and reflects the child's individuality.

Explanation

Every child has the right to surroundings in which it is both safe and functional for him/her to move around independently. It is important for the child's development and maintenance of self-esteem that he/she be given as much independence in functioning as possible. The individual identity of each child is important and must be supported.

Specific Recommendations

The health care setting should:

1. provide bathroom facilities, beds, tables, chairs, and doorknobs that are built in such a way that children can use them independently, without an adult's assistance.
2. if necessary, design, construct, or remodel all furniture and equipment so that it will be at the appropriate height for reach or grasp by a child.
3. encourage display of child's personal belongings or artwork.

D. Allowing the Child to Take Care of His/Her Own Needs

What the Health Care Setting Must Do

The health care setting should encourage the child to engage in his/her own daily care activities to the fullest extent possible, including bathing, feeding, toileting, dressing, and ambulating.

Explanation

When the child is allowed to take care of his/her own needs as far as possible, he/she will be better able to maintain self-esteem through continued control over those functions which have been mastered prior to hospitalization.

Specific Recommendations

The health care setting should:

1. instruct all staff to allow adequate time each day so that the child is able to bathe, feed, and dress himself/herself as far as possible.
2. ensure that staff encourages the child to continue using the daily care skills which he/she had achieved prior to hospitalization.
3. permit children to wear their own night clothes or play clothes when possible.

VI. PROMPT ATTENTION

What the Health Care Setting Must Do

The health care setting should ensure that each child is seen promptly. In addition, the facility staff should attend to the whole child, and not limit its attention to the ostensible reason for admission to that facility.

Explanation

A child needs to be attended to within a reasonable time-frame. His/her limited ability to comprehend concepts of time during periods of heightened anxiety or uneasiness make prompt health care attention an essential component of any care delivery system.

A child has the need for his/her special needs to be identified as soon as possible in order to prevent future disability and maximize the benefits of health care intervention and to make true comprehensive health care available to him/her. All children, insofar as possible, have the right to early detection of any abnormality or deviation in infancy (or as early as possible). They also have the right to immediate and continuing health guidance and comprehensive service until the maximum potential of the child is achieved.

Specific Recommendations

The health care setting should:

1. schedule appointments on a realistic basis.
2. assign staff so that periods of heavy usage are adequately covered.
3. encourage staff to explain when the system fails.
4. when appropriate, provide play opportunities for the child.
5. ensure that the child, a constantly changing individual, is evaluated by a multidisciplinary team at reasonable intervals.

6. ensure that suspicions about delays or gaps in cognitive, social, motor, and sensory development are pursued.
7. instruct each staff member to treat the whole child, and to review and discuss the child with other professionals through multidisciplinary meetings.

SUGGESTED READINGS

Adams, M.A. A hospital play program: Helping children with serious illness. *American Journal of Orthopsychiatry,* 1976, *46*(3).

Belmont, H.S. Hospitalization and its effect upon the total child. *Clinical Pediatrics,* 1970, 9.

Freud, A. The role of bodily illness in the mental life of children. *Psychoanalytic Study of the Child,* 1952, 7:69.

Gellert, E. (Ed.) *Psychosocial aspects of pediatric care.* New York: Grune & Stratton, 1978.

Glaser, H. The hospital as an environment. *Journal of the Association for the Care of Children in Hospitals,* 1974, *3*(1).

Haggerty, R.; Klaus, J.; Roghmann, J.; Pless, I.B. *Child health and the community.* New York: Wiley-Interscience, 1975.

Klaus, M., and Kennell, J. Maternal infant-bonding. St. Louis: C.V. Mosby, 1976.

Lawson, B.A. Chronic illness in the school-age child: Effects on the total family. *Maternal Child Nursing,* 1977, January-February.

Murphy, L.B. *The widening world of childhood: Paths toward mastery.* New York: Basic Books, Inc., 1962.

Petrillo, M., and Sanger, S. *Emotional care of hospitalized children,* 2nd edition. Philadelphia: J.B. Lippincott, 1980.

Plank, E. Working with children in hospitals. Chicago: Year Book Medical Publishers, 1971.

Prugh, D., et al. A study of the emotional reactions of children and their families to hospitalization. *American Journal of Orthopsychiatry,* 1953, 70.

Robertston, J. Young child in hospital. London: Tavistock Publications, 1970.

Robinson, M.E. Psychological impact of illness and hospitalization on the child: Birth through 12 years. Paper presented at a meeting of the Metropolitan-Washington affiliate of ACCH, May, 1972.

Rothenberg, M. Is there a national conspiracy against children in the United States? In Human Needs and Political Realities. Washington, D.C.: U.S. Government Printing Office, 1978.

Shore, M. Red is the color of hurting. Washington, D.C.: U.S. Government Printing Office, 1965.

Skipper, J.K., and Leonard, R.C. Children, stress, and hospitalization: A field experiment. *Journal of Health and Social Behavior,* 1965, 9.

Spitz, R. Hospitalism: An inquiry into the genesis of psychiatric conditions in early childhood. *Psychoanalytic Study of the Child,* 1945, 43.

Starfield, B., and Barkowe, S. Physician recognition of complaints made by parents about their children's health. *Pediatrics,* 1969, 43.

Study to quantify the uniqueness of children's hospitals. Wilmington, Del.: National Association of Children's Hospitals and Related Institutions, 1978.

Tisza, V., and Angoff, K. A play program and its function in a pediatric hospital. *Pediatrics,* 1957, 19.

Vardaro, J.A. Pre-admission anxiety and mother-child relationships. *Journal of the Association for the Care of Children in Hospitals,* 1978, 7(2).

Woler, J.A., and Visintainer, M. Pediatric surgical patients' stress responses and adjustments. *Nursing Research,* 1975, 24.

Resource Organizations

Action for Newborns
C/O Michael F. Shaunn
Albuquerque, New Mexico

Allergy Foundation of America
801 Second Avenue
New York, New York 10017

American Association of Mental Deficiency
5201 Connecticut Avenue, NW
Washington, D.C. 20015

American Cancer Society
219 East 42nd Street
New York, New York 10017

American Foundation for the Blind
15 West 16th Street
New York, New York 10011

American Medical Association
535 N. Dearborn Street
Chicago, Illinois 60610

American Diabetes Association
18 East 48th Street
New York, New York 10017

American Heart Association
7320 Greenville Avenue
Dallas, Texas 75231

American Lung Association
2851 Bedford Avenue
Pittsburgh, Pennsylvania 15219

American Speech and Hearing Association
9030 Old Georgetown Road
Washington, D.C. 20014

American Trauma Society
Arlington and Detroit Avenues
Toledo, Ohio 46615

Amyotrophic Lateral Sclerosis Foundation, Inc.
2840 Adams Avenue
San Diego, California 92116

Architectural and Transportation Barriers Compliance Board
Switzer Building
Washington, D.C. 20201

Arthritis Foundation
1212 Avenue of the Americas
New York, New York 10036

Association for Children with Learning Disabilities
2200 Brownsville Road
Pittsburgh, Pennsylvania 15210

Association for Education of the Visually Handicapped
1604 Spruce Street
Philadelphia, Pennsylvania 19103

Center for Sickle Cell Anemia
College of Medicine
Howard University
520 W. Street, NW
Washington, D.C. 20001

Children in Hospitals, Inc.
31 Wilshire Park
Needham, Massachusetts

CLOSER LOOK
The Special Education Information Center
Box 1492
Washington, D.C. 20013

Compassionate Friends
Post Office Box 1347
Oakbrook, Illinois 60521

Cooley's Anemia Blood and Research Foundation for Children, Inc.
Hyde Park
New York

Council for Exceptional Children
1920 Association Drive
Reston, Virginia 22091

Epilepsy Foundation of America
729 F. Street, NW
Washington, D.C. 20005

Foundation for Research and Education in Sickle Cell Disease
421–431 West 120th Street
New York, New York 10027

Friedreich's Ataxia Group in America, Inc.
Box 11116
Oakland, California 94611

Lupus Foundation of America, Inc.
11675 Holly Springs Drive
St. Louis, Missouri 63141

Muscular Dystrophy Associations of America, Inc.
1790 Broadway
New York, New York 10019

National Association of Sheltered Workshops and Homebound Programs
1522 K. Street, NW
Washington, D.C. 20006

National Committee for Prevention of Child Abuse
Box 2866
Chicago, Illinois 60690

National Cystic Fibrosis Research Foundation
521 Fifth Avenue
New York, New York 10019

National Easter Seal Society for Crippled Children and Adults
2023 West Ogden Avenue
Chicago, Illinois 60612

National Hemophilia Foundation
25 West 39th Street
New York, New York 10018

National Kidney Foundation
116 E. 27th Street
New York, New York 10018

National Multiple Sclerosis Society
257 Park Avenue South
New York, New York 10010

National Paraplegia Foundation
333 N. Michigan Avenue
Chicago, Illinois 60601

National Tay-Sachs and Allied Disease Association, Inc.
200 Park Avenue South
New York, New York 10003

Osteogenesis Imperfecta, Inc.
1231 May Court
Burlington, North Carolina 27215

Parent Information Center
407 S. Dearborn Street RM 680
Chicago, Illinois

Spina Bifida Association of America
104 Festone Avenue
New Castle, Delaware

United Cerebral Palsy Association, Inc.
321 West 44th Street
New York, New York 10036

United Ostomy Association, Inc.
1111 Wilshire Boulevard
Los Angeles, California 90017

Veterans Administration Prosthetics Center
Bioengineering Research Service
252 Seventh Avenue
New York, New York 10001

Vocational Rehabilitation Administration
Washington, D.C. 20201

Developmental Chart

The following developmental chart is meant to function as a set of guidelines for observing a child's abilities in a variety of areas. Each child develops at his/her own pace, and development is often uneven. These guidelines are meant to be general and should not be used to make formal developmental evaluations independent of other standardized measures.

Sources used in developing these guidelines were: Mt. Washington Pediatric Hospital physical therapy department checklist for gross motor skills, fine motor skills, and activities of daily living; Gesell's developmental milestones; E. Erikson's eight stages of man; J. Piaget's stages of development; I.C. Uzgiris and J. McV. Hunt's *Assessment in Infancy;* H. Perkins' *Human Development.*

DEVELOPMENTAL CHART

AGE	GROSS MOTOR	FINE MOTOR	ACTIVITIES OF DAILY LIVING	SPEECH AND LANGUAGE	COGNITION	SOCIAL/EMOTIONAL	SPECIAL ISSUES
1 month	lifts head briefly	reflex grasp; follows object to midline. Holds hands tightly fisted.	sucking and swallowing	crying due to discomfort, cooing, gurling.	regards dangling object	establishment of bond between caretaker and child.	totally dependent — needs physical contact to survive. birth — 2 years (sensori motor stage). ego-centric
2 months	lifts head recurrently supported sitting, head erect but bobbing.	retains toy briefly follows object past midline		social smile	follows moving person	development of trust	more alert
4 months	pulls to sitting with assist	follows object 180 hands together in midline mouths objects reaches.	recognizes bottle takes solids	spontaneous utterances, combinations of random syllables (ee, muh, gee)	plays with rattle if placed in hand; regards hands	responds to primary care taker in a special way.	becoming socially responsive. Begins to develop a sense of separation from mother.
6 months	rolls in both directions prone; goes forward sitting: leans forward on hands	transfers objects from hand to hand, reaches purpose-fully.	gums solids, introduced to cup	begins imitation syllable repetition (ba-ba) uses vocalizations to get attention	follows path of dropped object, plays peek-a-boo with cloth	recognizes self in mirror. Stretches arms up to be picked up. development of stranger anxiety more pronounced now.	
9 months	prone: assumes hand and knee position, trunk	Hits two objects together, shakes, pats, pokes,	Spoon to mouth independently, needs help filling	Jargon-inflected vocalizations. Must	Places string of beads around neck. Responds to simple		

DEVELOPMENTAL CHART

AGE	GROSS MOTOR	FINE MOTOR	ACTIVITIES OF DAILY LIVING	SPEECH AND LANGUAGE	COGNITION	SOCIAL/EMOTIONAL	SPECIAL ISSUES
	elevated. Sits without assistance. Pulls to stand.	points.	it. Drinks neatly from held cup. Finger feeds.	hear to reach this stage.	commands.		
10 months	cruises along furniture	removes blocks from container beginning good pincer grasp (11 months)	holds cup with a lot of assistance.	parrot speech pure imitation.	imitates patty-cake. deliberately drops objects. Lowers head when passing under obstacle.		
12 months (1 yr)	walks with one hand held; stands a few seconds with-out support.	one block brought over another. Rolls ball in imitation.	responds to "open your mouth" Cooperates with dressing.	Comprehension begins to show a spurt thru 18 months.	Stacks rings on pole in random order. Attempts to make things happen thru action. points to a variety of common objects.	Expresses anger, uses adults to obtain wants. Play is still solitary.	Fears strange people and places.
15 months	Walks with stability. Stops and starts.	Places blocks in container when asked.	lifts, replaces, drinks from cup. Fills spoon independently.	10-20 words used in one word sentences (thru 18 months)	hands over familiar object when named.	uses gestures, facial expressions words to show affection. Differentiates expressions on faces.	"into everything" - easily redirected, but needs more than verbal cues.
18 months	runs stiffly. creeps down stairs seats self in small chair.	builds 3 block tower, scribbles; pegs in hole hurls ball.	independent in feeding; starts to remove socks.		attends to book, turning 2-3 pages. Finds hidden objects where they "should" be. Extracts small objects from container. Uses foresight (stacks only rings with holes).	Gains attention by vocalizing with others Shows sustained interest and attention.	Separation from mother very difficult - separation anxiety present.

DEVELOPMENTAL CHART

AGE	GROSS MOTOR	FINE MOTOR	ACTIVITIES OF DAILY LIVING	SPEECH AND LANGUAGE	COGNITION	SOCIAL/EMOTIONAL	SPECIAL ISSUES
24 months (2 years)	runs well, walks up and down stairs. Jumps from bottom step.	Builds 6 block tower, 3 block train, strings 1" beads, turns pages one at a time.	unzips, can remove coat, shoes, pants. Toilet training likely to succeed	2 word sentences. 300 word vocabulary.	Follows 2 simple commands. points to 4-5 body parts. Puts simple puzzles together. Turns knob. Develops beginnings of symbolic activities. Recognizes constancy of external objects.	parallel play just beginning - has difficulty sharing.	beginning mastery of world. Beginning to learn rules, accepted patterns of the society. Ego-centricity is still central pattern.
2½ years	jumps with both feet in place. Walks up stairs alternating feet.		poor appetite shows a real interest in toileting, dressing skills.				beginning to be confused by choices. "Terrible two's" - difficulty with routines, changes. Tends to be rigid, inflexible, ritualistic, difference between "what I want to do" and can do" frustrating.
3 years	Stands on one foot. Uses tricycle with pedals and steering.	builds 3 block bridge. Copies a circle. Names 2 shapes (circle and square) Cuts gashes with scissor. Does 8-10 piece puzzles. Holds pencil in hand.	Removes all clothing, unbuttons easy buttons. Puts on socks, shoes, pants, coat. Feeds self independently. Washes and dries hands. Pours from open carton.	900-1000 word vocabulary. Short simple sentences. Over 90% of speech should be understood.	Recognizes common objects. Can tell a simple story. begins to differentiate big from small. begins to understand comparison of dissimilar objects.	Wants to please and conform, looks for adult approval. Begins imitative play. Continues parallel play, some sharing. Needs to explore, experiment with materials.	Difficulty in separating May begin to have bad dreams. Learning to relate to people outside the family. Beginning experiences in pre-school group settings. Pre-operational thought patterns.

DEVELOPMENTAL CHART

AGE	GROSS MOTOR	FINE MOTOR	ACTIVITIES OF DAILY LIVING	SPEECH AND LANGUAGE	COGNITION	SOCIAL/EMOTIONAL	SPECIAL ISSUES
4 years	Hops on one foot.	Copies a cross 12-16 piece puzzle. Cuts straight line with scissors. Catches and throws ball accurately.	Zips; begins lacing large buttons, uses fork, knife for spreading.	1500 word vocabulary. Uses more complex and compound sentences, grammatically correct.	Understands the function of common objects, body parts. Begins to categorize by similarity, draws a man with at least 2 parts.	Plays often with peers, tests anti-social behavior. Sets up small groups with "ins" and "outs". Curious, eager to learn, questioning. Quickly changing emotions, from anger, to beginnings of a real sense of humor.	Tends to be "out-of bounds" – experiments to test abilities. May develop fears of dark, animals. Needs external limit setting and controls. 2-4 year olds develop sense of use of symbols (words) to express things; sense of conceptualization will imerge at close of stage.
5 years	Skips. Walks downstairs alternating feet.	imitates a square. Shows hand preference, can cut out simple objects.	Can take care of daily routines independently.	2000 word vocabulary articulation at least 80%.	Can draw a recognizable figure.	is conscious of social routines, and wants to conform. Begins to see himself in relation to world-questions death, God, birth. Lives in the present just beginning to understand time concepts.	A period of calmness, security, cooperation. Feels more sure of himself.
6 years	jumps from 12"	Throws a small ball accurately. Copies diamond shape.	Cuts with knife. Uses telephone.	Most sentences correct. Uses irregular verbs, comparative adjectives.	draws a complete human figure, including clothes, neck, full body. Understands number concepts 1-10. Can copy symbols and shapes (alphabet) may be able to decode symbols (reading) is developing a "set" to	Changeable/emotional variations. Beginning to leave dominent home family for school, friends, community. Has trouble handling criticism; becomes easily frustrated. Enjoys dramatic play.	Beginning of independence outside the home setting. Beginning to turn to peer group for acceptance, estimates of self-worth.

DEVELOPMENTAL CHART

AGE	GROSS MOTOR	FINE MOTOR	ACTIVITIES OF DAILY LIVING	SPEECH AND LANGUAGE	COGNITION	SOCIAL/EMOTIONAL	SPECIAL ISSUES
6 years cont'd	CAN PERFORM ALL MOTOR	TASKS AND SELF	HELP SKILLS	NECESSARY TO	MEET PERSISTENT LIFE learn. Learns by concrete experiences and participation.	SITUATION	4-7 year old – pre-logical – perceptual reasoning, where child sees relationships but in a trial and error way. Things tend to be seen as having a single property or variable at a time (short fat glass holds a different amount of liquid as tall thin glass).

DEVELOPMENTAL CHART

AGE	COGNITION/MOTOR	SOCIAL/EMOTIONAL	SPECIAL ISSUES
7-9 years	Beginning of abstract thinking. Logical reasoning, still concrete, emerges. Can understand reversibility, can accept constarcy of physical objects despite changes in variables such as height, weight, size, volumn.	Learning to relate to adults outside the home. Attempts to win acceptance by peers. Learning to make ethical judgements to determine right and wrong.	Beginning to enter stage of concrete, operational thought. industry vs. inferiority is an important developmental task at this time.
9-11 years	Growth in use of abstractions; increased interest in organized sports.	Increased awareness of opposite sex and acceptance of own sex roles.	Peer influence is very important
12-14 years	Uses formal operational thought processes, deductive reasoning, logic adult thinking processes.	Asserting independence of adults. Forming relationships with adults and peers outside home.	Developing sense of identity.
14-18 years	Refining thinking processes, increasing knowledge.	Developing identity - body image and sex roles very important. Establishing meaningful heterosexual relationships.	Need for control, right to make independent decisions. Developing habits of work, responsibility. Developing a system of values and a life philosophy. Making career choices.

BIBLIOGRAPHY

Bee, H. *The developing child.* New York: Harper & Row, 1975.

Erikson, E.H. *Childhood and society.* New York: W.W. Norton, 1963.

Freud, A. *The psycho-analytic treatment of children.* New York: International Universities Press, 1946.

Gesell, A. *Studies in child development.* New York: Harper & Brothers, 1948.

Ilg, F.L., & Ames, L.B. *Child behavior.* New York: Harper & Row, 1955.

Perkins, H. *Human development.* Belmont, CA: Wadsworth Publishing Company, 1975.

Piaget, J. *The essential Piaget* (H.E. Gruber & J.J. Voneche, Eds. and trans.). New York: Basic Books, 1977.

Stone, L.J., & Church, J. *Childhood and adolescence* (3rd ed.). New York: Random House, 1975.

Uzgiris, I.C., & Hunt, J. McV. *Assessment in infancy.* Chicago: University of Illinois Press, 1975.

Glossary of Medical Terms

Abdomen. Portion of the trunk located between the chest and the pelvis.

Acetone. Ketone produced when fats are not properly oxidized, due to inability to oxidize glucose in the blood.

Adrenal gland. A triangular shaped body covering the superior surface of each kidney. It is a gland of internal secretion.

Albumin. One of a group of simple proteins widely distributed in plant and animal tissues.

Allergy. An acquired hypersensitivity to a substance (allergen) that does not normally cause a reaction.

Anoxia. Deficiency of oxygen.

Aplastic. Pertaining to the failure of an organ or tissue to develop normally.

Arthritis. Inflammation of a joint, usually accompanied by pain and frequently by changes in structure.

Aspirin. Acetylsalicylic acid; compound used to reduce pain and inflammation.

Asthma. Air hunger resulting in labored or difficult breathing accompanied by wheezing caused by a spasm of the bronchial tubes or by swelling of their mucous membrane.

Bacterial endocarditis. Inflammation of the lining membrane of the heart that begins abruptly and progresses rapidly. Usually caused by virulent organisms such as staphylococci or pneumococci.

Biopsy. Excision of a small piece of living tissue for microscopic examination. Usually performed to establish a diagnosis.

Brain stem. The stemlike part of the brain that connects the cerebral hemispheres with the spinal cord. Comprises the medulla oblongata, the pons, and the midbrain.

Bronchial tubes. The smaller divisions of the bronchi (the two main branches leading from the trachea to the lungs).

Bronchitis. Inflammation of mucous membrane of the bronchial tubes.

Carditis. Inflammation of the heart muscles. Usually involves two of the following: pericardium, myocardium, or endocardium.

315

Cerebellum. The large dorsally projecting part of the brain concerned especially with the coordination of muscles and of maintenance of body equilibrium, situated anterior to and above the medulla which it partly overlaps, and formed in main of two lateral lobes and a median lobe.

Cerebrum. The largest part of the brain consisting of two hemispheres separated by a deep longitudinal fissure. It is considered to be the seat of conscious mental processes.

Cerebral. Pertaining to the cerebrum.

Chemotherapy. In the treatment of a disease, the application of chemical reagents that have a specific and toxic effect upon the disease-causing organism.

Chorea. A nervous condition marked by involuntary muscular twitching of the limbs or facial muscles.

Cirrhosis. A chronic disease of the liver characterized by hardening caused by excessive formation of connective tissue followed by contraction.

Coma. An abnormal deep stupor occurring in illness, as a result of or due to an injury. The patient cannot be aroused by external stimuli.

Congenital. Present at birth.

Convulsions. A sudden periodic attack of involuntary muscular contractions and relaxations.

Corpus callosum. The connection between the cerebral hemispheres of the brain.

Cortex. The outer layer of an organ.

Cryoprecipitate. Separating a substance from a solution by use of very low temperatures.

Cystic fibrosis. An inherited disease of exocrine glands affecting the pancreas, respiratory system, and sweat glands. Usually begins at infancy and is characterized by chronic respiratory infection, pancreatic insufficiency, and heat intolerance.

Cystoscopy. Examination of the bladder with the cystoscope.

Desensitization. The reduction of sensitivity to an allergen by systematic administration of small doses of the allergen.

Dialysis. Process of diffusing blood across a semipermeable membrane to remove toxic materials and to maintain fluid, electrolyte, and acid-base balance in cases of impaired kidney function or absence of the kidneys.

Dilantin. An anticonvulsant used especially in treatment of epilepsy.

Edema (swelling). A local or generalized condition in which body tissues contain an excessive amount of tissue fluid.

EEG (electroencephalogram). The record obtained from the amplification, recording, and analysis of the electrical activity of the brain.

Electrophoresis. The movement of suspended particles through a fluid under the action of an electromotive force applied to electrodes in contact with the suspension.

Endocrine. Pertaining to a gland that secretes directly into the bloodstream.

Enzymes. Any of numerous complex proteins that are produced by living cells and catalyze specific biochemical reactions.

Epilepsy. A recurrent paroxysmal disorder of cerebral function characterized by sudden brief attacks of altered consciousness, motor activity, or sensory phenomena. Convulsive seizures are the most common form of attacks, but any recurrent seizure pattern is considered epilepsy.

Epithelium. Pertaining to the layer of cells forming the epidermis of the skin and the surface layer of mucous and serous membranes. Serves to enclose and protect the other parts of the body, to produce secretions and excretions, and to function in assimilation.

Etiology. The study of the causes of disease.

Exocrine gland. A gland (as a sweat gland or kidney) that releases a secretion external to or at the surface of an organ by means of a canal or duct.

Fontanel. An unossified space or soft spot lying between the cranial bones of the skull of a fetus or infant.

Friedreich's ataxia. An inherited degenerative disease with sclerosis of the dorsal and lateral columns of the spinal cord. Accompanied by ataxia, speech impairment, lateral curvature of the spinal column, and peculiar swaying and irregular movement, with paralysis of the muscles, especially of lower extremities.

Gangrene. A death of tissue, usually due to insufficient blood supply.

Glomerulonephritis. A form of nephritis in which the lesions involve primarily the renal glomeruli (which are small structures made up of capillary blood vessels).

Glycosuria. The presence of glucose in the urine.

Grand mal. A form of epileptic attack with or without coma. It is generalized and affects the entire brain. A sensation of sinking or rising in the epigastrium, the aura, is the start of the seizure. The seizure proceeds with loss of consciousness, falling, and tonic then clonic contractions of the muscles. Usually lasts 2-5 minutes.

Hematologist. Physician who specializes in diseases of the blood.

Hemodialysis. Removal of chemical substances from the blood by passing it through tubes made of semipermeable membranes. The tubes are continually bathed by solutions which selectively remove unwanted material. Used to cleanse the blood if one or both kidneys are defective or absent and to remove excess accumulation of drugs or toxic chemicals in the blood.

Hemolytic. Pertaining to the breaking down of red blood cells.

Hemorrhage. Abnormal internal or external discharge of blood. May be venous, arterial, or capillary from blood vessels into tissues, into or from the body.

Hemophilia. A hereditary blood disease characterized by greatly prolonged coagulation time. The blood fails to clot and abnormal bleeding occurs. It is a sex-linked hereditary trait, being transmitted by normal heterozygous females who carry the recessive gene. It occurs almost exclusively in males.

Hirsutism. Condition characterized by the excessive growth of hair or presence of hair in unusual places, especially in women.

Hydrocephalus. Increased accumulation of cerebrospinal fluid within the brain. This can be the result of developmental anomalies, infection, injury to the brain, or brain tumors.

Hydrotherapy. Scientific application of water in treatment of disease.

Hyperglycemia. Increase of blood sugar level, as in diabetes.

Hypertension. A condition in which a patient has a higher blood pressure than is judged to be normal.

Idiopathic. Pertaining to conditions without clear pathogenesis, or disease without recognizable cause, as of spontaneous origin.

Immunosuppressive. Substance that acts to suppress the body's natural immune response to an antigen (substance that induces the formation of antibodies).

Insulin. A hormone essential for the proper metabolism of blood sugar (glucose) and for maintenance of the proper sugar level. Produced in the islets of Langerhans in the pancreas.

Insulin shock. A condition resulting from an overdose of insulin, causing the blood sugar level to go below normal.

Islets of Langerhans. Cluster of cells in the pancreas. The cells are of three types: alpha, beta, and delta. The beta cells are found in greatest abundance and produce insulin.

Jaundice. A condition characterized by yellowness of the skin, white of eyes, mucous membranes, and body fluids due to deposition of bile pigment resulting from excess bilirubin in the blood. It may be caused by obstruction of bile passageways, excess destruction of red blood cells, or disturbance in functioning of liver cells.

Ketones. The ketone acids in the body are the end product of fat metabolism.

Kyphosis. Exaggeration of the normal posterior curve of the spine, resulting in a condition commonly known as "humpback" and "hunchback."

Legg-Calvé-Perthes Disease. Disease in which changes take place in bone at the head of the femur, with resulting deformity.

Meningomyelocele. Hernia of the spinal cord and membranes.

Metabolism. The sum of all physical and chemical changes that take place within an organism; all energy and material transformations that occur within living cells.

Metastasize. The transfer of disease from a primary focus to a distant one by conveyance of causal agents or cells through the blood vessels or lymph channels.

Mucous membrane. Membrane lining passages and cavities communicating with the air.

Muscular dystrophies. Diseases that result in the wasting away and atrophy (decrease in size) of muscles.

Nephron. The structural and functional excretory unit of the kidney. There are approximately 1 million nephrons in the kidney.

Nephrosis. Condition in which there are degenerative changes in the kidneys without the occurrence of inflammation. It is a disease that is characterized by fluid retention.

Orthopedic. Concerning the branch of science that deals with the prevention or correction of disorders involving the locomotor structures of the body, especially the skeleton, joints, muscles, and other supporting structures such as ligaments and cartilage.

Osteogenic sarcoma. Cancer arising from connective tissue in bone.

Osteogenesis imperfecta. An inherited disorder of connective tissue characterized by defective bone matrix (brittle bones).

Osteoporosis. Increased porosity of bones, leading to their softening.

Ostomy. Artificial opening, surgically created, which serves as an exit from the bowel or intestine to the outside. Usually situated on the patient's trunk area. Detachable, disposable bags are used to collect waste materials.

Paraplegia. Paralysis of the low portion of the body and both legs.

Paresis. A slight paralysis, incomplete loss of muscle power, or limb weakness.

Petit mal. Brief and general epileptic seizures with a 10-30 second loss of consciousness, eye or muscle flutterings, and sometimes loss of muscle tone.

Phenobarbital. A hypnotic, long-acting sedative and anticonvulsant. Used in treatment of epilepsy.

Platelets. Round or oval discs, 2-4 micrometers in diameter, found in the blood vertebrates. They play an important role in blood coagulation by adhering to each other and the edges of an injury, forming a plug that covers the area.

Pneumonia. Inflammation of the lungs caused primarily by bacteria, viruses, and chemical irritants.

Poliomyelitis. Inflammation of the gray matter of the spinal cord. Can cause paralysis or death. Active immunization has greatly reduced its incidence.

Portal hypertension. Increased pressure in the portal vein as a result of the flow of blood through the liver.

Prophylactic. Any agent or regimen that contributes to the prevention of an infection and disease.

Prosthesis. Replacement of a missing part by an artificial substitute such as an artificial extremity.

Psychogenesis. The origin and development of mind; to have a psychological origin.

Psychomotor. Concerning or causing physical activity associated with mental processes.

Pyelograms. An x-ray film of the renal pelvis and ureter.

Quadriplegia. Paralysis of all four extremities and usually the trunk.

Radiation. Emission of energy rays in all directions from a common center.

Radiation therapy. Ionizing radiation used for diagnostic or therapeutic purposes.

Remission. Lessening of severity or abatement of symptoms. Period in which symptoms abate.

Rheumatic fever. An inflammatory and nonsuppurative disease in nature and variable in severity and duration. It is sometimes followed by serious heart or kidney disease.

Rheumatoid arthritis. Form of arthritis with inflammation of joints, stiffness, swelling, and pain.

Rubella. Acute infectious disease resembling both scarlet fever and measles, but differing from these in short course and slight fever.

Scoliosis. Lateral curvature of the spine. Usually consists of two curves, the original deformity plus a compensating curve in the opposite direction.

Sickle cell anemia. A hereditary chronic form of anemia in which abnormal sickle or crescent-shaped red blood cells are present.

Spina bifida. Congenital defect in the walls of the spinal canal, caused by lack of connection between the vertebrae. As a result, the membranes of the spinal cord are pushed through the opening (see meningomyelocele).

Spina bifida occulta. Vertebrae fail to close, but spinal cord membranes do not protrude out.

Steroids. Any of numerous compounds containing the carbon ring system of the sterols and various hormones and glycosides.

Sympathetic nervous system. A division of the autonomic nervous system, concerned with involuntary body functions.

Temporal lobe. Lobe of the cerebrum located laterally and below the frontal and occipital lobes. Contains auditory receptive areas.

Thalamus. Area of the brain in which all sensory stimuli, with the exception of olfactory, are received and synthesized, associated and relayed to specific areas of the cortex. It is also the center for appreciation of primitive uncritical sensations of pain, crude touch, and temperature.

Tracheotomy. Operation of cutting into the trachea through the neck, usually for insertion of tube to overcome tracheal obstruction.

Transfusions. The injection of blood or a blood component into the bloodstream.

Trauma. A physical injury or wound caused by external force or violence. Also, an emotional or psychological shock that may produce disordered feelings or behavior.

Turner's syndrome. Congenital endocrine disorder caused by failure of ovaries to stimulate pituitary hormone. Results in short stature, possible swelling of the neck, and possible intelligence impairment.

Ureter. The tube that carries urine from the kidney to the bladder.

Uveitis. Inflammation of the iris of the eye, ciliary body, and choroid, or the entire area.

Vascular. Pertaining to or composed of blood vessels.

Vertebrae. The 33 bony segments of the spinal cord.

Virus. A minute organism not visible with ordinary light microscopy and a parasite dependent on nutrients inside cells for its metabolic and reproductive needs.

Index

A

Abdomen, defined, 315
Acceptance
  of death, 222
  of degenerative disease, 193
Accidents, 137
Acetone, defined, 315
Adaptation
  of equipment and materials, 165
  of games and activities, *170-174,*
    178
Adolescents
  anger, 181
  body image, 44-45
  with burns, 165
  with cystic fibrosis, 120
  with degenerative disease, 196-197
  denial of illness, 46
  with depression, 45-46
  with diabetes, 101
  with Friedreich's ataxia, 191
  hospitalized, 131-132, 180-183
  independence, 162
  normal development in, 30-31

psychological impact of disability
  on, *183-184*
response to illness, 36
with spina bifida, 161
with spinal cord injury, 142
stress in, 43
testing limits for, 46
vocational planning for, 182-183
Adrenal gland, defined, 315
Albumin, defined, 315
Alcohol, as cause of chronic illness, 6
Alcohol abuse, as response to illness,
  46
Allergens, in asthma attacks, 88, 89
Allergy, defined, 315
Amniocentesis, 6
Amputation
  in bone tumors, 211-212
  in prolonging life, 237, 238
Anger
  at impending death, 222, 224
  in parents, 53-54, 234
  as reaction to illness, 101, 141, 142,
    181, 226-227
  as reaction to injury, 141, 142

Note: Italicized page numbers include references to tables, figures, and exhibits.

H

About the Author

SUSAN KLEINBERG received her B.A. in psychology in 1961, her M.A. in special education in 1975, and is currently a Ph.D. candidate in human development. She has been the Director of Child Life and Education at Mt. Washington Pediatric Hospital for the past six years, and prior to that was employed by the Baltimore City Public School Home/Hospital Division. She has published an article concerning the infant-at-risk, has coauthored a booklet concerning the psychosocial needs of children in health settings, and has conducted numerous in-services relating to issues in educating chronically ill and hospitalized children.

As a professional and as a parent, Mrs. Kleinberg has been a committed advocate for the child with special needs in both school and hospital settings. She is dedicated to increasing public awareness and professional competency so that the special child's unmet needs can be addressed and mediated.